# Kid BY Kid, Skill BY Skill

*Teaching in a Professional Learning Community at Work*™

# ROBERT EAKER & JANEL KEATING

Solution Tree | Press

a division of

Solution Tree

555 North Morton Street

Bloomington, IN 47404

800.733.6786 (toll free) / 812.336.7700

FAX: 812.336.7790

email: info@solution-tree.com

solution-tree.com

Visit **go.solution-tree.com/PLCbooks** to download materials related to this book.

Printed in the United States of America

19   18   17   16                3   4   5

Library of Congress Cataloging-in-Publication Data

Eaker, Robert E.

  Kid by kid, skill by skill : teaching in a professional learning community at work / by Robert Eaker and Janel Keating.

      pages cm

  Includes bibliographical references and index.

  ISBN 978-1-942496-37-3 (perfect bound)  1.  Professional learning communities. 2. Teachers--In-service training. 3.  Academic achievement.  I. Keating, Janel. II. Title.

  LB1731.E128 2015

  370.71'1--dc23

                                     2015017782

**Solution Tree**
Jeffrey C. Jones, CEO
Edmund M. Ackerman, President

**Solution Tree Press**
*President:* Douglas M. Rife
*Associate Acquisitions Editor:* Kari Gillesse
*Editorial Director:* Lesley Bolton
*Managing Production Editor:* Caroline Weiss
*Copy Editor:* Ashante K. Thomas
*Proofreader:* Elisabeth Abrams
*Text and Cover Designer:* Rian Anderson
*Compositor:* Abigail Bowen

To Rick DuFour.

*A true friend freely advises justly,*

*assists readily, adventures boldly,*

*takes all patiently, defends courageously,*

*and continues a true friend unchangeably.*

—William Penn

It is with deep gratitude that I dedicate this book to Rick DuFour, my dearest, unwavering friend for nearly four decades. It is impossible to imagine my life, both personally and professionally, if Rick and I had never met. Rick and I have been partners in the truest sense of the word. I will be forever grateful for his friendship, not only to me, but to my entire family. We have traveled life's journey together, sharing both the happy times—of which there have been many—and the inevitable sad times. And, along the way, Rick remained a steady, generous, encouraging, and unwavering friend. Everyone should be so blessed!

—Bob Eaker


To Joyce Stewart.

*For there is no friend like a sister*

*In calm or stormy weather;*

*To cheer one on the tedious way,*

*To fetch one if one goes astray,*

*To lift one if one totters down,*

*To strengthen whilst one stands*

—Christina Rossetti

From the time I was a little girl, I looked up to, admired, and loved my sister, Joyce. She's an educator—an associate superintendent in the Everett School District. For over fifty years, she has been my constant source of support. Daily we motivate each other to create positive learning environments and a high standard of care for our administrators, teachers, and students. We also support each other as we work to be great mothers to our girls—Jodi, Jill, and Taylor.

—Janel Keating

# Acknowledgments

The ideas, concepts, and practices described in this book are based, to a great degree, on the work of Rick DuFour and Becky DuFour. Since Rick and Bob Eaker published *Professional Learning Communities at Work: Best Practices for Enhancing Student Achievement* in 1998, Rick and Becky have steadily continued to refine and advance the thinking about how to successfully improve schools—and school districts—and how to assist educators in their efforts to successfully re-culture schools into professional learning communities. We are indebted to them for their contributions and support, but more importantly for their encouragement and friendship.

Special thanks to Tracy Nelson and the English Language Arts Team, Scott Harrison, Cody Mothershead and the White River High School Math Team, Adam Uhler, Nick Hedman, Aaron Rummack, James Sims, Hugh Flint, Lisa Grace, Janis Heigl, and the White River High School Physical Science Team for your specific contributions to the book. Your examples and products greatly enhance this book.

Learning how to re-culture a school district into a high-performing professional learning community has been a challenging yet rewarding journey. We have been blessed to have our own laboratory. For over a decade, the school board, administrators, faculty, and support staff of the White River School District have been the perfect partners in our efforts to implement PLC practices throughout the entire district. It would be difficult, if not impossible, to overstate their professionalism and commitment to continuous improvement on behalf of kids. We owe the entire White River School District our sincere thanks and gratitude.

This book would not have been possible without the support of the outstanding professionals at Solution Tree. From our initial idea to final publication, we have enjoyed the encouragement, support, and professional advice from Douglas Rife, the president of Solution Tree Press, and our editor, Lesley Bolton. Their ideas, encouragement, hard work, and importantly, their friendship have been invaluable.

We would also like to acknowledge and thank Jeff Jones, the co-owner and CEO of Solution Tree. Jeff's commitment to the professional learning community concept and his leadership in disseminating PLC practices worldwide has served as an inspiration to us and has made our work, as well as the work of many others, possible. We are greatly indebted to Jeff for his continued support and unwavering friendship.

Last, we would like to acknowledge what we have learned from each other. Our thinking about how to re-culture school districts, schools, teams, and classrooms—kid by kid, skill by skill—has been enhanced by a decade of friendship and collaborative work. We are often asked how a "singleton" teacher (a teacher who is the only one teaching a grade level or subject) can be a member of a meaningful and productive team. Although one of us resides in the state of Washington and the other in Tennessee, we have proven that the lack of proximity does not rule out establishing rich collaborative partnerships. We each know more as a result of our teamwork than either of us would ever have learned individually.

Visit **go.solution-tree.com/PLCbooks**
to download materials related to this book.

# Table of Contents

CHAPTER 6

EPILOGUE

APPENDIX

# About the Authors

**R**obert Eaker, EdD, is professor emeritus in the department of educational leadership at Middle Tennessee State University, where he also served as dean of the College of Education and later as interim executive vice president and provost. He is a former fellow with the National Center for Effective Schools Research and Development, and in 1986, *Phi Delta Kappan* recognized him as one of North America's leaders in translating research into practice.

Bob has written widely on the issues of effective teaching, effective schools, helping teachers use research findings, and high expectations for student achievement, and he has coauthored with Richard and Rebecca DuFour numerous books and other resources on the topic of re-culturing schools and school districts into professional learning communities (PLCs).

In 1998, Bob was recognized by the governor of Tennessee as the recipient of Tennessee's Outstanding Achievement Award. Also in 1998, the Tennessee House of Representatives passed a proclamation recognizing him for his dedication and commitment to the field of education. In 2003, he was selected by the Middle Tennessee State University Student Government Association to receive the Womack Distinguished Faculty Award.

For over four decades, Bob has served as a consultant to school districts throughout North America and has been a frequent speaker at state, regional, and national meetings.

To learn more about Bob Eaker's work, visit allthingsplc.info.

**J**anel Keating is the superintendent of the White River School District in Buckley, Washington. An accomplished educator with more than thirty years of experience, Janel has served as an elementary and middle school teacher, elementary principal, director of student learning, and deputy superintendent. For eight years, Janel had the privilege of being the principal of Mountain Meadow Elementary School in Buckley, Washington. During her time there, Mountain Meadow was recognized as one of the highest academically performing elementary schools in the state. Janel has been named Principal of the Year in Pierce County, Washington. She presents at state and national events, is a coauthor with Rick DuFour, Rebecca DuFour, and Robert Eaker of *The Journey to Becoming a Professional Learning Community*, and coauthored with Robert Eaker the book *Every School, Every Team, Every Classroom*. She has written numerous articles on leadership and school improvement. She coauthored with Robert Eaker the lead chapter in the 2012 Yearbook of the National Council of Teachers of Mathematics. Janel was recently presented with the Carroll College 2013 Alumni Academic Achievement Award. The Alumni Academic Achievement Award is given to Carroll College alumni who have distinguished themselves academically.

Janel consults monthly with school districts throughout the United States. During the past ten years, Janel has shared her thinking to improve school systems, schools, teams, and classrooms with nearly 275 schools and school districts. She is past president of the Washington State Association for Supervision and Curriculum Development.

Janel earned a master's degree in educational leadership from the University of Idaho and a bachelor's degree in elementary education from Carroll College in Helena, Montana. She received a superintendent's certificate from Seattle Pacific University.

Janel's most important job is being the mother of Taylor Keating. Taylor is currently a junior at White River High School.

To book Robert Eaker or Janel Keating for professional development, contact pd@solution-tree.com.

# Introduction

Much has been written about the power of professional learning community (PLC) concepts and practices to positively impact the culture of school districts, schools, and classrooms in ways that significantly improve student achievement. Books, articles, and media products abound describing what PLCs are (and what they are not), how they should function, and how they differ from traditional schools. Likewise, much has been written about the role of effective leaders in the successful implementation of PLCs.

Remarkably, relatively little has been written about teachers in a professional learning community, with two exceptions: The fundamental structure of a PLC is the teacher team, and the literature is replete with information related to collaborative teaming. Likewise, the need for shared, or dispersed, leadership in a PLC has frequently been addressed. A number of researchers and writers have highlighted the need for developing teacher leaders and the importance of teacher leadership.

Here we bring teachers to the forefront. This is a book for teachers about teachers, about what it means to be a teacher in a professional learning community. Unless efforts to improve student achievement impact classroom teachers, good intentions and hard work will have little, if any, effect on student learning. After all, teachers are the heart and soul of any school, but especially schools that function as high-performing PLCs. We concur with Jon Saphier, Mary Ann Haley-Speca, and Robert Gower's (2008) observation:

> *Many things are important for good schools: curriculum is important; parental involvement is important; having a clean, safe building is important. But of all the things that are important to having good schools, nothing is as important as the teacher and what that person knows, believes, and can do. That is where the rubber meets the road in our business. (p. v)*

This book is for those who seek to gain a deep, rich understanding of the role teachers play in schools that function as a PLC. We wish to emphasize, however, that this book is not just for teachers. To be effective, we must be vicarious—that is, to possess the ability and willingness to look through the lenses of others. We believe it is helpful for leaders who aren't classroom teachers to reflect on what it means and looks like to be a teacher in a professional learning community, and therefore we encourage administrators and school leaders to read this book also. When we forget what it was like to be a student or a teacher, we end up doing things that are irrelevant to the very people whose behavior we hope to impact!

And importantly, we write this book to honor teachers and the heroic work they do day in and day out. At a time when teachers and the teaching profession are under constant attack, especially by many of our elected officials and those within the news media, it is important to reflect on the complexity and difficulty of what teachers are asked to do.

*When we forget what it was like to be a student or a teacher, we end up doing things that are irrelevant to the very people whose behavior we hope to impact!*

Think of the work of an elementary teacher who is expected not only to teach twenty-eight or more students to read, to write, to do mathematics, but also to help them become responsible learners and to ensure they acquire the social and interpersonal skills that will last them a lifetime. Many of these students come to teachers with special needs or English language deficiencies. On top of this, we want teachers to make our kids feel special by paying attention to their individual needs and by taking time to create a learning profile on each student.

Or imagine the critically important work of a middle school or high school teacher. It is common for these teachers to work with 150 or more students each day, teaching them at ever-increasing complexity and rigor levels, while all the time ushering them into adulthood. We must realize that we cannot have good communities without good schools and that we cannot have good schools without good teachers!

Teachers' work is not only complex and increasingly difficult, it is also honorable and should be valued, recognized, and celebrated. At the bare minimum, we should toss them a compliment periodically. Allen Mendler (2012), in his book *When Teaching Gets Tough,* reminds us that compliments go a long way in helping teachers feel affirmed in their work.

Teachers don't become teachers for the paycheck. It's all about those goose bump moments when a student connects with a concept that a teacher has been working on with the child for months. It's simply those moments and a few words of positive praise or feedback that a principal shares that can refuel a teacher. That's why they became teachers—to influence and feel it! Consider a strategy that Jeff Byrnes, principal at Mountain Meadow Elementary School, uses to provide praise and feedback to his staff.

Jeff uses feedback journals as a tool to celebrate all of the wonderful things he sees in classrooms on a day-to-day basis. This tool promotes all of the things we as educators want to observe in our classrooms every day from positive praise, to student engagement, to the rigorous work our kids are doing with the Common Core. He also records reflective questions, which typically lead to a conversation in the staff room or in the hallway. It's turned out to be a great way to open up dialogue as teachers see it as feedback, not evaluative. He uses this journal as well to leave personal notes such as "Have a great Thanksgiving" or "Congrats on the new grandchild." It is a chance for him to celebrate their work as teachers but also the big events in their lives. Let's take a look at an example.

Teacher to Jeff Byrnes regarding the feedback journals:

*Thank you for providing this journal opportunity for me, but, more importantly the rest of the Mountain Meadow staff. Your kind words and thoughtful praise will go a long way in building confidence in many folks. People will grow and become confident to do what they truly should do as teachers—take risks, make mistakes, fall down and get up, and through this process, they will create more meaningful and engaging ways to help kids reach their full learning potential.*

Jeff's note to teacher in the feedback journal:

*You always do such a wonderful job using academic vocabulary with your kids. By the way, your engagement rate was off the charts throughout the lesson!*

One teacher shared just how truly meaningful these journals have become: "I look forward to reading Jeff's comments each time he writes in it. His feedback is always positive, which boosts my spirits, makes me happy, and affirms that I am a great teacher! He focuses on different aspects of what he observes when in my room to include student accountability, engagement strategies, learning targets, classroom environment, pacing, student interaction, and more. Jeff knows that the key for us [teachers] to continue to grow is through feedback and thoughtful reflection. This starts with the positive comments he leaves in our journals, which spreads to the overall atmosphere and feel of the school. Because we have been 'built up' by positive comments, it is easy to discuss areas of growth that we need to work on to become an even more effective teacher, which in turn, positively affects student learning. Going back to my journal and being able to read and reflect on my teaching makes the tough days a little easier to handle and the great days more to celebrate."

It is unreasonable to ask teachers to successfully ensure high levels of learning for every student absent the resources and recognition they desperately need and deserve! We must realize that being a teacher means much, much more than achieving one year's worth of growth with one year's teaching. We prefer to see teachers through the lens of Henry Adams, who observes, "a teacher affects eternity; he can never tell where his influence stops" (as quoted in Chalfant & Wright, 2007, p. 20).

*It is unreasonable to ask teachers to successfully ensure high levels of learning for every student absent the resources and recognition they desperately need and deserve!*

Most of you probably agree that these are challenging times for teachers, to say the least. Never before have teachers been asked to accomplish so much in the rapidly changing and increasingly complex world of public schools and to do so with declining resources and support and under a seeming bombardment of negativity! It is little wonder that teachers are leaving the profession in droves. Results from the annual MetLife Survey of the American Teacher report teacher morale is at its lowest point in more than twenty years, with one in three teachers saying they are likely to leave the profession in the next three years. Teachers cite deep concerns over job security, effects of increased class size, and deep cuts in services and programs as having a negative impact on their morale and their willingness to remain in the profession (Santos, 2012).

But there is hope. More is known about how to improve student learning than ever before. Likewise, more is known about the kind of schools in which teachers can experience success and feel a sense of pride and accomplishment. Researchers and practitioners alike are calling for school cultures to reflect the practices of a professional learning community, not simply to raise student achievement, but also to provide a professional culture that will attract, develop, and keep excellent teachers. We must remember why we became teachers in the first place. Never once while Janel Keating was on the campus at Carroll College in Helena, Montana, did she state that she wanted to become a teacher to raise test scores. She wanted to be a role model for kids, to influence their lives and help them learn! Teachers flourish in schools and school districts that function as PLCs.

Consider this example: T. J. Suek, a fourth-grade teacher, sent Janel this note just before Christmas during his first year teaching: "Thank you for being so involved in the life of a first-year teacher. It's such a cool feeling to know the superintendent could swing by my room at any time and for me not to be nervous about it. I appreciate the collaboration time and community feeling that you've fostered throughout the district. I have great admiration for how this 'team thing' works! Thank you for all you do and so much more!"

## Teachers and the Power of PLCs

The concepts and practices that form the framework of a professional learning community offer our best hope for creating a school culture in which teachers can flourish, experience success, and gain a great deal of professional and personal satisfaction. The National Commission on Teaching and America's Future identifies the creation of schools as strong learning communities as one of the core strategies for improving both teaching and schools. The commission (2003) emphasizes:

> *Quality teaching requires strong, professional learning communities. Collegial interchange, not isolation, must become the norm for teachers. Communities of learning can no longer be considered utopian; they must become the building blocks that establish a new foundation for America's schools. (p. 17)*

The PLC concept is based on the belief that no program, no curriculum, no technology—and certainly no teacher-evaluation program, or loss of tenure, or loss of the right to enter into collective bargaining—will, in and of itself, be sufficient to meet the challenge of educating all students at high levels, no matter how honorable the intentions or how hard we try. We must recognize that for the most part these are *political* initiatives designed to meet long-term political goals, not necessarily *educational* initiatives to improve the learning levels of *all* students. Teachers remain the most important players in our efforts aimed at ensuring high levels of learning, and professional learning communities are structured to create conditions in which teachers are valued and where teachers can continue to grow and learn as professionals. It is no accident that the first word in the phrase "professional learning community" is the word *professional*!

The teacher's position is viewed differently in a school that functions as a PLC. In traditional schools, administrators are viewed as holding positions of leadership, and teachers are viewed more or less as holding implementation positions— implementing programs and initiatives that their administrative

> *We must recognize that teachers remain the most important players in our efforts aimed at ensuring high levels of learning.*

superiors or political appointees have selected and planned. PLCs break from this traditional norm and view teachers as the key transformational leaders in a school district. After all, who is in the best—and really *only*—position to enable students to successfully accomplish things they never thought they could possibly do? The answer is the classroom teacher!

PLCs not only focus on student learning, but on adult learning as well. Remember, the overall goal is more students learning more at higher levels. The kids won't learn more until the adults learn more. This focus on adult learning is reflective of a school culture in which teachers continually become more knowledgeable and skillful at doing the complex work of their profession. The culture of a PLC fosters conditions in which teachers continually improve and constantly review and analyze the results of their teaching. Thus, teachers *know* they are increasingly effective because they constantly—and importantly, collaboratively—review the results of their efforts. They are able to validate what strategies work with their students. This is a critical piece of the continuous improvement cycle.

The word *community* is especially powerful within the PLC context. The desire to belong, to be part of a successful endeavor, is an innate human desire, and we believe this desire is especially strong among teachers. PLCs break down the traditional barriers that lead to isolation, loneliness, and in many cases, a feeling of helplessness, by capturing the power of collaborative teaming. As a result of teachers working together doing critically important work, PLCs become places of mutual support, respect, interdependence, and importantly, mutual accountability. Schools move from places where teachers are asked to do seemingly impossible tasks by themselves in isolation from their colleagues to collaborative workplaces where educating all students at high levels seems inherently doable.

Last, schools that function as PLCs provide a culture of hope. Robert Evans (1996) argues, "Of all the factors vital to improving schools, none is more essential or vulnerable—than hope" (p. 290). Richard DuFour, Rebecca DuFour, Robert Eaker, and Thomas Many (2010) note:

> *Professional learning communities set out to restore and increase the passion of teachers by not only reminding them of the moral purpose of their work, but also by creating the conditions that allow them to do that work successfully. The focus is on making a positive difference in the lives of kids rather than raising test scores. . . . They make heroes of staff members by weaving a never-ending story of committed people who touch both the minds and the hearts of their students. (p. 264)*

By focusing on the learning of each student, teachers in a PLC are constantly coming face to face with the "why" question: Why are we doing this work? The answer lies in the data and the student faces; it lies in meaningful conversations that elicit the dreams for the kids, schools, or school district. Simon Sinek (2009) in his book *Start With Why*, highlights that Dr. Martin Luther King Jr. was absolute in his conviction. He knew change had to happen in the United States. His clarity of why, his sense of purpose, gave him the strength and energy to continue his fight against seemingly insurmountable odds. He gave the "I Have a Dream" speech, not the "I Have a Plan" speech. Ask: "What is your dream?" It's our hope that the ideas embedded in this book will help you fulfill your dreams for your school and your students.

## About This Book

Effective educators, whether they are teachers or administrators, have the ability to see the big picture, to tie everything together, to connect the dots. Chapter 1, "Looking Inside a Professional Learning Community," takes an inside look at what it is like to teach in a school that functions as a professional learning community from the teacher's standpoint.

We believe being a highly effective teacher starts on the inside, with one's most basic beliefs and assumptions. Being a teacher in a PLC involves much more than being a member of a collaborative team or assuming an expanded leadership role within the school or school district. To put it as succinctly as possible, because teachers are called on to behave differently in a PLC, they must reflect on their most cherished beliefs, assumptions, attitudes, and behaviors in ways that go to the very core of what it means to be a teacher. Chapter 2, "Being a Teacher in a Professional Learning Community," gives focus to the beliefs, assumptions, attitudes, and behaviors that we believe are prerequisite for being an effective teacher in a professional learning community.

Schools have become so complex it is almost impossible for even the best teachers to successfully ensure that all of their students are learning at high levels when they work by themselves. The power of collaborative teaming enhances virtually every major factor related to teacher effectiveness. Chapter 3, "Working in Collaborative Teams," explores what teachers *do* in a collaborative team by providing sample products that teams create. Importantly, the chapter also provides a deep discussion of the assumptions, attitudes, and commitments teachers must have if they, and their teams, are to be successful.

More is known now than ever before about the relationship between teacher behaviors in the classroom and student achievement. Few areas have been as widely researched—and misused—as research findings related to effective instructional practices. Chapter 4, "Using the Effective Teacher's Toolbox,"

> *The power of collaborative teaming enhances virtually every major factor related to teacher effectiveness.*

makes a case for increasing teacher effectiveness by enhancing the instructional practices of teachers within the framework of collective inquiry—seeking out and utilizing best practices.

The quantity and quality of student learning is linked to how students behave. Effective teachers realize that reacting to student misbehavior isn't nearly as effective as managing to prevent student misconduct. Chapter 5, "Managing Classroom Behavior," provides specific, research-based examples of how teachers can better manage their classrooms in order to reduce student misbehavior and increase student learning.

A school that functions as a professional learning community reflects an intense and passionate focus on results. Chapter 6, "Teaching in a Results-Oriented Culture," describes how a focus on results is reflected in the practices of individual teachers and teacher teams in a PLC.

The epilogue ties it all together and reflects the powerful impact teachers make in their students' lives—day in and day out!

One last note about this book: The term *professional learning communities* has become enormously popular throughout the world, especially in North America—so much so that the term has come to mean many different things to different people. We want to be clear. The concepts and practices described in this book are based on the Professional Learning Communities at Work™ framework DuFour and Eaker (1998) developed in their book *Professional Learning Communities at Work*, and later revised in *Revisiting Professional Learning Communities at Work* (DuFour, DuFour, & Eaker, 2008).

There are many schools throughout the world achieving unprecedented results because they function as a professional learning community. Parents and their children deserve such schools. Equally important, teachers deserve to experience success both personally and professionally. It is our sincere hope that this book provides a useful framework for how teachers are viewed and how they view themselves. After all, our students and the teachers who teach them deserve nothing less.

# Chapter 1
# Looking Inside a Professional Learning Community

*There is no more powerful engine driving an organization toward excellence and long-range success than an attractive, worthwhile and achievable vision of the future, widely shared.*

—Burt Nanus

The professional learning community (PLC) concept is based on the overarching assumption that the purpose of public schools is to ensure that all students learn at high levels. The big learning is the work layered under the four critical questions and how to operationalize the work in classrooms, teams, schools, and the district:

1. What do we want students to learn?

2. How will we know if they've learned it?

3. What will we do if they haven't learned it?

4. What will we do if they've demonstrated proficiency?

The commitment to ensuring that students learn rather than merely being taught has huge ramifications for all stakeholders—especially teachers. As Richard DuFour, Rebecca DuFour, Robert Eaker, and Thomas Many (2010) observe:

> *Every educator—every teacher, counselor, principal, central office staff member, and superintendent—will be called upon to redefine his or her role and responsibilities. People comfortable working in isolation will be asked to work collaboratively. People accustomed to hoarding authority will be asked to share*

> *it. People who have operated under certain assumptions their*
> *entire careers will be asked to change them. (p. 248)*

These changes manifest themselves in multiple ways, both structurally and culturally, but most significantly in the expectation that administrators and teachers are mutually accountable for enhancing student learning and that they must provide mutual support to each other in doing so.

## A Simultaneous Loose-Tight Framework

Teachers who teach in a PLC are part of a school (and hopefully a district) culture of mutual accountability that is simultaneously loose and tight. When Tom Peters and Robert Waterman (1982) studied some of America's best-run companies in order to determine what practices they had in common, they discovered these companies reflected a culture that was both loose (encouraging experimentation, autonomy, creativity) and tight (non-negotiable in such areas as the mission, vision, and core values). They observe:

> *Having a culture that is simultaneously loose and tight is in*
> *essence the co-existence of firm central direction and maximum*
> *individual autonomy. Organizations that live by the loose-tight*
> *principle are on the one hand rigidly controlled, yet at the same*
> *time allow (indeed insist on) autonomy, entrepreneurship, and*
> *innovation from the rank and file. (p. 318)*

The efficacy of a culture that is both loose and tight has also been documented in research related to effective school districts. For example, Timothy Waters and Robert Marzano (2006) refer to the concept as "defined autonomy" (p. 8). Other writers, such as Eaker and Keating (2012), refer to such a culture as "simultaneous top down and bottom up" (p. 15). Whatever the term, the implications for teachers cannot be overemphasized. Successful teachers who work collaboratively in a PLC are constantly experimenting, trying out new approaches, and making decisions, but all within a clearly defined framework of a collaboratively developed mission, vision, and clearly articulated shared commitments. Teachers who resent any top-down direction and seek to work in a school with few, if any, boundaries will struggle in a school that functions as a professional learning community.

## Mutual Accountability and Support

Balancing this culture of tightness in which there are clear expectations about the framework within which everyone works is a culture of support. This support is reflected in many ways, most notably being the support from fellow team members. Teachers aren't asked to go it alone; additional support is provided culturally. This culture of mutual support is reflected in the concept of reciprocal accountability—direction from the top will be accompanied by a corresponding level of support. PLC leaders recognize they have an obligation to provide staff with the resources, training, mentoring, and support to help them successfully accomplish what they have been asked to do. Richard Elmore (2006) defines the obligation this way: "For every increment of performance I demand of you, I have an equal responsibility to provide you with the capacity to meet that expectation" (p. 93).

The mutual accountability and support culture is reflected every day as teachers work together to enhance the success of their school, each other, and their students. Teachers in PLCs are supportive of each other. The concepts of interdependence, common goals, and mutual accountability drive collaborative teamwork.

The foundation of an accountability culture that is both loose and tight is a clearly articulated mission—the core purpose that drives everything that happens, every day. DuFour et al. (2008) point out:

> *Clarity of purpose and a willingness to accept responsibility for achieving that purpose are critical to school improvement. Unfortunately, however, many educators interpreted our advocacy for shared mission as a call to write a new mission statement. . . . There is an enormous difference between writing a mission statement and* living *a mission. (p. 114)*

Being a teacher in a school that functions as a true professional learning community means *living* a school's mission of ensuring high levels of student learning for all students.

It is impossible for teachers to be accountable for embedding a mission of ensuring student learning in their work without being clear on what such work would look like. If a school successfully embeds its written mission statement into its day-to-day practices, what would it look like? Janel helped administrators, faculty, and staff in her district clarify this question by asking them to collaboratively specify what would take place in the district if they really meant it when they said they wanted all students to learn at high levels: What would people see us doing? DuFour et al. (2008) propose the following eleven actions that someone would routinely see in a school that really means it when it advocates a learning mission.

> *Being a teacher in a school that functions as a true professional learning community means* living *a school's mission of ensuring high levels of student learning for all students.*

> 1. *Every teacher is engaged in a process to clarify what each student is to learn in each grade level, each course, and each unit of instruction.*
>
> 2. *Every teacher is engaged in a process to clarify consistent criteria by which to assess the quality of student work.*
>
> 3. *Every teacher is engaged in a process to assess student learning on a timely and frequent basis through the use of teacher-developed common formative assessments.*
>
> 4. *Every school has a specific plan to ensure that students who experience initial difficulty in learning are provided with*

*additional time and support for learning during the school day in a timely and directive way that does not cause the student to miss any new direct instruction.*

5. *Every school has a specific plan to enrich and extend the learning of students who are not challenged by the required curriculum.*

6. *All professionals are organized into collaborative teams and are given the time and structure during their regular workday to collaborate with colleagues on specific issues that directly impact student learning.*

7. *Every collaborative team of teachers is called upon to work interdependently to achieve a common SMART goal for which members of the team are mutually accountable.*

8. *Every teacher receives frequent and timely information regarding the success of his or her students in learning the essential curriculum and then uses that information to identify strengths and weaknesses as part of a process of continuous improvement.*

9. *Building shared knowledge of best practice is part of the process of shared decision making at both the school and team level.*

10. *Every practice and procedure in place in the school has been examined to assess its impact on learning.*

11. *School leaders are held accountable for ensuring all of the above happen. (pp. 116–117)*

A PLC depends on a faculty composed of teachers who embrace (through their beliefs, attitudes, and behavior) the parameters reflected in the characteristics listed previously. It's not enough that a teacher is willing to teach in a school that lives a learning mission; he or she must be excited about getting to teach in a school that is tight about a passionate and persistent focus on improving the learning of every student.

## Collective Commitments

A culture of mutual accountability means much more than pursuing the promise of a school's mission and vision. Teachers in a PLC enthusiastically engage in processes with their colleagues that lead to specific shared commitments and values for both the team and the school. Importantly, teachers engage in this process with fidelity—absolutely believing that developing shared commitments is important and can have a significant impact on student success. John Kotter notes that the central challenge of changing culture is "changing people's behavior" (Kotter & Cohen, 2002, p. 2). Engaging in a collaborative process to develop collective commitments is one of the most powerful activities for shaping values that can ultimately transform the culture of a school or district.

It is critical that teachers understand the connection that ties values and commitments together. Collective commitments are shaped by the school's values, just as the school's values are displayed in the commitments people are willing to make. As Ken Blanchard (2007) writes:

> *Values provide guidelines on how you should proceed as you pursue your purpose and picture of the future. They need to be clearly described so that you know exactly what behaviors demonstrate that the value is being lived. Values need to be consistently acted on, or they are only good intentions. (p. 30)*

But articulating core values is never enough. The question that flows from articulated values is: If these are the things we value, what, then, are we prepared to do?

For example, the White River School District in Buckley, Washington, has used the power of collective commitments by asking all staff members to consider the questions: What would it look like if we really meant it when we said we embrace learning as our fundamental purpose, or we will build a collaborative culture, or we will use evidence of results to respond to student needs and improve our practice? What commitments are we prepared to make to every student who walks into our schools this fall? What commitments are we prepared to make to one another as we attempt to create a professional learning community? Educators at all levels are asked to participate in a deliberate effort to identify the specific ways they will act to improve their organizations and then commit to one another that they will act accordingly.

While focusing on improving reading achievement, one elementary school in the district, Mountain Meadow, made a collective commitment that "the children *most in need* will receive the *most help* from the *most skilled staff.*" In order to fulfill this commitment, a school-leadership team started by making adjustments to the master schedule to ensure the schedule reflected meeting the students' needs, and collaborative teacher teams began reviewing formative assessment results together and making timely instructional changes to meet each student's needs. They developed plans to provide students who were experiencing difficulty with additional time and support within the school day, and they began reporting student progress to parents on a weekly basis. These practices represented a seismic cultural shift from the days when kids most in need received help from paraprofessionals who had minimal training and little direct guidance from a classroom teacher or when parents only received formal progress reports every nine weeks.

A word of caution: Collective commitments should not be confused with developing a shared vision for a school. Vision describes an attractive future for the organization, but its focus is on the organization and the future: "Someday we hope our school will be a place where . . ." Collective commitments clarify how each individual can contribute to the work, and they have a much more immediate focus: "This is what I can do today to help create the school we want." We can think of collective commitments as a series of "if-then" statements. For example:

- *If* we are to be a school that ensures high levels of learning for all students, *then* we must commit to monitor each student's learning on a timely basis using a variety of assessment strategies and create systems to ensure they receive additional time and support as soon as they experience difficulty in their learning.

- *If* we are to create a collaborative culture, *then* we must commit to be positive, contributing members to our collaborative teams and accept collective responsibility for the success of our colleagues and our students.

Another example of collective commitments is provided in figure 1.1.

---

The **vision** of Mountain Meadow Elementary School is to provide leadership, professional staff development, alignment of curriculum, assessment, and instruction in a caring learning environment and to build parent and community partnerships.

The **mission** of Mountain Meadow Elementary School is to ensure high levels of learning for each child, preparing them for future success.

We have established the following **collective commitments** in order to accomplish our mission and make our vision a reality. They represent our shared purpose and will guide us daily as we interact with our learners, peers, and community.

**The Mountain Meadow Learning Community will . . .**

1. Respectfully collaborate around revising and informing our instruction based on learning data and standards.

2. Proactively and intentionally work with all learners and provide extra time and support.

3. Make learning targets clear to help each learner achieve standard and reach the target.

4. Model lifelong learning and the commitment to quality work with continual growth.

5. Actively involve parents and community in the learning process.

---

Figure 1.1: Mountain Meadow Elementary vision, mission, and collective commitments.

*Source: White River School District. Used with permission.*

## Being a Contributing Member of a Collaborative Team

The most visible structural and cultural dynamic you witness in a school truly functioning as a PLC is teachers working with their colleagues in collaborative teams. Teacher teams are the engines that drive PLC work. They are the heart and soul of "how things are done."

What is a collaborative team, and what do teachers do as members of a high-performing team? DuFour et al. (2008) write:

> *Collaboration is a means to an end, not the end itself. In many schools, staff members are willing to collaborate on a variety of topics as long as the focus of the conversation stops at their classroom door. In a PLC, collaboration is a systematic process*

*in which teachers work together, interdependently, to analyze and impact professional practice in order to improve results for their students, their team, and their school. (pp. 15–16)*

What would it be like to teach in a school that functions as a high-performing PLC? Unlike in traditional schools where teachers often work in isolation, teachers in a PLC are expected to be contributing members of collaborative teams, and the collaboration is purposeful. Great care is given to the makeup of each team, with the primary organizing idea being that team members should teach, generally, the same content. For example, an elementary teacher may be on the third-grade team or a member of a prekindergarten–second-grade vertical team.

At the middle school or high school level, a teacher might be a member of the mathematics team, or in a larger school, he or she may be a member of the mathematics team but spend the majority of time with a course-specific team such as an algebra team or a geometry team. The point is, teachers have a shared purpose for being on a collaborative team, and that purpose is to improve student learning!

*Teachers have a shared purpose for being on a collaborative team, and that purpose is to improve student learning!*

## Foundations for Future Work

What collaborative team members do in a PLC goes far beyond collaborative conversations. Early on, the team develops foundational pieces for its future work. For example, team members collaboratively develop team norms—guidelines for how the team will do its work day in and day out. They frequently refer to the norms, using them to guide the quality of their interactions.

Determining what students should be taught by clarifying and adding meaning to standards is the basic foundation piece of a collaborative team's work. The team engages in a deep, rich study of the state and national standards. In traditional schools, it is generally left to individual teachers to interpret what the standards mean and the relative importance of each standard. In PLCs, collaborative teams of teachers become students of the standards, clarifying the meaning of each standard and developing common pacing guides to ensure adequate time is being given to the essential learning outcomes—or as Doug Reeves (2002) refers to them, the "power standards."

Through the work of collaborative teams, teachers develop what Marzano (2003) refers to as a "guaranteed and viable" curriculum. Simply put, students are guaranteed the same curriculum regardless of the teachers they are assigned or the school they attend. Additionally, because teacher teams collaborate about the amount of time needed to effectively teach each standard and for students to learn each standard, the curriculum is viable. A word of caution: care should be given not to let commercially prepared materials become the guaranteed and viable curriculum.

Once teams, and ultimately the entire district, develop a guaranteed and viable curriculum, the teams then begin to drill deeper into their work. They focus their discussions on questions such as, What would student work look like if this particular standard is met? In more traditional schools, even when teachers align their instruction to the standards, there can be a wide disparity among teachers' expectations for high-quality student performance.

*Once teams, and ultimately the entire district, develop a guaranteed and viable curriculum, the teams then begin to drill deeper into their work.*

Developing rubrics for high-quality student work naturally leads to the discussion of common scoring of student products and about reporting student progress. The collaborative team is continually engaged in rich dialogue around what is essential for all students to know and be able to do—sharpening the content in order for students to learn in deeper and more meaningful ways.

### Common Formative Assessments

The team next moves to the rather logical question, How will we know if our students are learning? Collaborative teams in PLCs develop common formative assessments to monitor each student's learning, skill by skill, on a frequent and timely basis. Collaborative teams aren't content with merely clarifying what students must learn. They pursue a cultural shift from an almost exclusive reliance on summative assessments to more frequent, collaboratively developed, common formative assessments. Simply put, teachers in a PLC recognize that students are more apt to perform well on high-stakes summative assessments if the quality of their learning is regularly monitored along the way—especially when the results of the formative assessments are used to provide students with additional time or support, or to extend the learning of students who demonstrate proficiency.

This also helps teachers and leaders understand the answer to these questions: Don't we do a lot of assessing already? What assessments are the most important? The common formative assessments closest to the student and teacher are the most important. These assessments, such as quick checks for understanding, are more responsive in nature. This means the teacher and the student can respond to the data *tomorrow*. The next most important assessments are the team-created common assessments, including the common end-of-the-unit assessments. These assessments give the teacher and student data regarding the learning of the specific standards in a particular unit. There is tremendous power in the combination of quick checks for understanding and common formative assessments—especially the end-of-unit common assessment. Effective teachers and teams realize that if you frequently check for understanding, you are able to catch kids who are struggling along the way and provide them with specific and focused time and support. There will be fewer kids who need additional time and support at the end of the unit.

You might ask, "What about the district benchmark assessments?" Many districts administer benchmark assessments three times a year, especially in reading and math. These assessments give more general information to see if students are making progress on grade-level standards and if curriculum resources are effective. Think about it. There should be no surprises regarding how a student does on the state assessment. If a student does well on his or her daily and weekly checks for understanding, the common formative assessments, the end-of-unit assessments, and the benchmark assessments, and receives focused time and support, the student will likely do well on the state assessment.

### Student Learning Data

The power of formative assessments lies in how they are utilized. During team collaboration time, teachers collaboratively analyze student learning data, as well as examples of student work. They discuss assessment results, item by item, and the effectiveness of the assessment itself. Teachers highlight strengths in student learning and identify areas of concern. They share instructional strategies that were used, learning from each other's strengths. They monitor the learning of each student, skill by skill. Most importantly, they plan together, collaboratively deciding on appropriate interventions for students, planning units of instruction, sharing instructional strategies and materials, reflecting on the effectiveness of instructional practices that were utilized, and setting goals. In short, they drill deep into their kids' learning and their effectiveness as a team—both short term and long term.

The very act of collaboration around student learning data is a perfect example of job-embedded staff development. The process forces teachers to reflect on and sharpen their understanding of two critical questions: (1) What do we want students to learn, and (2) How will we provide additional time and support and extend the learning of our students who demonstrate proficiency once we have collaboratively analyzed the results? The collaborative analysis of learning data also forces teachers, both individually and as a team, to reflect on the effectiveness of their instructional practices and forms a basis for discussions for improving lessons the next time the unit is taught. This is an example of the continuous improvement cycle in action.

> *The power of formative assessments lies in how they are utilized.*

Effective teams keep this information on the share drive and review the information prior to teaching the same unit the next year. They want to be sure to use the same effective strategies, and they want to remember where students struggled. They don't want students to struggle with the same content or skills next year. They will know to build in additional time, possibly provide more scaffolding, or use a different strategy or resource. This information is also very helpful the following year to any new member of this team.

## Additional Time and Support

Since students learn at different rates and in different ways, teachers in a school that functions as a PLC recognize that some students, even their best students, struggle with specific skills. When they do, they need additional time and support— as well as encouragement. In more traditional schools, teachers are left to fend for themselves when they realize some kids just aren't getting it. There is only so much the best intentioned and talented teachers can do by themselves. The number of students who need additional time and support is often too great, and the range of needs is often too wide. The absence of a schoolwide systematic plan to provide struggling students with additional time and support sets both students and teachers up for failure. On the other hand, teachers in a PLC have the benefit of a systematic schoolwide plan of layered interventions that provide students with help when they experience difficulty in their learning. If a school does everything else at a high level of quality but fails to provide additional time and support when students experience difficulty, the school's effectiveness will decline.

Further, schools that function as professional learning communities recognize it is their moral obligation to help struggling students. As DuFour et al. (2010) observe, "It is disingenuous for any school to claim its purpose is to help all students learn at high levels and then fail to create a system of intervention to give struggling learners additional time and support for learning" (p. 104).

What does additional time and support look like in a PLC? Following the advice of DuFour et al. (2010), first and foremost, it follows a systematic plan that is timely and directive, rather than merely invitational. Because the plan is composed of a series of sequential layers, students benefit from ever-increasing focused support based on their level of need. Initially, most interventions occur within the classroom. For example, a teacher simply might reteach a particular skill set. Perhaps students who demonstrate proficiency assist students who are struggling. However, some students may need the benefit of more intense interventions such as a tutor or time in a mathematics lab or a specific language program. In a PLC, students have the benefit of planned interventions designed to help them learn each essential skill.

*In a PLC, students have the benefit of planned interventions designed to help them learn each essential skill.*

Of course, not all students need additional time and support. Many students demonstrate proficiency in their learning, and they could learn more. All schools have students who make excellent grades but are "under learning." In most schools, it is left up to individual teachers to develop ways to enrich or extend student learning. Again, there is only so much even the most dedicated teachers can do by themselves. Being a teacher in a PLC means having the benefit of a schoolwide plan to enrich and extend student learning, stretching them far beyond proficiency.

## Homework and Grading

Teachers in a PLC have deep discussions about topics that are rarely addressed in traditional schools yet have a huge impact on student learning. For example, teams discuss issues such as grading and homework. They study the research about effective grading and homework policies and practices. They work to gain shared knowledge by referring to resources such as John Hattie's (2009) review and synthesis of literally hundreds of research studies. They collaboratively address such questions as: What is the purpose of homework? How much homework is appropriate? How much weight will homework have in grading? What happens when students do not complete their homework or if it is completed incorrectly? In traditional schools, these questions—and many more like them—are left almost entirely to the discretion of individual teachers. Teaching in a PLC means that *teacher teams* tackle important and complex issues that have a huge impact on student learning.

Importantly, teaching in a PLC also means that teachers benefit from collaborative planning. In addition to clarifying and adding meaning to state and national standards, team members engage in rich discussions around unit planning. For example, they collaboratively review the standards, discuss preassessment ideas and share instructional strategies and materials, develop common scoring rubrics and quick checks for understanding, and share ideas about how to provide students with appropriate practice and high-quality feedback. In a PLC, student success is impacted by collaborative planning that occurs in collaborative teams.

## Adult Learning

What about the learning of adults in a PLC? Schools that function as professional learning communities embrace the assumption that improved *student* learning is inexorably linked to improved *adult* learning, and adult learning can best be accomplished by doing the work of a high-performing collaborative team. As Jeffrey Pfeffer and Robert Sutton (2000) observe:

> *The answer to the knowing-doing problem is deceptively simple: Embed more of the process of acquiring new knowledge in the actual doing of the task and less in the formal training programs that are frequently ineffective. If you do it, then you will know it. (p. 27)*

Thus, teachers engage in professional growth experiences that flow up from the learning needs of their students and their team rather than down from arbitrary and random ideas about what they need or what they might enjoy. Their learning is truly job-embedded.

Consider this example from the White River School District. Effective professional development can begin with a conversation. A team looks at data—maybe from the previous year, maybe from a unit they just completed—and realizes there are some gaps in their instructional practices. This occurred recently when a fourth-grade teacher contacted the English language arts teacher on special assignment with a request for some help with opinion writing for her team. Her team knew this was an area in which they had not done as well as they wanted during the previous year, because it was such a new focus in writing as Common Core State Standards rolled out. With a districtwide, three- to five-team-leader English language arts (ELA) meeting approaching, the ELA teacher on special assignment asked the rest of the team to share what their team needs might be looking ahead to the next unit. Others voiced a need for more work around opinion writing. Work on clearly understanding the academic vocabulary related to the upcoming unit was also suggested as a need.

With this in mind, the professional development / common learning time focused on these two areas. Grade-level team leader teams first worked through the process of identifying the common academic vocabulary for the unit ahead. The teams spent time looking more deeply into their opinion writing standard—how it connected to the anchor standard, what the same standard asked learners to do at the grade level before and grade level after, and how the standard could be repacked into day-by-day learning targets to help learners achieve mastery of the standard by the end of the unit. With this common thinking in place, instructional strategies and materials were shared to help build teachers' and teams' capacity to provide quality instruction around the standard.

Since each building had a representative at each grade level, the learning flowed back to the building teams through the team leaders. Professional development such as this can strengthen teachers' and teams' daily lesson planning for particular units of instruction. This is an example of need-based, real-time/real-life professional development.

Numerous researchers and practitioners have endorsed the efficacy of job-embedded professional development such as the previous example. DuFour et al. (2008) summarize these findings by noting:

> *The message is consistent and clear. The best professional development occurs in a social and collaborative setting rather than in isolation, is ongoing and sustained rather than infrequent and transitory, is job-embedded rather than external, occurs in the context of the real work of the school and classroom rather than in off-site workshops and courses, focuses on results (that is, evidence of improved student learning) rather than activities or perceptions, and is systematically aligned with school and district goals rather than random. In short, the best professional development takes place in professional learning communities. (pp. 369–370)*

Some of the best job-embedded learning occurs when there are glitches along the way. Dealing with issues that appear unexpectedly can lead to new learning for a team and individuals within the team. The work of a team, if it is the right work and is monitored and enhanced, is the most effective form of staff development because it is job-embedded and focuses on the real world of classroom teachers.

## Recognition and Celebration

Imagine teaching in a school where faculty and staff's efforts and achievements are publicly recognized and celebrated. In schools that function as professional learning communities, there is the recognition that effectively ensuring that all students learn is a difficult, complex, and incremental endeavor, and that the improvement process can only be sustained, over time, if those who are doing the work day in and day out know their hard work and incremental success are recognized and appreciated. As James Kouzes and Barry Posner (2006) note, "There are few if any needs more basic than to be noticed, recognized, and appreciated for our efforts . . . extraordinary achievements never bloom in barren and unappreciative settings" (p. 44). PLC leaders do not leave recognition and celebration to chance or to the goodwill of others. They shape the school's culture, and ultimately the behavior of those within it, through planned, purposeful, and most importantly, sincere and meaningful recognition and celebration of the behaviors they value the most.

> *PLC leaders do not leave recognition and celebration to chance or to the goodwill of others.*

# Chapter 2

# Being a Teacher in a Professional Learning Community

*The key to ensuring that every child has a quality teacher is finding a way for school systems to organize the work of qualified teachers so they can collaborate with their colleagues in developing strong learning communities that will sustain them as they become more accomplished teachers.*

—National Commission on Teaching and America's Future

Being a great teacher is about so much more than test scores or instructional strategies. While instructional strategies and methodology are certainly important, we do not believe these are the first things that should be examined when discussing teachers, teaching, or the teaching profession—especially when discussing what it means to be a teacher in a PLC. The place to start is with the core beliefs, assumptions, and attitudes that every teacher brings to the table. Instructional strategies—as important as they are—only take a teacher so far. Ultimately, the fundamental beliefs, values, and assumptions that drive the way the teacher thinks and, by extension, behaves determine his or her effectiveness. Taken together, they determine the lens through which teachers view the world of schools and students. They determine the nature and quality of teachers' interactions with their colleagues, administrators, parents, and most important, their students.

*Ultimately, the fundamental beliefs, values, and assumptions that drive the way the teacher thinks and, by extension, behaves determine his or her effectiveness.*

It is important for each of us to reflect on the assumptions we hold dear. For many of us, our basic assumptions go largely unexamined since they were acquired incrementally over time. Such reflection can help us drill deeper into the real world of teachers and what underlies the hundreds of decisions teachers make each day. While there is no one correct checklist, we believe the following areas form the basis for self-reflection—and group discussion—regarding the beliefs, assumptions, and attitudes central to being an effective teacher in a PLC.

- Enthusiasm for the opportunity to teach
- Focus on learning
- Teacher expectations
- School effects and high expectations
- Self-efficacy
- Reflection on how students learn best
- An effort-based classroom
- Parent involvement
- Continuous professional development

## Enthusiasm for the Opportunity to Teach

Being an effective teacher is hard work in any school, but this is especially true in a professional learning community. In addition to creating a safe, orderly, and supportive environment in which students are made to feel special, teachers in PLCs are asked to work collaboratively with their colleagues and parents to ensure high levels of learning for all students, kid by kid, skill by skill. This intense and persistent focus on the learning of each student requires energy, enthusiasm, and a positive attitude—the kind of attitude exhibited by Margaret Ann Smith, who taught Latin and English literature at Providence Christian Academy in Murfreesboro, Tennessee. Mrs. Smith taught until her health forced her retirement when she was well into her eighties! Even in her last year of teaching, she simply gushed with excitement and enthusiasm about her students and going to school each day. She shared with everyone how much she loved teaching Latin and her students. Mrs. Smith saw teaching as a wonderful opportunity, rather than merely a job she had to do. In other words, she reflected the attitude and enthusiasm of a "get to" teacher ("I *get to* do this job!") rather than a "have to" teacher ("I *have to* go to work today").

*Teachers in PLCs are asked to work collaboratively with their colleagues and parents to ensure high levels of learning for all students, kid by kid, skill by skill.*

We believe Mrs. Smith provides an excellent example of the first question teachers need to ask themselves, "Am I a have-to teacher, or am I a get-to teacher?" It is unreasonable to think that students will be more energetic, enthusiastic, or demonstrate a more positive attitude about learning than their teacher. Furthermore, it is virtually impossible for a have-to teacher to successfully accomplish the high-quality collaborative work that is expected of teachers in a PLC. Approaching teaching as a job with an "August is over; I've got to go back to work" attitude really has no place when it comes to being a role model and improving learning for our kids.

## Focus on Learning

Of course, looking inside ourselves requires much more than simply examining the motivation that drove us to be teachers in the first place. At the very core of what we do each day as teachers is our fundamental belief about what it means to be a teacher—the very work we signed on to do. Grant Wiggins (2010) argues that fundamental school reform "begins with a serious ongoing and in-depth dialogue about the essential question of teaching: what's my job as a teacher *really*?" (p. 28).

As simple as this question may seem, there is a wide range of teacher views regarding the most basic, fundamental role of a teacher. For example, most of us, at one time or another, has heard a teacher proclaim, "It's my job to teach, but it's the student's job to learn!" At the core of this attitude is a belief that many teachers hold—that is, the fundamental role of a teacher is to teach. Teachers who hold this belief place great emphasis on getting the content covered. They feel they have fulfilled their responsibility once the content has been taught.

Teachers in a PLC are asked to make a fundamental shift—a shift from a primary focus on teaching to a focus on the learning of each individual kid, skill by skill. Teaching is seen as a means to this end, rather than an end in itself. The fundamental questions that drive teachers in a professional learning community are, Have the students learned, and how do we know? rather than Have I taught the content; did I get it all covered?

This shift from a focus on teaching to a focus on learning is much more than mere semantics. It goes to the very heart of what it means to be a teacher, simply because teachers' beliefs about the fundamental purpose of schools and what it means to be a teacher drive how they think and ultimately what they *do*! The action verbs matter!

Teachers in a PLC also know that being a teacher involves much, much more than ensuring one year's growth in student achievement with one year's instruction. They impact the lives of their students in ways that are immeasurable, almost impossible to describe, and maybe even unrecognizable at the time. Consider Bob Eaker's experience in his English class during his junior year in high school.

Mr. Pearson was perhaps the most highly respected teacher at Ringgold High School in rural North Georgia. He had high expectations of his students but was also viewed as being friendly and fair. He was calm, yet it was obvious he was passionate about literature. One day at the end of the period, Mr. Pearson called Bob to his desk. He said something to the effect of, "Bobby, you are a good student, but you should be reading more than the things we read in school. You should expand your mind. Here, take this and read it, and then I want to talk with you about it."

> *Being a teacher involves much, much more than ensuring one year's growth in student achievement with one year's instruction.*

After all these years, Bob still remembers the title—*A Moon and Sixpence* by W. Somerset Maugham. Bob points out that it was not the particular book that changed his life that day, but the fact that Mr. Pearson thought he was special and that he could be more than what was traditionally expected of students in that small North Georgia community. And importantly, Bob developed a lifelong love for reading. To this day when asked what he is reading, Bob will invariably answer by naming at least three or four titles. Mr. Pearson also taught Bob another valuable lesson: Being a teacher and ensuring students learn is about so much more than instructional strategies. It's about having a positive impact on student lives that lasts a lifetime.

Because it is so basic, it's often overlooked, but perhaps the most important question a teacher should ask when looking inside—regardless of whether they are just entering the profession or a seasoned veteran—is, "What does it *really* mean to be a teacher?"

## Teacher Expectations

This leads us to a particular aspect of how teachers view their students, and themselves, that warrants special attention. The expectation lens is of critical importance in a school that functions as a PLC since teachers in such a school accept the proposition that it is their school's core purpose to ensure that *all* students learn at high levels. Obviously, it will be impossible to fulfill this core purpose if teachers hold low expectations for some students or if they do not have confidence in their own ability to ensure their students learn.

Simply put, some teachers operate from the idea that it is the natural order for only some of the students to learn. Such teachers believe that some students won't learn and others will excel simply because learning is directly linked to ability, and ability is unequally distributed among the population—*and ability is unalterable*. And since they cannot alter the ability of students, it's only natural that some get it and some don't. Further, it is the teachers' role to maintain high standards so that the cream will eventually rise to the top. This belief has played a dominant role in education for decades, even centuries.

George Bernard Shaw (1916/2003) captured the power of expectations in his play *Pygmalion*. In Act V of the play, Liza Doolittle tells Colonel Pickering how he differs from Professor Henry Higgins.

> *Liza: ". . . But do you know what began my real education?"*
>
> *Pickering: "What?"*
>
> *Liza: "Your calling me Miss Doolittle that day when I first came to Wimpole Street. That was the beginning of self-respect for me. And there were a hundred little things you never noticed, because they came naturally to you. Things about standing up and taking off your hat and opening doors—"*

*Pickering: "Oh, that was nothing."*

*Liza: "Yes. Things that showed you thought and felt about me as if I were something better than a scullery-maid; though of course I know you would have been the same to a scullery-maid if she had been let into the drawing room. You never took off your boots in the dining room when I was there."*

*Pickering: "You mustn't mind that. Higgins takes off his boots all over the place."*

*Liza: "I know. I am not blaming him. It is his way, isn't it? But it made such a difference to me that you didn't do it. You see, really and truly, apart from the things anyone can pick up (the dressing and the proper way of speaking, and so on), the difference between a lady and a flower girl is not how she behaves, but how she is treated. I shall always be a flower girl to Professor Higgins, because he always treats me as a flower girl, and always will; but I know I can be a lady to you, because you always treat me as a lady, and always will." (pp. 94–95)*

Since the publication of Robert Rosenthal and Lenore Jacobson's (1968) *Pygmalion in the Classroom*, few areas of education have been as widely researched—and misunderstood—as the role teacher expectations play in student learning. The power of teacher expectations in classrooms and schools is well documented. And, increasingly, research has moved beyond simply focusing on the effects of teacher expectations on student learning to include the role that expectation plays on adults within the school district as well.

Thomas Good and Jere Brophy (1980) define teacher expectations as inferences that teachers make about the future academic achievement of students (the key word here is *future*)—the assumptions that teachers hold about whether or not certain students are capable of learning specific knowledge or skills. Some researchers such as Harris Cooper and Thomas Good (1983) differentiate between two types of expectations: (1) the sustaining expectation effect and (2) self-fulfilling prophecies.

The sustaining expectation effect reinforces and maintains existing behaviors and can be an important factor in the prevention of change. A classic example of the sustaining expectation effect (low expectations) is recorded in Alex Haley's (1965) *The Autobiography of Malcolm X*. In the book, Malcolm shares a conversation he had with his high school English teacher.

> *He told me, "Malcolm, you ought to be thinking about a career. Have you been giving it thought?"*
>
> *The truth is, I hadn't. I never figured out why I told him, "Well, yes, sir, I've been thinking I'd like to be a lawyer." Lansing certainly had no Negro lawyers—or doctors either—in*

*those days, to hold up an image I might have aspired to. All I really knew for certain was that a lawyer didn't wash dishes, as I was doing.*

*Mr. Ostrowski looked surprised, I remember, and leaned back in his chair and clasped his hands behind his head. He kind of half-smiled and said, "Malcolm, one of life's first needs is for us to be realistic. Don't misunderstand me, now. We all here like you, you know that. But you've got to be realistic about being a nigger. A lawyer—that's no realistic goal for a nigger. You need to think about something you* can *be. You're good with your hands—making things. Everybody admires your carpentry shop work. Why don't you plan on carpentry? People like you as a person—you'd get all kinds of work." (p. 43)*

Many years later, Malcolm still remembered the disappointment, hurt, and anger from this conversation.

Self-fulfilling prophecies, on the other hand, encourage change rather than prevent it. In self-fulfilling prophecies, once expectations are held, the individual tends to behave according to those beliefs. Eventually, the behavior may cause the expectations to become a reality—for example, Eliza Doolittle in George Bernard Shaw's *Pygmalion*.

Cooper and Good (1983) point out that while self-fulfilling prophecies are the more dramatic and visible form of expectations, they may occur infrequently in classrooms. Sustaining expectation effects (low expectations) are subtler, but they occur quite frequently. The implication for teachers in a PLC is clear. It makes little sense to proclaim a mission of learning for all and yet have low expectations for some students.

*It makes little sense to proclaim a mission of learning for all and yet have low expectations for some students.*

## Best Practices

Teachers in a PLC are constantly seeking best practice. What is known about teacher expectations and the impact on student learning? What information does a cursory review of the research provide? In the 1960s when considerable attention was being focused on the problems of poverty, disadvantaged youth, and desegregation, much research was completed that supported the contention that many teachers held lower expectations for students from lower socioeconomic levels (Deutsch, 1963; Passow, 1963; Wilson, 1963). Actually, there were data from earlier studies with the same implications (Becker, 1952; Davis & Dollard, 1940; Warner, Havinghurst, & Loeb, 1944). Kenneth Clark, in A. H. Passow's (1963) *Education in Depressed Areas*, captures the essence of the findings from these studies, noting:

*One may assume that if a child is not treated with the respect which is due him as a human being, and if those who are charged with the responsibility of teaching him believe that he cannot learn, then his motivation and ability to learn may become impaired. If a teacher believes that a child is incapable of being educated, it is likely that this belief will in some way be communicated to the child in one or more of the many forms of contact inherent in the teacher-pupil relationship. (pp. 147–148)*

The apparent danger, which Clark highlights, is that some disadvantaged kids might be victims of low teacher expectations, which can have a negative effect on their learning. John Hattie (2009) offers this advice:

*Based on the evidence, teachers must stop over emphasizing ability and start emphasizing progress (steep learning curves are the right of all students regardless of where they start), stop seeking evidence to confirm prior expectations but seek evidence to surprise themselves, finds ways to raise the achievement of all, stop creating schools that attempt to lock in prior achievement and experiences, and be evidence-informed about the talents and growth of all students by welcoming diversity and being accountable for all (regardless of the teachers' and schools' expectations). (p. 124)*

## The Self-Fulfilling Prophecy

Rather than preventing students from reaching their potential (the sustaining expectation effect), can teacher expectations actually have a *positive* impact on student academic performance (the self-fulfilling prophecy)? This question forms the basis for one of the most famous studies in American education. In 1964, Robert Rosenthal of Harvard University and Lenore Jacobson of the South San Francisco Unified School District conducted an experiment designed to test the proposition that within a given classroom those children for whom the teacher *expected* greater academic growth would, in fact, show a greater increase in learning than other students within the same classroom.

The researchers attempted to influence teacher expectations by claiming that a test that had been given to students in grades 1–6 could identify intellectual late bloomers. The teachers were told the names of specific students who could be expected to bloom intellectually and as a consequence show unusual gains in achievement during the coming school year. Actually, the students had been selected randomly. The test that had been administered previously was not a test to identify late bloomers; it was a general standardized achievement test. Thus, there was no real basis to expect unusual gains of these students. However, another standardized achievement test was administered at the end of the school year and showed that the students who had been identified as late bloomers learned more than the other students. Rosenthal and Jacobson (1968) reason that the expectations for success that were created in the teachers' minds caused the teachers to treat these students differently.

In his 1970 study, Wilburn Schrank conducted a similar experiment but with one major difference. In this study, the instructors *knew* the students had actually been grouped by random selection, but Schrank asked the teachers to teach the class as if they had been grouped by ability. No differences between the groups were found.

Schrank's research, as well as the research of others such as Elyse Fleming and Ralph Anttonen (1971), provides us with an important clue about the self-fulfilling prophecy. For expectations to become a reality, there must be genuine belief in the expectations. Good and Brophy (1978), in *Looking in Classrooms (Second Edition)*, comment on the importance of genuine expectations. They write:

> *The negative results in studies using induced teacher expectations should not necessarily be taken as disproof of the self-fulfilling prophecy idea. The negative results are more likely due to failure to induce the desired expectations in teachers than to failure of teacher expectations to affect teacher behavior. Naturalistic studies using teachers' real expectations about their students have often shown that high and low teacher expectations are related to differential teacher behavior (Cornbleth, David, and Button, 1972; Brophy and Good, 1974). These studies suggest that teachers' expectations may have self-fulfilling prophecy effects, causing the teachers to behave in ways that tend to make their expectations come true. (p. 69)*

*For expectations to become a reality, there must be genuine belief in the expectations.*

In the same work, Good and Brophy emphasize that it is not merely the existence of expectations that causes the self-fulfilling prophecy effect. It is the behaviors that the expectations produce that form the link between teacher expectations and student behavior. They describe the process as working in the following manner.

1. The teacher expects a specific behavior and achievement from particular students.

2. Because of these different expectations, the teacher behaves differently toward different students.

3. This treatment tells the students what behavior and achievement the teacher expects from them and affects their self-concept, achievement motivations, and level of aspiration.

4. If this treatment is consistent over time, and if the students do not resist or change it in some way, it will shape their achievement and behavior. High-expectation students will be led to achieve high levels, while the achievement of low-expectation students will decline.

5. With time, students' achievement and behavior conform more and more to that originally expected of them.

In what ways do teachers differentiate their behavior toward students who they perceive as high achievers or low achievers? Good and Brophy (1980) report twelve of the more common ways teachers treat high- and low-expectation students differently.

1. Seating low-expectation students far from the teacher or seating them in a group

2. Paying less attention to low-expectation students in academic situations (smiling less often and maintaining less eye contact)

3. Calling on low-expectation students less often to answer classroom questions or to make public demonstrations

4. Waiting less time for low-expectation students to answer questions

5. Not staying with low-expectation students in failure situations (for example, providing fewer clues, asking fewer follow-up questions)

6. Criticizing low-expectation students more frequently than high-expectation learners for incorrect public responses

7. Praising low-expectation students less frequently than high-expectation learners after successful public responses

8. Praising low-expectation students more frequently than high-expectation learners for marginal or inadequate public responses

9. Providing low-expectation students with less accurate and less detailed feedback than high-expectation students

10. Failing to provide low-expectation students with feedback about their responses as often as high-expectation students

11. Demanding less work and effort from low-expectation students than from high-expectation students

12. Interrupting low-expectation students' performance more frequently than high-expectation students'

Cooper and Good (1983) emphasize that an important outcome of this research is that not all teachers treat high- and low-expectation students differently. In fact, Brophy and Good (1974) estimate that approximately one-third of the classroom teachers who have been observed in related research have shown important differences in their behavior toward high and low achievers. Another important point is that different behaviors toward high and low achievers do not necessarily represent inappropriate behavior. This point is essential. The issue is not one of merely treating students differently. Rather, the question is, Are teachers' behaviors toward students based on informed educational judgments about individual students, or are the behaviors the result of expectations that are grounded in certain biases regarding race, gender, cleanliness, student demeanor, quality of English usage, or participation in class, as a few examples?

## School Effects and High Expectations

Teachers, administrators, support staff, and students work together in a social system—a school. This is why a teacher must understand and hold beliefs and assumptions that are congruent with the culture of a school that functions as a PLC. How do the expectations that exist outside the classroom—in the larger school culture—affect what goes on in the inside? Much has been written about the school effectiveness research and the role expectations play in effective schools. Let's take a quick look at some of the research.

Larry Lezotte (2005) provides an excellent summary of the effective schools research. Based on his own research and the finding of other researchers, Lezotte identifies seven correlates of an effective school, one of which is high expectation for student achievement. (The other correlates are instructional leadership, clear and focused mission, safe and orderly environment, frequent monitoring of pupil progress, positive home-school relations, and opportunity to learn and time on task.)

George Weber, in a frequently cited 1971 study, focuses on the characteristics of four inner-city schools in which reading achievement was clearly successful for poor children based on national norms. Weber reports that all four schools had high expectations for their students.

In 1974, the New York State Office of Education Performance Review published a study that has findings similar to Weber's study. However, the New York study differs in methodology in that it focuses on two New York City public schools, one high achieving and the other low achieving, each serving prominently poor students. The New York City study attempts to identify the differences that seem most responsible for achievement variation between the two schools. One of the findings deals with the different expectations in the two schools. The study shows that many professional personnel in the less-effective school attributed students' reading problems to non-school factors and were pessimistic about their ability to have an impact, creating an environment in which kids failed because they were not expected to succeed. However, in the more effective school, teachers were less skeptical about their ability to have an impact on students' achievement.

Beverly Caffee Glenn's (1981) case studies of four urban elementary schools support many of the findings previously mentioned. Her findings, too, emphasize the importance of schools having high expectations for student achievement.

The California State Department of Education's (1980) study of eight improving schools and eight schools where reading scores were decreasing finds that one characteristic of the schools with increasing scores is high expectations for student learning.

Wilbur Brookover and Lawrence Lezotte's (1979) study of eight elementary schools in Michigan focuses on characteristics that differentiated schools with increasing fourth-grade reading scores from those with decreasing reading scores. They identify ten characteristics of schools with increasing scores, two of which are:

(1) a belief by most teachers that most students can master basic skills objectives and (2) high expectations for the educational accomplishments of the students. Brookover, Beady, Flood, Schweitzer, & Winsenbaker (1979) in an analysis of two pairs of public elementary schools find substantive differences in a number of areas, one of which is expectations for student achievement.

Rutter, Maughan, Mortimore, and Ouston's (1979) study differs from the previous studies discussed in that it is a longitudinal study conducted from 1970 to 1974. The study examines twelve inner-city secondary schools in London, England. Three findings are of particular relevance to this discussion. One, in the more effective schools, there is a general attitude and expectation for academic success, coupled with specific actions emphasizing those attitudes and expectations. Two, there are clearly recognized principles and guidelines for student behavior, and three, effective schools treat students in ways that emphasize their success and potential for success.

The effective schools research should be viewed in a broader context than mere lists of effective schools' characteristics. Stewart Purkey and Marshall Smith (1982), in a review of the effective schools research, caution that the research should not be viewed as simply a recipe for school improvement. Rather, the real value of the research is that it provides important clues for better understanding the culture of an effective school with high expectations for students and staff.

## Self-Efficacy

Having high expectations for student success is much more complicated than merely expecting students to do well. Effective teachers believe they have the knowledge, skills, and persistence to ensure their students learn. In other words, not only do they hold high expectations for their students, but they also have high expectations for themselves. We earlier made mention of Shaw's (1916/2003) play *Pygmalion*. It's tempting to say that the play is about the expectations that Professor Henry Higgins has for the flower girl, Eliza Doolittle. However, the real secret to Henry Higgins's success is his belief in himself and his own abilities. When Colonel Pickering offers a wager as to whether Professor Higgins can teach Eliza to speak well enough that she can pass as a duchess, Henry Higgins accepts the challenge by declaring, "Yes. In six months—in three if she has a good ear and a quick tongue—I'll take her anywhere and pass her off as anything" (p. 29).

Bob recalls a striking example of the power of self-efficacy he observed while serving as the interim provost and executive vice president at Middle Tennessee State University. Students were required to pass a course in college algebra as a graduation requirement. One particular student had passed all of his courses, except the algebra course, which he had attempted numerous times. There was no getting around it; the student could not graduate unless he passed the course. The student told Bob there was simply no way he could ever pass the course

*Effective teachers believe they have the knowledge, skills, and persistence to ensure their students learn.*

and asked if there was an alternative. There was no alternative, but Bob knew of the reputation of a particular professor in the department of mathematics, Frances Stubblefield. Bob called Stubblefield and explained the situation. Stubblefield said, "Just send him over to me. I'll make sure he learns algebra," and she did. The student did just fine in the course and graduated on time. Professor Frances Stubblefield, like Professor Henry Higgins, had full confidence in her ability to ensure that her students learned.

We don't have to look to professors for examples of teacher self-efficacy. Janel witnessed an example of self-efficacy at a registration night for prospective kindergarten students. Imagine the excitement. All of these little kids in one room with their parents signing up to start school! Most of the students were nicely dressed and on their best behavior. Many were shy, not knowing what to expect. However, one little girl was just a ball of energy. She showed up in her pajamas and flip-flops! She was standing on a chair just oozing excitement and enthusiasm. One teacher remarked to Janel, "Oh goodness! I hope I don't get that one. What would I ever do with her?" Later, Janel was chatting with another teacher who spotted the little girl and said, "Look at that! What I could do with that girl! I'm going to go tell her that if I'm her teacher it'll be the best day of her life!"

## Teacher Teams and Teacher Self-Efficacy

Teacher self-efficacy is greatly enhanced when teachers are contributing members to a high-performing collaborative team. Being a highly effective teacher has become increasingly difficult. Perhaps there was a time when individual teachers could work in isolation by themselves and successfully ensure their students learned. However, today's schools—and society in general—have become so complex, it is virtually impossible for an individual teacher to be highly successful. Certainly every school has pockets of excellence, but in every school, there is only so much an individual teacher can do. They soon come to see it as an invisible ceiling. And, unfortunately, many succumb to despair. More and more teachers are leaving the profession each year.

However, there is hope. Since the 1960s, organizations of all types have tapped into the power of collaborative teaming. Collaborative teaming is especially powerful in the complex world of schools and school districts. While an individual teacher may come to feel overwhelmed with all that is expected, he or she can gain a sense of confidence knowing he or she is not alone, that there is help and support within the team. Virtually everyone agrees that schools need to enhance teacher effectiveness. This can never happen unless teachers have a sense of confidence and a belief that they can, in fact, ensure that all their students learn at high levels. This sense of self-efficacy, which is so critical to teacher effectiveness, is greatly enhanced when teachers work in teams rather than by themselves and when the team is doing the right work, for the right reasons, with specificity and fidelity.

### Student Self-Efficacy

Perhaps the greatest gift a teacher can give a student is the student's belief in him- or herself. Unfortunately, many students do not believe they can be successful in school. Teachers in a PLC work collaboratively to help students develop the mindset that they can not only learn, but learn at high levels.

Teachers increase self-efficacy in their students in distinct ways. They are purposeful in their teaching, aligning their lessons directly to the high-stakes essential standards and then breaking down each standard into daily learning targets. In addition to utilizing common formative assessments that the teacher team has developed, teachers in PLCs create ways for students to monitor their own learning on a regular basis. Teachers and students monitor the acquisition of each skill— skill by skill. Teachers plan for appropriate student practice along with specific, focused feedback. Most important, when students struggle, they receive additional time and support within the school day—regardless of the teacher to whom they are assigned. In other words, teachers keep working with each student, skill by skill, incrementally until he or she reaches a predetermined proficiency level, and this incremental success is coupled with genuine recognition and celebration.

Teachers in PLCs also work to create a classroom culture characterized by encouragement and caring. They constantly send the message, "You can do this, and I won't give up on you because I care!" Because they realize the power of developing positive relationships, they touch students on an emotional level.

Hattie (2009) summarizes the importance of creating strong, helpful, caring relationships:

> *The power of positive teacher-student relationships is critical for learning to occur . . . It requires them [teachers] to believe that their role is that of a change agent—that all students can learn and progress, that achievement for all is changeable and not fixed, and that demonstrating to all students that they care about their learning is both powerful and effective. (p. 128)*

## Reflection on How Students Learn Best

Since continuously improving the learning of every student is the primary focus of a school that functions as a professional learning community, we should recognize that all teachers have fundamental beliefs and attitudes about learning—what students should learn, how they learn, and what should happen when students don't learn, as well as when they do learn. Teacher attitudes, the lens through which they view these questions, shape not only how they approach teaching, but also the nature and quality of their day-to-day interactions and relationships with students, colleagues, administrators, and parents.

At the heart of any serious introspection about student learning are teacher attitudes about how students learn best and the teacher's role in student learning. In virtually every school, there are a wide range of teacher beliefs and attitudes regarding student learning, but the belief that is central to teachers in a PLC is reflected in the answer to these fundamental questions: "Do I believe students learn at different rates and in different ways, and, if so, how is this belief reflected in my behavior?"

Teachers who answer the first part of this question in the affirmative—and if they really mean it—are much more likely to help students who experience difficulty, providing specific feedback to students and insisting that they continue to redo their work until it reflects proficiency. Teachers also provide other ways of giving very powerful feedback such as student-to-student feedback and self-assessing. This involves a teacher teaching the kids how to provide meaningful feedback by modeling what it looks like and sounds like (star/celebration and next steps), practicing together using student samples (anchor papers, anonymous student samples, examples right from the classroom) and success criteria connected to the focus standard/target. Once students have had practice, they are able to analyze their work, or the work of others, and provide constructive feedback to move the learning forward. A teacher can share suggestions over and over again, but often there is great power in hearing it from a peer and, even more so, recognizing the next steps in learning on their own.

Also, because these teachers believe students learn in different ways, they realize that when it comes to instructional strategies, one size doesn't fit all. Quite naturally, then, they view differentiated instruction as an essential element to virtually every unit of instruction.

Teachers who are part of a PLC also understand the importance of student practice, coupled with appropriate, focused feedback and encouragement. Of course, most teachers recognize the common sense associated with the importance of student practice. However, teachers in PLCs realize that practice alone is seldom enough, and inappropriate practice can be detrimental to learning. And, they make decisions about appropriate practice in collaboration with their team. For example, decisions about the most appropriate homework for a particular lesson or unit are an important aspect of team planning.

*Teachers who are part of a PLC also understand the importance of student practice, coupled with appropriate, focused feedback and encouragement.*

So, the first question teacher teams tackle when it comes to student practice is simply this: Practice what? Quite obviously students shouldn't practice just anything. Teachers in PLCs, much like coaches and music teachers, align student practice with the skills and knowledge for which students will be held accountable.

Teachers in a PLC realize the importance of connecting appropriate practice to specific, focused feedback, coupled with genuine encouragement. Simply having students practice a skill is never enough. If a student makes a mistake, it is of little help to simply mark the problem incorrect and give the student a grade. (This is often referred to in research as *product feedback*.) Rather, teachers in a PLC see their role, in part, as showing students where they made a mistake and how to do the work correctly (*process feedback*).

The point is this: The lens through which teachers view student practice, feedback, and encouragement is of critical importance when it comes to student learning. If teachers view their role as merely assigning and grading student work, they will do little to impact improvement. On the other hand, teachers who see their job as one of working with their colleagues to plan appropriate student practice assignments linked to standards and then providing students with specific, focused feedback and encouragement will see far more success in student learning.

## An Effort-Based Classroom

Another important assumption related to student learning that often goes unexamined is what teachers view as the primary determinants of student academic success, or lack thereof. This is a critical lens, since some teachers tend to see student academic success primarily linked to ability, while others see student success as being primarily associated with effort. Teachers in PLCs work to create effort-based classrooms—classrooms in which student effort is encouraged, expected, supported, and rewarded.

However, looking through an effort lens can be woefully misleading and even harmful. It is seldom enough to simply say to students, "You can do this if you just put forth the effort!" If students are to learn more, their effort must be coupled with help—additional time and support. This is only common sense. There are many, many things in life that we cannot do, no matter how much effort we put forth. What most people need when it comes to improving performance is for someone to help them, to show them how to get better. Consider the following story of Janel's brother Ray Kuntz.

### Time and Support

Ray received a special recognition from his alma mater, Carroll College. In his acceptance speech, Ray recalled that although he attended a small, rural high school with a limited curriculum, at Carroll he double-majored in mathematics and economics. However, in his first college calculus class, engineering calculus, he struggled. The other students had taken calculus in high school, but calculus was not offered in the small high school that he attended. His first grade was very low, as was his second grade, and his professor, Al Murray, wrote a note on Ray's test paper instructing Ray to come see him.

Ray was expecting the professor to urge him to drop the course, given his poor test scores. At their meeting, the professor asked, "Do you know why I wanted to meet with you?" Attempting to add some levity to the situation, Ray responded, "Well, I suppose you think I should drop the class. I may not be doing well on the calculus tests, but I do know the average of my test scores."

Murray then proceeded to interview Ray. He was doing what we know now as getting a learning profile on Ray. The professor said, "Ray, you didn't have calculus in high school, did you?" Ray replied, "No. I went to a small high school in North Dakota." Then the professor said just the right thing. "Ray, although you haven't done well on the first two exams, I've watched you work in class and put forth an effort. And you are getting better. You just started further behind than the others in the class. I don't want you to drop the class. Instead, I want you to come by and see me on a weekly basis, and we'll get you caught up. You can do this!"

Ray graduated from Carroll College with a double major in mathematics and economics. Ray's success required a lot of effort. However, effort alone was not enough. Ray, like each of us, has had a lot of help along the way in order to make his effort pay off. Ray would tell you that Al Murray valued him. Murray looked for *potential* in him and didn't want to lose Ray from the mathematics department.

An interesting aspect of Ray's story is that the professor went beyond recognizing the importance of Ray putting forth the effort to succeed and helping him do so. The professor also recognized the importance of encouragement and caring, of establishing a personal relationship with Ray in order to help him succeed. The professor actually pulled up a chair next to Ray and helped him. The noted psychologist Carl Rogers (1961) observes:

> *Change appears to come about through experience in a relationship. . . . If I can provide a certain type of relationship, the other person will discover within himself the capacity to use that relationship for growth, and change and personal development will occur. (p. 33)*

What would such a relationship look like according to Rogers? In addition to being genuine and real with students, he emphasizes the importance of communicating a sense of empathy and understanding coupled with an acceptance and genuine liking toward individual students with whom teachers are working. Rogers (1961) further notes:

> *By acceptance I mean a warm regard for him as a person of unconditional worth—of value no matter what his condition, his behavior or his feelings. It means a respect and liking for him as a separate person, a willingness for him to possess his own feelings in his own way. It means an acceptance of and regard for his attitudes of the moment, no matter how negative or positive, no matter how much they may contradict other attitudes he has held in the past. This acceptance of each fluctuating aspect of this other person makes it for him a relationship of warmth and safety, and the safety of being liked and prized as a person sees a highly important element in a helping relationship. (p. 34)*

As teachers reflect on their assumptions about student ability versus student effort and their core beliefs about helping students through an encouraging and caring relationship, the issue of "Do I basically like students?" must be a core question of personal self-reflection. The answer to this question is powerful simply because how students perceive their teacher views them has a huge impact on students' behavior, attitude, and ultimately, their learning.

The lens through which teachers view effort and help will be critical to their success in a PLC since central to the PLC concept is the belief that schools must have a systematic schoolwide plan to provide students with additional time and support when they struggle. Teachers who view learning through a lens of *effort, help, encouragement, and care* will be much more likely to see the value in planning for schoolwide systematic additional time and support than teachers who believe, deep down, that student learning is primarily linked to individual student ability.

## Student Motivation

Any discussion of the lens through which teachers view student learning must include the topic of how effective teachers motivate students to learn. Do teachers see blame and punishment as the primary motivators for getting students to learn more? Do teachers really believe that the threat of a low grade will motivate low-achieving students? Or do teachers look through the lens of encouragement and caring? Teachers in a PLC constantly send the message, "I am insisting that you learn this, because it is important for you, and because it is so important, I will help you. I will not give up on you, because I care!" Teachers should reflect on the assumptions they hold regarding what motivates students to try harder.

Teachers who view student motivation and learning through the lens of encouragement and caring recognize that a classroom culture of encouragement and caring is inextricably linked to recognition and celebration. It is difficult for teachers to convince students (and parents) that they believe in encouraging students to learn more if they don't recognize and publicly celebrate learning when it occurs. Consider the following scenario.

Mary, an eighth-grade student, generally makes low Bs on her report card. The teacher encourages her to do better, to work harder. The teacher tells Mary that she can become an A student if she will put forth the effort, and the teacher promises to help her. Additionally, Mary is an only child and receives considerable help and encouragement from her parents. They take an interest in her schoolwork, and they check her work

> *It is difficult for teachers to convince students (and parents) that they believe in encouraging students to learn more if they don't recognize and publicly celebrate learning when it occurs.*

each night to make sure it is done correctly and explain concepts and skills with which Mary might struggle. How many points, at most, will Mary have to overcome to become an A student in a typical school, and equally important, how do schools generally celebrate students who make As? We would suggest that in a typical school the most points that Mary would have to overcome would be ten or less. Also, if she is successful, she makes the Principal's List, the Honor Roll, or some similar recognition.

Now, let's compare Mary's experience with Jean's. Jean is in the same classroom, but her situation at home is very different than Mary's. Jean's parents are divorced, and her mom works two jobs, trying to make ends meet. Jean has two younger sisters, whom she helps her mom look after. Jean doesn't get a lot of help with her homework from her mom and does not turn in some assignments for which she receives a zero. Because of her zeros, she makes a significant number of Fs on her report card. She typically has an average grade of around 20. But her teacher encourages her to do better and provides her with help. How many points on average will Jean have to overcome simply to become a D student? Obviously, the answer is forty or more, which is virtually impossible to overcome. But, let's say that through some Herculean effort Jean does overcome such a big deficit and moves from making Fs to making Ds, how will her efforts be recognized and celebrated in a typical classroom and school?

The lens through which teachers view this scenario tells a lot about the beliefs and assumptions they hold about students and student motivation—as well as what they really and truly value. If teachers say they value improvement but then fail to recognize and celebrate it when it occurs, soon they will lose all credibility with both students and their parents. Terrence Deal and Allan Kennedy (1982) in *Corporate Cultures* remind us that in the absence of rituals and ceremonies, important values lose all meaning.

Recognizing and celebrating even small, incremental improvements that students make—not only in their learning, but in their behavior and attitudes as well—is critical if teachers are to move students from a framework of despair ("I can't do this!") to one of increased success and self-confidence ("I *can* do this!"). Harvard professor and author Rosabeth Moss Kanter (2006) in her book *Confidence* provides an example of how encouragement, recognition, and incremental celebration can contribute to stopping "downward spirals, reverse negative trajectories, unwind doom loops, end bad habits, and lay the foundation for confidence" (p. 146). She cites the example of Bruce Walker, a teacher at Booker T. Washington High School in Memphis, Tennessee.

> *Walker helped students change into winners. At one point, he took aside a student troublemaker who had a group of loyal followers and told him, "You take that same savvy you use to be a bully, and put it into school! You're a natural leader." The boy didn't believe him at first, but he started trying a little bit every now and then. By eleventh grade he won the school's Most Improved Student Award. "He had a different kind of swagger coming down from the stage after receiving that award," Walker observed. His new demeanor influenced his followers to*

*change. In his senior year that student was voted Mr. Booker T.
Washington High, the school's highest honor. (p. 252)*

Teachers in a PLC do not leave recognition and celebration to chance. They collaboratively develop plans to ensure students are recognized and celebrated for their incremental improvements along the way. For example, as principal of Mountain Meadow Elementary School in Buckley, Washington, Janel worked with her teachers to develop monthly assemblies in which every teacher recognized three students whose behavior, attitude, or schoolwork had improved. As teachers called the name of each student, he or she came before the entire student body to have a medal placed around his or her neck. This tradition still continues at Mountain Meadow, and every student knows that his or her efforts to improve will be recognized and publicly celebrated.

In your school, do you celebrate the things you say you value? Do you value excellent schoolwork? Do you value improvement? Do you value effort? Do you value a great attitude? Do you value excellent behavior? If so, all of these things must be recognized and celebrated when they occur, or others will not believe you.

Recognition and celebration are not just for the kids. Teachers deserve to be recognized and celebrated as well. Start by recognizing something great that a student or group of students accomplished. Then recognize the teacher or team that helped the student or students. Now here's where everyone benefits: highlight what the teacher or team actually did! Emphasize the strategies the teacher or team deployed to help the student or students. Everyone will learn from the success and examples of these teacher leaders.

## Parent Involvement

Since a school that functions as a professional learning community is committed to ensuring the learning of each student, the lens through which teachers view parents is of particular importance. DuFour et al. (2008) observe:

> *Parent involvement increases when schools welcome parents into
> the teaching and learning process, communicate the importance
> of the parent's role in student success, and provide explicit strategies for parents to become involved in their children's learning.
> Teachers promote deeper parent involvement in the education
> of their children when they reach out to parents on a regular
> basis, make them aware of learning goals and the pacing of the
> curriculum, clarify expectations, and solicit parent perspectives
> on their children's interest and aptitudes. (p. 385)*

When Janel was principal at Mountain Meadow, the school was recognized for its partnership and strong relationships with parents. In *Revisiting Professional Learning Communities at Work* (DuFour et al., 2008), Janel describes how such strong relationships were established and pointed to the fact that they viewed parents as partners.

> *The most important step we took in this effort to strengthen our partnership with parents was to demonstrate a sincere interest in giving them a voice in the education of their children. We knew parents had important insights about their own children, and we committed to including them in our planning and respecting them as "the experts" where their children were concerned. Our mantra became, "When in doubt, ask mom or dad." Each year we ask parents to complete a form indicating their child's interests, strengths, and weaknesses as learners, and any information that will help us create the best educational opportunity for their child. (p. 404)*

In the White River School District, systems are created to engage students, parents, and teachers in celebrating student successes and setting goals for future success. Figure 2.1 is a sample form that parents, students, and teachers fill out together at spring conferences to set goals for the rest of the year and over summer. Kids love to celebrate what they have accomplished with their parents and set realistic goals to show the most growth possible before the end of the school year. Such collaborative goal setting processes can help prevent the "summer slide," which is prevalent in many classrooms.

Quite obviously, the beliefs and assumptions of individual teachers will impact the capacity of schools to develop strong partnerships with parents. In a PLC, teachers are expected to operate from the assumption that all parents, regardless of socioeconomic background, race, ethnicity, or education level, want their children to do well in school. It is impossible to create a school culture such as the one at Mountain Meadow unless individual teachers view parents through a positive lens and see working with parents as a normal, commonsense aspect of being a good teacher.

*Teachers work with parents to help students learn but at the same time accept the responsibility themselves for ensuring that all kids learn at high levels regardless of a parent's contribution.*

However, teachers in a PLC do not *depend* on parents for the education of students. Let's face it, students do not get to pick their parents, and some kids simply are not fortunate enough to live in a home with parents who are willing and able to help them with their learning. Teachers work with parents to help students learn but at the same time accept the responsibility themselves for ensuring that all kids learn at high levels regardless of a parent's contribution. The focus of teachers and teacher teams is on what they can control during the school day!

**Spring Progress Report and Plan 2015**

Mrs. Grace's Fourth and Fifth Grade Class

Student Name: Jerry

Current Data

| Reading | Writing | Math |
|---|---|---|
| CBM: 235/1<br><br>STAR GE: 5.1<br><br>AR: 30 books @ 80% or better!!! Wowza!<br><br>(Goal was 13 books @ 80% or better by March 31, 2015) | Scored "Meets Standard" for vocab and style, as well as conventions. Scored "Approaching Standard" for purpose and organization, and elaboration. | Unit 4: Meets standard for<br><br>5.NBT.5–7 (17.5/18 pts)<br><br>5.NF.4a (4/4 pts)<br><br>5.OA.2 (4/4 pts)<br><br>Weekly checkups: averaging 80% or better |
| Goals: Read seventh-grade-level books and record in AR. Raise STAR GE to 6.0 by June 2015. | Score "Meets Standard" for purpose and organization on opinion writing piece "The Lorax" and "Screen Time" by May 2015. | Finish Daily Math on time. Meet standard on Units 5 and 6, and score 80% or better on weekly assessments. |
| Plan: Read books at higher end of ZPD level—seventh grade. Provided with seventh-grade AR list by teacher. | Write short informational reports and opinion essays using ReadWriteThink.org and learnzillion.com over the summer. | On grade level with math. Use ixl.com to maintain status quo, and practice in *Spectrum Math* book for grade 5 review prior to starting sixth grade. |

Figure 2.1: Sample goal-setting form students review with parents.

*Source: White River School District. Used with permission.*

## Continuous Professional Development

Adult learning is another important aspect of looking inside and examining your beliefs about learning. A focus on learning as a PLC isn't just about student learning. A *learning* community focuses heavily on the learning of adults as well, and as professionals, the adults in a PLC are constantly learning about best practices and are open to trying different approaches to enhance their effectiveness.

Teachers in a PLC learn in a number of ways. They are constantly analyzing the effectiveness of their own instruction through the lens of student learning. Teacher teams are engaged in the process of examining the results of common formative assessments, along with student work, and then learning from one another. They also become engaged in a collaborative process with their colleagues to seek best practices. In short, they are committed to improving student learning by improving their own learning. Teachers in a PLC realize it is unrealistic to think that students will be more enthusiastic about learning than their teachers.

Although teacher beliefs, attitudes, and expectations are powerful, they only have impact if they cause teachers to do something. Teacher assumptions and the expectations are central to a school functioning as a PLC and form the basis for commitments to behave in certain ways—to *do* certain things. Teacher pronouncements will have little impact on student learning unless they become embedded into day-to-day school culture—particularly at the classroom level.

# Chapter 3

# Working in Collaborative Teams

*Collaboration, cooperation, and coordination are the three dynamics supporting the practice of team medicine at Mayo Clinic. These dynamics drive the delivery of personalized care for patients, although staff members—from physician to custodian—become active team players to serve patients' needs because treating complex illnesses requires the diverse expertise available from all personnel and supporting infrastructure. To work at Mayo is to be on the team.*

—Leonard Berry and Kent Seltman

Since the 1980s, virtually every major organization throughout the world has structured itself to capture the power of collaborative teaming. The use of collaborative teams becomes such a way of life in most organizations that the efficacy of organizing into collaborative teams is rarely debated—except in public education. In many, if not most, schools across the United States, the norm still reflects an individual teacher facing increasing expectations and scrutiny, with fewer resources in an increasingly complicated, complex, and challenging environment of today's public schools. It is unreasonable to think that an individual teacher can successfully ensure that all of his or her students are learning at high levels. Schools that function as professional learning communities are organized, both structurally and culturally, to provide teachers with support and benefits that can be achieved through collaborative teaming.

The power of collaborative teams is captured by Daniel James Brown in the book *The Boys in the Boat* (2013), a book about the 1936 Berlin Olympics and nine Americans' quest for the gold medal. He writes,

*Great crews may have men or women of exceptional talent or strength; they may have outstanding coxswains or stroke oars or bowmen; but they have no stars. The team effort—the perfectly synchronized flow of muscle, oars, boat, and water; the single, whole, unified, and beautiful symphony that a crew in motion becomes—is all that matters. Not the individual, not the self.*

*The psychology is complex. Even as rowers must subsume their often fierce sense of independence and self-reliance, at the same time they must hold true to their individuality, their unique capabilities as oarsmen or oarswomen or, for that matter, as human beings. Even if they could, few rowing coaches would simply clone their biggest, strongest, smartest, and most capable rowers. Crew races are not won by clones. They are won by crews, and great crews are carefully balanced blends of both physical abilities and personality types. In physical terms, for instance, one rower's arms might be longer than another's, but the latter might have a stronger back than the former. Neither is necessarily a better or more valuable oarsman than the other; both the long arms and the strong back are assets to the boat. But if they are to row together, each of these oarsmen must adjust to the needs and capabilities of the other. Each must be prepared to compromise something in a way of optimizing his stroke for the overall benefit of the boat—the shorter-armed man reaching a little farther, the longer-armed man foreshortening his reach just a bit—so that both men's oars remain parallel and both blades enter and exit the water at precisely the same moment. This highly refined coordination and cooperation must be multiplied out across eight individuals of varying statures and physiques to make the most of each individual's strengths. Only in this way can the capabilities that come with diversity— lighter, more technical rowers in the bow and stronger, heavier pullers in the middle of the boat, for instance—be turned to the advantage rather than disadvantage. . .*

*Good crews are good blends of personalities: someone to lead the charge, someone to hold something in reserve, someone to pick a fight, someone to make peace, someone to think things through, someone to charge ahead without thinking. Somehow this all must mesh. That's the steepest challenge. Even after the right mixture is found, each man or woman in the boat must recognize his or her place in the fabric of the crew, accept it, and accept the others as they are. It is an exquisite thing when it all comes together in just the right way. (pp. 178–180)*

## Teaming: It's Just How We Do Things Here

Teachers in a PLC are expected to be a contributing member of a team—in fact, probably more than one team. For example, an elementary teacher may be a member of a horizontal team that meets often and also a member of a vertical team that meets less frequently. A middle school team may meet regularly by content areas but periodically as interdisciplinary teams. A high school teacher may be a member of the larger departmental team (the English team, for example) but also a member of a course team (perhaps those who teach ninth-grade English).

For teachers who are new to a school that functions as a professional learning community, their first experience with collaborative teaming occurs even before they are employed. Since they are being hired into a specific team rather than the more generic school, the team plays an important role in the interview and recommendation process. Being an effective team member involves much more than possessing the correct credentials. The central questions are: What kind of team member will a prospective team member be? What does he or she bring to the team in terms of experiences and skill set? And, how will he or she strengthen the team as it pursues the goal of increasing student learning?

This issue of being a positive, contributing member of a team is one example of why teachers need to look inside regarding their beliefs, assumptions, and attitudes. What will be a new teacher's attitude about working closely with colleagues? Is the teacher excited about sharing ideas, materials, and learning data in order to improve not only student learning, but also his or her own professional practice? Is the teacher excited that he or she gets to work in a school that is organized in teacher teams, or does he or she feel that working in a team is a chore?

Teaching in a PLC differs from teaching in a traditional school in that teacher teams engage in a collaborative process designed to clarify and add meaning to the most essential standards. The team addresses the question, "What would this standard, if met, look like in student work?" Additionally, the team addresses issues such as identifying learning targets, proficiency, pacing, and common scoring; teachers become students of the standards by working in concert with their fellow team members. In more traditional schools, individual teachers generally address these issues. This does not mean a school that functions as a PLC is a cookie-cutter school in which everyone is teaching and going about her or his work the same way; rather, collaborative team planning is an excellent example of tight on the *what*, but loose on the *how*.

The quality of collaboration depends, to a great degree, on the beliefs and assumptions that individual teachers hold regarding working interdependently with their fellow teachers, administrators, and the support staff. Do teachers view all the students as *our* kids, or do they believe they only have responsibility for the students who are assigned to them? The answer to this question, along with many more, reflects the lens through which a teacher views working in a collaborative culture with his or her colleagues.

Clarity about what teams must do is of critical importance. Unless there is clarity about what teachers will be called on to do as members of a collaborative team, it is doubtful the team will be able to function at a level of quality and fidelity that is needed to be successful. Of course, a teacher's core beliefs and assumptions regarding collaboration with colleagues will affect how well he or she functions as a team member.

For example, does each teacher believe that it is preferable to collaboratively study the standards with his or her fellow team members in order to clarify what the standards mean, identify which ones are absolutely essential, and discuss what the standard looks like in student work? Or, deep down, do some teachers prefer to be left alone to make these decisions? The same goes for pacing out the year in order to ensure enough time is devoted to the essential or power standards. Do some teachers believe that monitoring student learning is best left to the discretion of each individual teacher, or does every teacher believe this can best be done in a collaborative team? Should whether or not a student receives additional time and support be left up to individual teachers, or can this best be accomplished through a collaborative process? And the same question holds true for extending and enriching the learning of students who demonstrate proficiency. These kinds of activities, along with unit planning and many other issues related to student learning, are the things teachers are asked to undertake as part of a collaborative team in a professional learning community, and a teacher who prefers to be left alone to teach his or her own students cannot be successful in such a setting. Further, he or she will have a negative effect on the work of the entire team.

While the lens through which teachers view their colleagues is of critical importance, it is also important that teachers look inside themselves regarding how they view administrators and the support staff. A PLC's success depends on teachers who view their colleagues as people who are dedicated to ensuring that all students learn at high levels. Teachers who hold an adversarial view of administrators detract from the effectiveness of the school. A we-versus-them attitude simply will not work in a school that seeks to function as a professional learning community. The same holds true for how teachers view the support staff. Do teachers see the support staff as critical contributors to student learning? Do they value support staff's role and the contributions they make? Needless to say, the principal plays a vital role in developing a school culture in which the contributions of each role are valued, but the core beliefs and assumptions of teachers are also critically important.

*A PLC's success depends on teachers who view their colleagues as people who are dedicated to ensuring that all students learn at high levels.*

## Setting Team Norms

Teachers are expected to adhere to collaboratively developed team norms—a mutual commitment to how the team will normally operate as they go about their work of enhancing the learning of each student. Daniel Goleman, Richard Boyatzis, and Annie McKee (2002) articulate the importance of collaboratively developed team norms by noting:

> *When self-managed norms are explicit and practiced over time, team effectiveness improves dramatically, as does the experience*

*of team members themselves. Being on the team becomes reward-*
*ing in itself—and those positive emotions provide energy and*
*motivation for accomplishing the team's goals. (p. 182)*

The format for team norms isn't nearly as important as the norms themselves and the personal commitment each teacher makes to adhere to them. The norms should be created by each team, focused on behaviors rather than beliefs, periodically reviewed and evaluated, and few in number (DuFour et al., 2010).

Figure 3.1 is an example of a fourth-grade team's norms.

---

**Fourth-Grade Team Norms**

* * We will start and end each meeting on time.
* * We will make decisions based on consensus, after listening to all ideas.
* * We will come prepared for the agreed-on task.
* * We will support each other, both professionally and emotionally.
* * We will advocate for all fourth-grade students.
* * We will keep confidential our discussions and comments.
* * We will share responsibilities fairly.
* * We will keep all discussions student driven, data driven, or both.

**Accountability Protocol**

* * We agree to quickly go over the norms at the beginning of each meeting and self-assess.
* * We agree to hold each other accountable by bringing the concern to the team member's attention and asking them how we can support him or her.

---

Figure 3.1: Fourth-grade team norms at Mountain Meadow Elementary.

*Source: White River School District. Used with permission.*

In addition to norms is the accountability protocol the team collaboratively agrees on. The accountability protocol is simply the agreement the team makes regarding the procedures the team will follow when either an individual is not meeting the team norms or the team as a whole seems to be floundering.

It is unreasonable to think that no one will ever violate, either consciously or unconsciously, team norms, and failure to deal with violations of team norms can quickly undermine the entire team's effectiveness. Realizing that violations will occur from time to time and that they will range in frequency and severity, teams do not wait for incidents to occur to figure out what should be done. Instead, teams collaboratively develop protocols for how they will deal with norm violations when they occur. Typically, the protocols are arranged in a pyramid of ascending order, based on the severity and frequency of the violations. For example, initially a team may simply review its norms, emphasizing the need for everyone to recommit to the collaboratively agreed-on behavior, or perhaps the team leader may meet privately with the team member involved, reminding him or her of the importance of following the norms and offering help and support. If the behavior continues, the team leader may ask the principal to meet with the entire team or the individual. Regardless of the exact protocol, the important point is that team members anticipate possible violations and agree on the appropriate responses in advance of their occurrence.

Ken Williams (2010) in "Do We Have Team Norms or 'Nice to Knows'"? states that unprepared teams don't have a process for answering the question:

> *What is our process for holding each other accountable in a respectful and dignified manner? Unanswered, this question is a definite team-dynamic derailer. Without this process in place, teams will end up with a list of "nice to knows," rather than effective team norms.*
>
> *When teams establish a process for holding each other accountable when someone violates a norm, then unnecessary confrontations and unspoken tensions are avoided. It's a given that violations will occur, and collaborative teams that have a predefined process for dealing with them will be the ones that become highly effective. Teams that don't engage in this very important step will often end up with a list of "nice to knows" instead of effective team norms and commitments. Teams that do address the question, "What happens when?" create the kind of safety and predictability on their team that serves to accelerate the collaborative culture.*

The overarching idea communicated to each teacher is this: "Our focus at this school is on ensuring that all of our students are learning, and to achieve this purpose, we work in *collaborative* teams that do specific things for specific reasons. As a member of one of these teams, you are responsible, not only for your students, but for all of our students. In short, you must be excited about being a contributing member of your collaborative team!"

## Getting Started

Of course, being a contributing member of a collaborative team in a professional learning community means much more than merely being genuinely excited or even working well with your colleagues. The goal isn't to just be a member of a team. The goal is to be a contributing member of a high-performing team. A team's effectiveness is a reflection of what it does daily, the decisions it makes, the impact it has on student learning. It's time we recognize it's not the home these kids come from but the school they go to and the teachers and team to whom they are assigned that have a direct impact on learning year after year. Let's be clear, an *effective team improves student learning.*

In addition to a clear understanding of the schoolwide commitments and team norms that each teacher is expected to embrace, all teachers must have a clear grasp of what teacher teams do in a professional learning community—

*The goal isn't to just be a member of a team. The goal is to be a contributing member of a high-performing team.*

what products teacher teams generate, what the work is. In the broadest sense, the work of a teacher team is centered on the four critical questions of learning (DuFour et al., 2010). Simply put, if we want all of our kids to learn, we as a team—and as individual teachers—must be clear about the work that's layered under the four critical questions and the products the team needs to generate to improve student learning (Eaker & Keating, 2012).

1. **What do we want all of our students to learn and be able to do in each course and unit?** Common Core State Standards, Career and Technical Education Standards, Next Generation Science Standards, essential outcomes or power standards, learning targets, pacing, clarifying the meaning of each standard, what the standards look like in student work, depth of knowledge (DOK) attached to each standard, learning progression of the standard, instructional/engagement strategies

2. **How will we know if they have learned and can do these things?** Responsive assessments to include quick checks for understanding, common formative end-of-unit assessments, benchmark assessments, state assessments, results analysis

3. **How will we respond when students experience difficulty in their learning?** Classroom-based differentiated instruction, interventions tied to core instruction, team-based interventions, response to intervention (RTI) process, positive behavioral interventions and supports (PBIS), multitiered system of support (MTSS)

4. **How will we celebrate and extend and enrich the learning of students who demonstrate proficiency in their learning?** Differentiated instruction, use of technology, students working in teams or individually on in-depth research

By focusing their work on the essential questions surrounding student learning, teachers benefit from clear and consistent expectations. For example, some of the very first documents a new teacher to a PLC receives are the essential learning standards for each course or subject, unit by unit or chapter by chapter, and the common formative assessments that the team has developed in order to monitor student learning on a frequent and timely basis. Importantly, the team goes far beyond merely providing new members of the team with these documents. They engage new teachers in deep, rich discussions about how the standards were agreed on, clarifying what each standard means; determining what the standard, if met, would look like in student work; reviewing the learning targets for each standard; reviewing the common formative assessments the team has developed; and previewing the process of how the team reviews the results from formative assessments. All of these documents are contained in team member binders and can be found on the district computer server or share drive by grade level and content area.

> *Each year is a process of revisiting, refining, and getting better—a culture of continuous improvement!*

One of the distinct advantages of being a teacher in a PLC is that team members have copies of their team's work from previous years, as well as access to other teams' work. Each year is a process of revisiting, refining, and getting better—a culture of continuous improvement!

## Determining Essential Standards and Learning Outcomes

The White River School District is an excellent example of a school district that has successfully embedded PLC work into each school and each team, ensuring a guaranteed and viable curriculum for each student regardless of the school he or she attends or the teacher to whom he or she is assigned. For example, the math department at White River High School continually engages in deep, rich discussion about the essential outcomes that every student should know or be able to do. Consider this example from Cody Mothershead, of the team's collaborative work for unit 1 in algebra (figure 3.2). After agreeing on the power standards for the unit, the team collaboratively developed learning targets for students. See the appendix for more examples of learning targets (pages 187–188).

---

**Power Standards for Unit 1 (From Common Core State Standards)**

HSN.Q.A.1 Use units as a way to understand problems and to guide the solution of multi-step problems; choose and interpret units consistently in formulas; choose and interpret the scale and the origin in graphs and data displays. (Claims 1, 2, 4)

HSN.Q.A.2 Define appropriate quantities for the purpose of descriptive modeling. (Claims 1, 2, 4)

HSN.Q.A.3 Choose a level of accuracy appropriate to limitations on measurement when reporting quantities. (Claims 1, 2, 4)

HSA.SSE.A.1 Interpret expressions that represent a quantity in terms of its context. (Claims 1, 2)

HSA.CFD.A.1 Create equations and inequalities in one variable and use them to solve problems. (Claims 1, 2, 4)

HSA.CED.A.4 Rearrange formulas to highlight a quantity of interest, using the same reasoning as in solving equations. (Claims 1, 2, 4)

HSA.REI.A.1 Explain each step in solving a simple equation as following from the equality of numbers asserted at the previous step, starting from the assumption that the original equation has a solution. (Claims 1, 3, 4)

HSA.REI.A.3 Solve linear equations and inequalities in one variable, including equations with coefficients represented by letters. (Claims 1, 2, 4)

HSA.REI.A.4 Solve quadratic equations in one variable.

    b. Solve by taking square roots. (Claims 1, 2, 4)

*Since there are so many standards in this unit, the team decided to group them into two power standards: Solving Equations and Solving Inequalities. Students will receive a score in each of these topics.*

*After agreeing on the power standards for a particular unit, the team collaboratively developed learning targets for students.*

**Learning Targets for Unit 1**

**Solving Equations**

2.1: I can solve one-step equations for a single variable by adding or subtracting—1 day

2.2: I can solve one-step equations for a single variable by multiplying or dividing—1 day

2.3: I can solve two-step equations for a single variable by multiple inverse operations—2 days

2.4: I can solve equations with a single variable on both sides of the equation—2 days

2.5: I can solve a formula for a given variable and solve other literal equations—3 days

2.6: I can solve equations in one variable that contain absolute value expressions—2 days

2.7: I can write and use rates, ratios, and unit rates to solve proportional problems—1 day

**Solving Inequalities**

3.1: I can identify and graph solutions of inequalities in one variable—1 day

3.2: I can solve one-step equations for a single variable by addition and subtraction—1 day

3.3: I can solve one-step equations for a single variable by multiplication and division—2 days

3.4: I can solve multi-step equations for a single variable by multiple inverse operations—2 days

3.5: I can solve inequalities that contain a variable on both sides—2 days

3.6: I can solve compound inequalities in one variable and graph their solution sets—2 days

3.7: I can solve inequalities in one variable involving absolute value expressions—1 day

Figure 3.2: Example of collaboratively developed power standards and learning targets.

*Source: White River School District. Used with permission.*

Once the algebra team agreed on the power standards for unit 1, it was then able to focus its discussions on such topics as pacing, what student work would look like if the standards were met, appropriate homework assignments, common scoring, and assessment formats and conditions.

## Developing and Utilizing the Results of Common Formative Assessments

Clarifying and adding meaning to mathematics standards is the basic foundation piece of the work of a collaborative team. The algebra team next moved to the rather logical question, "How will we know if our students are learning?" Collaborative teams in professional learning communities develop common formative assessments in order to monitor the learning of each kid, skill by skill, on a frequent and timely basis.

The algebra team reorganized their assessments to help focus the conversations on student learning and level of understanding instead of retaining points to earn a score. The team committed to not have point values on their assessments; instead, the team has four levels of questions for each group of standards. The level of understanding, as noted on the four-point scale, depends on the knowledge demonstrated on the different levels of questions. The conversations now are about the level of understanding and the gap in their knowledge instead of needing one more point to get a four. By restructuring the assessment, the team has been able to differentiate and scaffold for students more easily by focusing on lower-level questions and then building from that point.

As a result of their collaborative analysis of the results of their formative assessments and an examination of student work, Mr. Mothershead noted that the algebra team at White River High School collaboratively identified specific areas in which students struggled, as well as identified why they seemed to struggle (figure 3.3).

---

### Algebra Team: Student Struggles in Unit 1

- Difference between combining like terms on the same side of equal sign and combining like terms on different sides of equal sign
- Mathematical operations of positive and negative numbers
- Identifying like terms when dealing with same variable but different exponents

### Why Kids Struggled

- Looking at item analysis to determine if it was the wording of the question, students got things mixed up with other concepts, or students just did not know
- Did not fully understand role of equal sign when solving and what it meant
- Misunderstanding of what subtraction meant when subtracting positive and negative numbers
- Misconception that the answer is always the sign of the larger number when dealing with operations of positive and negative numbers

---

Figure 3.3: Identification of areas of struggle.

*Source: White River School District. Used with permission.*

## Providing Intervention

Since students learn at different rates and in different ways, in a PLC there is the recognition that some students will struggle with specific skills. When they do, they need additional time and support—as well as encouragement. At the White River High School, students benefit from such a schoolwide, systematic plan for additional time and support. As part of this plan, algebra students are supported in their learning because the algebra team has collaboratively developed a plan to help students when they experience difficulty (figure 3.4).

Of course, not all students need additional time and support. The schoolwide plan includes ways to enrich and extend student learning, as well, stretching them far beyond proficiency.

**Algebra Team: Extra Help and Intervention**

- Throughout the unit, we will use the data from the quick checks for understanding to guide our intervention and determine which students need extra help.

- The initial help for students will be provided in individual classrooms. (For example, if most students miss the same problem or part of a problem, the teacher will simply reteach, or perhaps the teacher will use various forms of grouping so that students can help each other.)

- Before- and after-school help will be available (scheduled time for individual teachers to be available for students before and after school).

- STAT time for directed intervention for students. (STAT time at White River High School is a specific period within the school day in which all students receive additional time, support, or enrichment.)

- Collaborative group work in which students will go through corrections, example problems, and explain their reasoning to support their work.

- After-unit activities to review main points of power standards.

    * Use Algebra Tiles to conceptualize solving equations and combining like terms.

    * Use deck of cards and number lines for operations of positive and negative numbers.

    * Use items such as brooms, jars, and blocks to emphasize idea of combining like terms.

- Online textbook resources such as tutorials, and practice quizzes.

- Extra support through Algebra Support class for those enrolled. Algebra Support uses preteaching and reteaching models and supports student learning based on data from algebra assessments.

- Co-teaching model to support students who receive services.

- Specific learning activities connected to learning targets with opportunities for extensions for those who got it.

- Performance Task connected to standards and learning targets.

Figure 3.4: Intervention plan.

*Source: White River School District. Used with permission.*

## Planning Units of Instruction

Collaborative teams in a PLC emphasize how they *think* about planning a unit of instruction (see figure 3.5, page 56). They are much more concerned about focusing on the right questions than they are about a correct format. In one sense, collaborative unit planning is a perfect example of the simultaneous loose-tight framework in action. The team collaboratively agrees on a number of things that it will be tight about regarding each unit, but be loose regarding teacher methodology or instructional approaches. Teachers in a PLC are constantly reminded that teacher autonomy and creativity are not only allowed but, in fact, encouraged—within the set parameters of collaboratively developed units of instruction. While there is no one right way to teach, teacher teams engage in deep discussions about instructional effectiveness, reflecting on notes that were kept from previous years regarding what seemed to work and what didn't work so well, and then share these instructional ideas and materials.

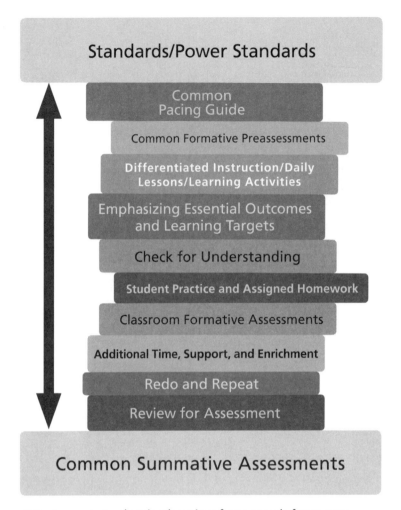

**Figure 3.5: A conceptual unit planning framework for teams.**

*Source: Adapted from Ainsworth & Viegut (2006).*

### Unit Rationale: The Why—Leaders Always Explain the Why

Let's take a look at an example of the rationale behind the creation of a unit plan:

The purpose of the White River School District English language arts (ELA) unit plans, common assessments, and pacing guide is to design a clear and coherent instructional and professional development district plan for ELA instruction in grades 3–5 for the school year. In other words, *What do we want our students to know/learn and be able to do?* Essentially, deliver a guaranteed and viable curriculum across the district.

At the district level, a guiding coalition identified the three priority standards (Key Ideas) in Reading and Writing. In Reading, these include both literary and information standards. In Writing, these include opinion pieces, informational/explanatory texts, and narratives. The ELA units of study 1–3 will be based on the Imagine It themes, target one reading and writing standard per unit, and then repeat for units 4–6. A minimal unit template has been initiated for grades 3–5. Site-based grade-level teams are empowered to further develop these unit plans based on student needs and instructional resources. To ensure that students learn the Reading Foundations standards, teachers are expected to teach the explicit phonemic, phonic, and fluency concepts for each lesson (green section).

Each unit will have grade-level-created common assessments, pre and post. The purpose of these assessments is to inform grade-level teams of their students' knowledge and skills and determine the next instructional steps. At the district level, these assessments will help inform our district practice, resource allocation, and professional development plan. In other words, *How will we know our students learned?* Several units will have grade-level-created performance tasks. The purpose of the performance tasks is to challenge students to apply their knowledge and skills to respond to complex real-world problems. They can best be described as collections of questions and activities that are coherently connected to a single theme or scenario. These activities are meant to measure capacities such as depth of understanding, writing and research skills, and complex analysis, which cannot be adequately assessed with traditional assessment questions.

First and foremost, the common assessment helps teams make learning decisions about their students, but it is also a common tool to communicate student learning on standards reflected on the report card. The team made some decisions about what the logical learning progression in ELA is using the Common Core State Standards, and those are reflected on the report card. During the 2014–15 school year, the ELA team will continue to work on the assessments, unit by unit, to ensure that every student has the opportunity to show their progression on those critical standards and that every teacher has enough information at hand to be able to accurately report on each student's growth.

In order to better support the transition to the Common Core State Standards at the district level, it is important that the professional development be targeted. The ELA units of study are identically sequenced in grades 3–5 so collaborative inquiry and training can be coordinated. Each unit is six to seven weeks.

At the end of each unit, school and district teams will score each assessment together, use the TACA form to analyze the results, provide additional time and support and extensions, and adjust the unit plan based on the results.

### *Unit Scope and Sequence*

### *Units 1 and 4*

*CCRA.R.1—Read closely to determine what the text says explicitly and to make logical inferences from it; cite specific textual evidence when writing or speaking to support conclusions drawn from the text.*

*CCRA.W.1—Write arguments to support claims in an analysis of substantive topics or texts using valid reasoning and relevant and sufficient evidence.*

**Units 2 and 5**

*CCRA.R.2—Determine central ideas or themes of a text and analyze their development; summarize the key supporting details and ideas.*

*CCRA.W.2—Write informative/explanatory texts to examine and convey complex ideas and information clearly and accurately through the effective selection, organization, and analysis of content.*

**Units 3–6**

*CCRA.R.3—Analyze how and why individuals, events, or ideas develop and interact over the course of a text.*

*CCRA.W.3—Write narratives to develop real or imagined experiences or events using effective technique, well-chosen details and well-structured event sequences.*

## The Unit Plan

Figure 3.6 is an example of a unit plan created for a districtwide third-grade ELA unit. Visit **go.solution-tree.com/PLCbooks** and the appendix (page 187) for another example.

As you can see, there are a number of important things the team should address during the collaborative planning process. Figure 3.7 (page 67) provides a visual depiction of the essential topics teams should think about and address as team members plan together. (Note that multiple checks for understanding should occur throughout the unit, including commonly developed formative performance assessments, products that will be scored by rubrics, pencil-and-paper exercises, oral questioning, and observation.)

Teams in White River understand the PLC way of thinking as it applies to their work, especially when they are engaged in crafting unit plans, designing assessments, analyzing data, and providing additional time, support, and extensions in core instruction for all kids. Sometimes we hear, "Are you talking about special education kids getting core instruction too?" Yes! Special education kids are general education kids first. They deserve core instruction with support *plus* Tier 2 and Tier 3 support. It's unethical to ask students to take a state assessment that assesses their knowledge on grade-level standards when teachers have never given them an opportunity to interact with the grade-level standards. Worse than that, we occasionally must then send the parents a letter telling them that their child didn't meet the standard. If we were perfectly honest, we would add a footnote telling the parents that their child was never taught the grade-level standards!

Grade Level: 3    Time Period: Jan. 12 – Mar. 13    Content Area: ELA    Unit Name: Unit 3 – Communities Across Time

## Standards Addressed in This Unit

| **Big Ideas: How do people affect their environment? How does the environment affect people?** | **Essential Questions:** |
| --- | --- |
| | How will students be able to identify a character and describe his or her physical and emotional traits? |
| | How will students be able to explain how characters' actions cause events to happen in a certain order or sequence in a story? |
| | How will students be able to tell about the time, sequence, and cause and effect of a historical event? |
| | • Of scientific ideas? |
| | • Of steps in a procedure? |
| | How will students be able to produce clear and coherent opinion writing? |

| **Reading Standards for Informational/ Literary Text:** | **Writing/Language Standards:** | **Speaking & Listening Standards:** |
| --- | --- | --- |
| RL.3.3—Describe characters in a story (e.g., their traits, motivations, or feelings) and explain how their actions contribute to the sequence of events. | W.3.1—Write opinion pieces on topics or texts, supporting a point of view with reasons. | SL.3.3—Ask and answer questions about information from a speaker, offering appropriate elaboration and detail. |
| RI.3.3—Describe the relationship between a series of historical events, scientific ideas or concepts, or steps in technical procedures in a text, using language that pertains to time, sequence, and cause/effect. | a. Introduce the topic or text they are writing about, state an opinion, and create an organizational structure that lists reasons. | |
| **Ongoing:** | b. Provide reasons that support the opinion. | |
| CCSS Reading Foundations | c. Use linking words and phrases (e.g., *because, therefore, since, for example*) to connect opinion and reasons. | |
| CCSS Vocabulary | d. Provide a concluding statement or section. | |
| | **Ongoing:** | |
| | **CCSS Language** | |
| | **CCSS Writing** | |
| | W.3.4—organization and purpose | |
| | W.3.5—revision and editing | |
| | W.3.6—technology in writing | |

Continued ↓

Figure 3.6: Third-grade unit plan.

*Source: White River School District. Used with permission.*

## Standards Addressed in This Unit

**Learning Progression:**

RL.2.3—Describe how characters in a story respond to major events and challenges.

RI.2.3—Describe the connection between a series of historical events, scientific ideas or concepts, or steps in technical procedures in a text.

W.2.1—Write opinion pieces in which they introduce the topic or book they are writing about, state an opinion, supply reasons that support the opinion, use linking words (e.g., *because, and, also*) to connect opinion and reasons, and provide a concluding statement or section.

SL.2.3—Ask and answer questions about what a speaker says in order to clarify comprehension, gather additional information, or deepen understanding of a topic or issue.

RL.4.3—Describe in depth a character, setting, or event in a story or drama, drawing on specific details in the text (e.g., a character's thoughts, words, or actions).

RI.4.3—Explain events, procedures, ideas, or concepts in a historical, scientific, or technical text, including what happened and why, based on specific information in the text.

W.4.1—Write opinion pieces on topics or texts, supporting a point of view with reasons and information.

Introduce a topic or text clearly, state an opinion, and create an organizational structure in which related ideas are grouped to support the writer's purpose.

Provide reasons that are supported by facts and details.

Link opinion and reasons using words and phrases (e.g., *for instance, in order to, in addition*).

Provide a concluding statement or section related to the opinion presented.

SL.4.3—Identify the reasons and evidence a speaker provides to support particular points.

**Common Core Essential Element:**

EE.SL.3.3—Ask or answer questions about the details provided by the speaker.

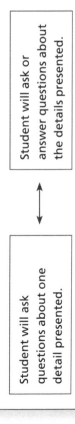

| Student will ask questions about one detail presented. | Student will ask or answer questions about the details presented. | Student will select one detail from a text presented. |
| --- | --- | --- |
| More Complex | | Less Complex |

## Standards Addressed in This Unit

**Washington State English Language Proficiency (ELP) Standards:**

www.k12.wa.us/MigrantBilingual/ELD.aspx (Visit this link for Specific ELA Leveled Skills—"Jump to a Section" for your grade level within categories of information.)

CCSS—RL.3.3, RI.3.3, W.3.1, SL.3.3 (See above)

ELP Standards aligned with this unit

ELP.2–3.1—Construct meaning from oral presentations and literary and informational text through grade appropriate listening, reading, and viewing . . .

ELP.2–3.4—Construct grade appropriate oral and written claims and support them with reasoning and evidence . . .

ELP.2–3.6—Analyze and critique the arguments of others orally and in writing . . .

ELP.2–3.9—Create clear and coherent grade-appropriate speech and text (temporal words in stories) . . .

ELP.2–3.10—Make accurate use of standard English to communicate in grade-appropriate speech and writing . . .

**Key Vocabulary**

| | | | |
|---|---|---|---|
| cause | effect | drawing conclusions | trait | fact |
| opinion | claim | evidence | passage | source |
| character | introduction | conclusion | sequence | |

Continued →

| Student-Friendly Learning Targets | Assessments/Evidence |
|---|---|
| **RL.2.3**—Describe how characters in a story respond to major events and challenges.<br>• I can identify a character in a story.<br>• I can describe physical traits.<br>• I can describe/infer emotional traits and support with text evidence.<br>• I can draw conclusions about characters/events in my reading.<br>• I recognize cause.<br>• I recognize effect.<br>• I understand how cause and effect relate to each other.<br>• I can explain how characters' actions cause events to happen in a certain order or sequence in a story (cause/effect).<br><br>**RL.3.3**—Describe characters in a story (e.g., their traits, motivations, or feelings) and explain how their actions contribute to the sequence of events.<br><br>**RI.2.3**—Describe the connection between a series of historical events, scientific ideas or concepts, or steps in technical procedures in a text.<br>• I can sequence events.<br>• I can sequence procedures or steps.<br>• I understand how cause and effect relate to each other.<br>• I can use language, transitions that show time, sequence, cause/effect when describing text.<br>• I can tell about the time, sequence, and cause and effect of a historical event/scientific ideas/steps in a procedure orally.<br>• I can tell about the time, sequence, and cause and effect of a historical event/scientific ideas/steps in a procedure in writing.<br><br>**RI.3.3**—Describe the relationship between a series of historical events, scientific ideas or concepts, or steps in technical procedures in a text, using language that pertains to time, sequence, and cause/effect. | **Preassessments**<br>• Informational—"Walking Tall"<br>• Literary—"My Community"<br><br>**Formative Assessments**<br>• Building Team—Generated<br><br>**Writing**<br>Prompt—In a several-paragraph essay, convince an animal lover which kind of pet is best. A cat or a dog? See daily plans for materials.<br><br>**Post-Assessments**<br>• Informational—"Walking Tall"<br>• Literary—"My Community"<br>• Performance Task—Changes to a Small Town (This PT will also take care of the writing portion of the social studies CBA "Humans and the Environment.") |

| Student-Friendly Learning Targets | Assessments/Evidence |
|---|---|
| **W.2.1**—Write opinion pieces in which they introduce the topic or book they are writing about, state an opinion, supply reasons that support the opinion, use linking words (e.g., *because, and, also*) to connect opinion and reasons, and provide a concluding statement or section. | |
| • I know the difference between fact and opinion. | |
| • I understand that I can have an opinion about facts. | |
| • I can determine my opinion or point of view about something that I have read. | |
| • I can support my opinion with details from the text. | |
| • I can research a topic to support my opinion using multiple sources. | |
| • I can make claims and provide evidence to support my opinion and claims. | |
| • I can organize information supporting my opinion on a graphic organizer. | |
| • I can connect the claims and evidence with words like: *because, therefore, since, and for example*. | |
| • I can write an opinion piece with an introduction, supporting reasons (claims and evidence), and a concluding statement/section. | |
| **W.3.1**—Write opinion pieces on topics or texts, supporting a point of view with reasons. | |
|   a.  Introduce the topic or text they are writing about, state an opinion, and create an organizational structure that lists reasons. | |
|   b.  Provide reasons that support the opinion. | |
|   c.  Use linking words and phrases (e.g., *because, therefore, since, for example*) to connect opinion and reasons. | |
|   d.  Provide a concluding statement or section. | |
| **SL.2.3**—Ask and answer questions about what a speaker says in order to clarify comprehension, gather additional information, or deepen understanding of a topic or issue. | |
| • I can… | |
| **SL.3.3**—Ask and answer questions about information from a speaker, offering appropriate elaboration and detail. | |

Continued →

**Differentiated/Daily Lessons – Developed by Building Teams**

| Reading | Writing |
|---|---|
| **Ongoing:**<br><br>• Green Section of *Imagine It!*<br>• Tier II vocabulary work using literature of teacher's choice from the unit and grade level vocab books.<br><br>**Daily Learning**<br><br>• Model using non-fiction feature with diagrams and close-ups including entries in lit log.<br>• Learning about non-fiction features—this lesson will take multiple days. A variety of non-fiction text at varied reading levels will be needed. Look over the books you select to make sure the features the kids will be studying are included in the books they will be working from (see lit log for the complete list of features the kids will be working on). These lessons can be done in combination with lessons that follow to save time.<br><br>*Smart Words Scholastic Animals* along with other animal informational text is a great option.<br><br>• Reading Procedures Lessons—CLOSE read with a procedure of your choice or one listed below. What are the parts? How are they arranged? What comes before? What comes after? How could the procedure be written in a paragraph with transitions?<br>   * "Here Comes the Sun"—Short functional selection to read<br>   * "How to Make an Eggshell Chalk"<br>   * "Peanut Butter Fudge"—Short functional selection to read<br>   * Up Goes a Skyscraper—old Scholastic<br>• Option—Write own procedure for something they know how to do (old Scholastic).<br>• Drawing conclusions—Complete drawing conclusions/making inferences information chart (see student lit log) and Drawing Conclusion PowerPoint.<br>• Drawing conclusion—Model lesson with box graphic organizer (2 to choose from in lit log) and *The Mary Celeste, Roanoke, Fly Away Home, The Stranger, I am the Dog, I am the Cat* or a read-aloud of your choice.<br>• *The Wreck of the Zephyr*—old reading series—Drawing Conclusions graphic organizer<br>• Student strong work examples and repeat as needed—reading materials to choose from—ReadWorks—"In Memory of Dr. King" and "Saving the Animals," and so on | **Daily Learning**<br><br>• Intro—YouTube videos (see email) and *Hey, Little Ant*<br>• Write your own fact or opinion when given a topic (object draw activity).<br>• Super Teacher Worksheets<br>• Identify fact or opinion in reading selections —graphic organizers—Fact Opinion Tree Diagram or two-column fact and opinion<br>• "Junk Food Attack" and "Junk Food Battles," readworks.org—short passages connected to fact and opinion<br>• Smart Exchange (SMART Board activities)<br>• Imagine It Unit 5 Lesson 3? "Earthquakes" fact and opinion<br>• SU—Lesson 9–2 Fact (evidence) vs. Opinion—Pull opinion writing samples from other sources.<br>• Opinion sentence writing in writing journals with kids learning that an "I" statement becomes part of topic paragraph<br>• SU—Lesson 9–1 opinion writing words (see opinion writing signal word list)<br>• Read articles—"Why cats make…" "Why dogs make…" articles leaving a trail of your thinking<br>• Form opinion and two-column notes from article<br>• *National Geographic*—Dogs vs. Cats—text features to read specific sections to beef up notes. Teacher models with one section. |

| Reading | Writing |
|---|---|
| * What conclusion can be drawn about MLK's impact on civil rights?<br><br>* What conclusion can be drawn about the students at Public School 48?<br><br>• Drawing conclusions—"The Case of the Missing Mascot" PowerPoint<br><br>• Model lesson cause and effect—*If You Give a Mouse a Cookie, Jimmy Boa's and the Big Splash Birthday Bash*… read-aloud of your choice—read and discuss with some strong examples on flowchart<br><br>• *Tomorrow's Alphabet*—read and write activity for cause and effect<br><br>• Imagine It, Unit 5 Lesson 4 *The Disappearing Island*, Imagine It Unit 5 Lesson 5, *The House on Maple Street*, Imagine It Unit 5 Lesson 3 *Earthquake*—use one, some, or all for cause and effect practice<br><br>• Extra Practice—What Is the Cause? Find the Effect? Super Teacher<br><br>• Timelines—Biographies—find and record important events, sequence events on a timeline, write a paragraph with transitions to support timeline from notes taken using two-column notes and researching main ideas about the topic (person) of their choice<br><br>• Another option for research and text features—Continent Poster project—see old Non-fiction Features materials for information (not in lit log)<br><br>• *Molly's Pilgrim*—Introduce content vocab/ partner read 1st half of book.<br><br>• *Molly's Pilgrim*—Review vocab, read second half of book with Cause/Effect Review.<br><br>• ReadWorks—"The Chimp's Champ" Character Analysis and Tier 2 vocab<br><br>• *Molly's Pilgrim*—Reread as necessary for evidence to support character idea/claim.<br><br>• Character explanatory paragraph—Model with a MM teacher of the kids' choice.<br><br>• *Molly's Pilgrim*—Write character expository paragraph for Elizabeth, or Molly pre-write and paragraph.<br><br>• What if… How might the story be different?—Supply kids with options for the characters from *Molly's Pilgrim* to act in a different way to discuss and write about how this would affect the story in a different way. Example: What if Elizabeth had smiled at Molly the first time they met? What if Molly's mother had let Molly stay home from school?, and so on.<br><br>• Additional materials to use as needed—*The Matchbox Diary and ReadWorks "A Rally Against Poverty"* | • Select two ideas or claims from notes and complete opinion essay following direction and prompt.<br><br>• Read, note taking, draft, revise and edit, conference, and publish over a five-day period<br><br>• Self-assessing and peer assessing using district-developed kid-friendly rubric<br><br>• Review teacher feedback. |

Continued ↓

**Intervention Plan—Developed by Building Teams**

| Intensive | Strategic | Good to Go |
|---|---|---|
| Two Groups | Two Groups | Three classroom groups—working on personalized reading goals: |
| Reading Mastery A (2 groups) | Corrective Reading B1 (2 groups) | Fluency |
| Corrective Reading A | Corrective Reading B2 | Motivation |
| | AND Fluency Goal work using pre-teach of Classroom CORE materials | Comprehension |
| | | And enrichment connected to CORE Lessons |
| Level 1 non-fiction—non-fiction features and independent reading (choosing a topic) | Level 1 and 2 non-fiction—features and independent reading (choosing a topic) | Tween Tribune—CLOSE reading |
| | | Procedure writing—Google Docs |
| | | Hannah's Journal—Novel Study |
| | | Biography research and timeline |

*Visit **go.solution-tree.com/PLCbooks** for a blank version of this figure.*

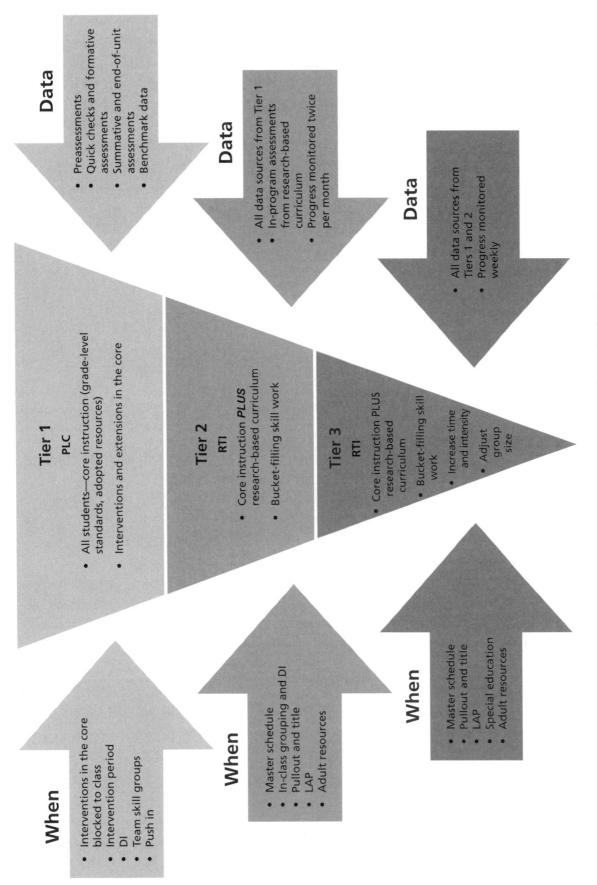

**Data**
- Preassessments
- Quick checks and formative assessments
- Summative and end-of-unit assessments
- Benchmark data

**Data**
- All data sources from Tier 1
- In-program assessments from research-based curriculum
- Progress monitored twice per month

**Data**
- All data sources from Tiers 1 and 2
- Progress monitored weekly

**Tier 1**
PLC
- All students—core instruction (grade-level standards, adopted resources)
- Interventions and extensions in the core

**Tier 2**
RTI
- Core instruction *PLUS* research-based curriculum
- Bucket-filling skill work

**Tier 3**
RTI
- Core instruction PLUS research-based curriculum
- Bucket-filling skill work
- Increase time and intensity
- Adjust group size

**When**
- Interventions in the core blocked to class
- Intervention period
- DI
- Team skill groups
- Push in

**When**
- Master schedule
- In-class grouping and DI
- Pullout and title
- LAP
- Adult resources

**When**
- Master schedule
- Pullout and title
- LAP
- Special education
- Adult resources

Figure 3.7: Grades 3–5 ELA team, White River School District, essential topics for unit planning.

*Source: White River School District. Used with permission.*

Occasionally, a teacher asks, "By having us plan together, study the standards together, and use the same assessments, aren't you wanting us to be cookie-cutter teachers—all teaching the same thing the same way at the same time?" Nothing could be further from the truth! The standards for the course, content area, and grade level don't change. After all, fourth grade is fourth grade, Title I school or non–Title I school. At the secondary level, biology is biology—same standards, same assessments, and same state end-of-course assessment, regardless of the school or teacher. When kids take the state assessment, the state doesn't care who the kids' parents are, where they live, or where they go to school. They care if kids meet the standard. That's what counts.

> *When kids take the state assessment, the state doesn't care who the kids' parents are, where they live, or where they go to school. They care if kids meet the standard.*

Here's what changes: Unit by unit between the standards and the assessment process, teachers provide the appropriate scaffolding that their students need to be successful. They make decisions about the lessons they will teach in an effort to ensure kids meet the standards along with the specific learning targets attached to those lessons. They make decisions about the homework they will assign and the additional time and support they will provide. They make decisions about the assessment process that will be in place to inform their teaching.

## Using Examples

Examples for students, teachers, and teams are always helpful. The following are examples of the work of teams in the White River School District at the elementary, middle, and high school levels. More examples can be found online at **go.solution -tree.com/PLCbooks** and in the appendix (page 187).

Exemplary work benefits teacher teams in a number of ways. It speeds up the process. By examining the work of others, teams can see what the finished products look like. And, since the examples should be excellent examples, teams can see what really good work will look like in the end. Examples send the message, "This can be done." The fact that other teams have successfully worked collaboratively to create excellent products can serve as a motivator to others.

### Clarifying and Articulating Essential Learning

Figure 3.8 is an example of a checklist style of articulating essential learning. Using this, students can see exactly what they must achieve in each area of sixth-grade math. We'll take a look at just one area here.

---

### Expressions and Equations

Apply and extend previous understandings of arithmetic to algebraic expressions (6.EE.1, 6.EE.2, 6.EE.3, 6.EE.4):

- ❑ I can write and evaluate numerical order of operations expressions involving whole number exponents.
- ❑ I can translate between words and math using variables.
- ❑ I can identify parts of an expression using mathematical terms.
- ❑ I can view one or more parts of an expression as a single entity.
- ❑ I can evaluate expressions that arise from formulas used in real-world problems.
- ❑ I can evaluate expressions, given the values for the variables, using order of operations.
- ❑ I can generate equivalent expressions.
- ❑ I can identify when two algebraic expressions are equivalent regardless of the value of the variable.

---

Figure 3.8: Grade 6 mathematics expectations checklist.

*Source: White River School District. Used with permission.*

## Creating Common Formative Assessments

Figure 3.9 (pages 70–73) is an example of a collaboratively created common formative assessment for a mathematics lesson on functions. See the appendix (page 187) for another example of a common assessment.

## Planning for Additional Time, Support, and Extension

There are no "correct" models for additional time and support—the issue is whether they are working. Following are a few examples of additional time and support from the White River School District.

### Secondary Co-Teaching Model

If students must meet the standards, they must first interact with the standards! That's why the co-teaching model is so powerful. The old model of having resource teachers, who were not endorsed in math, combined with the core replacement curriculum, which did not meet grade-level standards, was not an effective formula for our students who struggled the most to be successful. This model is designed to have a highly qualified and trained mathematics teacher partnered with an experienced teacher specializing in accommodations and who also understands how a student's disability impacts his or her ability to learn. The co-teaching model enables you to have the best of both worlds.

**Directions:** On every problem, show supporting evidence for ALL of your answers.

1. Circle the letter of all relations that are functions.

   A. $y = \frac{1}{2}x + \frac{1}{3}$

   B.

   | x | y |
   |----|----|
   | 3 | -9 |
   | 0 | -6 |
   | -1 | -3 |
   | -1 | 0 |
   | 4 | 3 |

   C.

   D. { (-2, 2), (-1, 1), (0, 0), (1, 1) }

2. Circle the letter of all ordered pairs that satisfy the function $y = -5x + 6$.

   A. (-4, -14)

   B. (-1, 11)

   C. (3, -9)

   D. (5, -31)

3. The volume of water, in gallons, in a water tower, depends on the time (t), in hours, and can be modeled by the function $y = -50t + 3000$.

   Circle the letter of all of the ordered pairs that satisfy the function.

   A. (2500, 10)

   B. (10, 2500)

   C. (0, 3000)

   D. (3000, 0)

4. Can the table of values be represented by the function $y = 3x + 2$? Explain.

   | x | y |
   |----|-----|
   | -4 | -10 |
   | -3 | -7 |
   | -2 | -4 |
   | -1 | -1 |
   | 0 | 2 |

5. Michael wrote the table of values to represent the function, $y = x^2$. Find and fix all of his mistakes.

| x | y |
|---|---|
| -10 | 100 |
| -7 | -14 |
| -4 | 16 |
| -2 | -4 |
| 0 | 0 |

6. Andrea's health club has a $75 enrollment fee. It also costs her $27.50 per month to keep her membership active.

Select the equation that models the relationship between the amount of money (A), in dollars, that she spends after m months.

A.  A = 75m + 27.50

B.  A = -75m + 27.50

C.  A = 27.50m + 75

D.  A = -27.50m + 75

7. Create a story that could completely represent the data table.

| x | y |
|---|---|
| 0 | 4 |
| 2 | 12 |
| 4 | 20 |
| 6 | 28 |

8. This table shows the relationship between the monthly cell phone cost from Company A and the number of minutes used within a month.

| Time (min) | Cost (dollars) |
|---|---|
| 0 | 50.00 |
| 2 | 50.20 |
| 4 | 50.40 |

The following equation shows the relationship between the monthly cell phone cost (c) for Company B and the number of minutes used within a month (m).

c = 39 + 0.05m

The flat fee is defined as the monthly cost for the phone when 0 minutes are used. What is the difference, in dollars, between the flat fee for Plan B and the flat rate for Plan A?

Continued →

Figure 3.9: Common formative assessment and grading rubric.

*Source: White River School District. Used with permission.*

9. Manuela had 2 dollars in her wallet and saved another dollar every two days. She modeled her data on a graph.

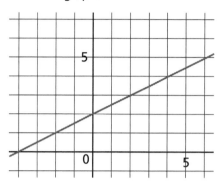

Select the equation represented by the graph.

A. $y = \frac{1}{2}x + 2$

B. $y = -\frac{1}{2}x + 2$

C. $y = 2x + 2$

D. $y = -2x + 2$

10. Several relations are represented in the table. Determine whether each relation is linear or nonlinear.

| Relation | Linear | Nonlinear |
|---|---|---|
| $y = \frac{3}{4}x + 2$ | | |
| <table><tr><td>x</td><td>y</td></tr><tr><td>-2</td><td>2</td></tr><tr><td>-1</td><td>1</td></tr><tr><td>0</td><td>0</td></tr><tr><td>1</td><td>1</td></tr><tr><td>2</td><td>2</td></tr></table> | | |
| 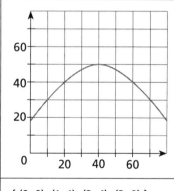 | | |
| { (0, 0), (1, 1), (2, 4), (3, 9) } | | |

## Evaluating Functions Test

Name _____          Period _____

| List of Skills | Minimal Understanding 1 | Nearing Mastery 2 | Demonstrated Mastery 3 |
|---|---|---|---|
| I can determine whether the relation is a function. (#1) | | | |
| I can determine which points satisfy the equation. (#2, 3, 4, 5) | | | |
| I can choose the rules that represent the scenario. (#6, 9) | | | |
| I can analyze data. (#7, 8) | | | |
| I can determine whether the relation is linear. (#10) | | | |

| Grading Rubric | | |
|---|---|---|
| 4.0 | A+ | 15 |
| 3.75 | A | 13–14 |
| 3.5 | B | 12 |
| 3.25 | B+ | 11 |
| 3.0 | C | 10 |
| 2.75 | D+ | 8–9 |
| 2.5 | D- | 7 |
| 2.0 | F | 0–6 |

### Algebra and Geometry Support Classes

These are additional math classes for students who struggle in either algebra or geometry. They are scheduled into a regular algebra or geometry class and an algebra support or geometry support class. The support class provides a smaller class size, gives students extra time to finish tests, allows time to preteach and reteach specific concepts differently, provides extra time to work on skill gaps, and provides a time for struggling learners to ask questions. Most struggling learners will sit back and not ask questions or even know what questions to ask. Just a side note: Last year White River had 69 percent of our support kids pass the Algebra Washington State End of Course assessment (which is a graduation requirement) compared to 39 percent the year before.

### Walk to Learn (Ongoing)

The building schedule provides a daily time set aside for teams to provide intervention for students. This might be a block anywhere from thirty to fifty minutes during which no core instruction occurs and time is specifically set aside for intervention. Because the schedule has been developed at a building level, paraprofessional schedules can often be aligned to this schedule to provide even more instructional support. An example of this is an ongoing ELA intervention block. A group of three teachers and three paraprofessionals might provide instruction that meets the needs of learners— from kids still needing word structure and phonics work to kids interacting with text beyond their grade level. This model still allows access to core instruction for all kids but also provides a chance to further their skills in a just-right way for each learner.

### Walk to Learn (Flexible)

Teams set aside a time in the daily schedule to have kids move to a particular spot to focus on a targeted learning need. This might be a decision a team makes after looking at common assessment data that were brought to the table showing apparent areas of focus for groups of kids that can be better met over multiple days with a thirty- to forty-minute block of time to concentrate on specific learning needs. It might last a few days, a week, or beyond. An example of this is a third-grade team shortening their core instructional block in math two days a week for a walk to math focused on standards relating to a fractions unit they are working on. One group might be kids who need backfilling, work on previous standards to help them better access the new learning. One group might be kids who have a basic understanding of the content standards relating to fractions but need more time applying these basic understandings to higher-level skills. Another group might be kids in need of enrichment like accessing the standards at the next level up or a project-based scenario to apply the skills they have.

## *Differentiated Instruction in the Classroom*

These groups happen within the normal flow of one classroom. As students are working on a learning activity, a teacher might pull a group together for fifteen to twenty minutes to work on a target skill. This might happen based on a team discussion of a common formative assessment or from checks for understanding teachers are using within their classrooms. These groups are not long-lived and provide students with another approach or another practice opportunity to master a skill. The group might be focused on an enrichment opportunity or a reteach of a basic skill. Picture a full class involved in opinion writing during a writer's workshop. A teacher might invite a group of kids to meet as a group that is focused on understanding how to use text-based evidence to support their opinions.

## Pacing the Learning

Figure 3.10 (pages 76–77) is an example of a grade 3 scope and sequence.

## Teaming in Action: The Story of the White River High School Social Studies Team

*By Scott Harrison, Assistant Principal, White River High School*

Periodically throughout the year, PLC visitors come to White River to observe the work of our teams during the Monday morning PLC time. This is followed by a breakout session designed to build shared knowledge about the work of our teams, answer important implementation questions that visitors might have, and share specific implementation resources that they can use as they return to their schools and continue their journey. While each visitor has his or her own story, there are two common themes that emerge when working with these incredibly dedicated educators.

The first group represents the classroom teacher who is generally an innovator by nature and has dedicated a significant amount of time and energy into his or her professional growth. Most of them have attended a PLC Institute and have come away invigorated and ready to implement the research-based practices of professional learning communities so that they can improve student learning for the students they serve. However, most of them express frustration and disenchantment when they return to their school and receive immediate pushback from their colleagues. This frustration is soon directed toward the administrator, and many of them want to know what our principals do to lead the work and ensure success.

The second group consists of building and district administrators who have worked tirelessly for several years and committed significant resources toward the goal of implementing a culture of collaboration and shared ownership of student learning that are indicative of a professional learning community. They too have grown frustrated by the lack of progress and seek to understand the systems and

**Grade 3 Scope and Sequence 2014–15**

**Ongoing Practices:** CLOSE Reading and Text-Dependent Questions (RL.3.1 and RI.3.1); Word Study—Imagine It! Green (Reading Foundational Skills); Vocabulary (RL.3.4 and L.3.4); Fluency (RF.3.4); Comprehension / Text Complexity (RL.3.10 and RI.3.1)

| Unit Theme | Unit Dates and Duration | Common Assessments | Essential Questions | Reading: Literature | Reading: Informational Text | Writing | Speaking and Listening |
|---|---|---|---|---|---|---|---|
| 1 Friendship | Sept. 2 – Oct. 17 (8 weeks) | Literature Informational PT | **What does it take to be a good friend?** How will students be able to read closely to determine what the text says explicitly? How will students use specific evidence from the text to support their answer? How will students produce clear and coherent narrative writing? | **RL.3.1**—Ask and answer questions to demonstrate understanding of a text, referring explicitly to the text as the basis for the answers. | **RI.3.1**—Ask and answer questions to demonstrate understanding of a text, referring explicitly to the text as the basis for the answers. | Narrative **W.3.3**—Write narratives to develop real or imagined experiences or events using effective technique, descriptive details and clear event sequences. | **SL.3.1**—Engage effectively in a range of collaborative discussions (one-on-one, in groups, and teacher-led) with diverse partners on grade 3 topics and texts, building on others' ideas and expressing their own clearly. |
| 2 Science in Our World | Oct. 27 – Dec. 19 (8 weeks) | Literature Informational PT | **How do scientists use evidence to support an argument?** How will students be able to read closely to determine the main idea of a text? How will students be able to recount the key details to support the main idea? How will students explain how key details support the main idea? How will students be able to recount stories? How will students explain the central message/lesson/moral? How will students explain how key details support the central message/lesson/moral? How will students produce clear and coherent explanatory writing? | **RL.3.2**—Recount stories, including fables, folktales, and myths from diverse cultures; determine the central message, lesson, or moral and explain how it is conveyed through key details in the text. | **RI.3.2**—Determine the main idea of a text; recount the key details and explain how they support the main idea. | Informational **W.3.2**—Write informative/explanatory texts to examine a topic and convey ideas and information clearly. | **SL.3.2**—Determine the main ideas and supporting details of a text read aloud or information presented in diverse media and formats, including visually, quantitatively, and orally. |

| Unit Theme | Unit Dates and Duration | Common Assessments | Essential Questions | Reading: Literature | Reading: Informational Text | Writing | Speaking and Listening |
|---|---|---|---|---|---|---|---|
| 3 Communities Across Time | Jan. 12 – Mar. 13 (9 weeks) | Literature Informational PT | **How do people affect their environment? How does the environment affect people?**<br><br>How will students be able to identify a character and describe their physical and emotional traits?<br><br>How will students be able to explain how characters' actions cause events to happen in a certain order or sequence in a story?<br><br>How will students be able to tell about the time, sequence, and cause and effect of a historical event?<br><br>• Of scientific ideas?<br>• Of steps in a procedure?<br><br>How will students be able to produce clear and coherent opinion writing? | **RL.3.3—**Describe characters in a story (e.g., their traits, motivations, or feelings) and explain how their actions contribute to the sequence of events. | **RI.3.3—**Describe the relationship between a series of historical events, scientific ideas or concepts, or steps in technical procedures in a text, using language that pertains to time, sequence, and cause/effect. | Opinion<br>**W.3.1—**Write opinion pieces on topics or texts, supporting a point of view with reasons. | **SL.3.3—**Ask and answer questions about information from a speaker, offering appropriate elaboration and detail. |

Continued ↓

Figure 3.10: Example scope and sequence.

*Source: White River School District. Used with permission.*

| Unit Theme | Unit Dates and Duration | Common Assessments | Essential Questions | Reading: Literature | Reading: Informational Text | Writing | Speaking and Listening |
|---|---|---|---|---|---|---|---|
| 4<br><br>Reading With Purpose | Mar. 23 – May 29<br><br>(9 weeks) | Literature<br>Informational<br>Brief Write<br>Interim | **What does the text tell a reader? How do readers interact with different types of text?**<br><br>How will students be able to read closely to:<br><br>• Determine the main idea of a text?<br>• Recount the key details to support the main idea?<br>• Explain how key details support the main idea?<br><br>How will students be able to recount stories?<br><br>How will students explain:<br><br>• The central message/lesson/moral?<br>• How key details support the central message/lesson/moral?<br><br>How will students be able to identify a character and describe their physical and emotional traits?<br><br>How will students be able to explain how characters' actions cause events to happen in a certain order or sequence in a story?<br><br>How will students be able to tell about the time, sequence, and cause and effect of a historical event?<br><br>• Of scientific ideas?<br>• Of steps in a procedure?<br><br>How will students be able to revise and edit writing to improve it for their audience? | **RL.3.2**—Recount stories, including fables, folktales, and myths from diverse cultures; determine the central message, lesson, or moral and explain how it is conveyed through key details in the text.<br><br>**RL.3.3**—Describe characters in a story (e.g., their traits, motivations, or feelings) and explain how their actions contribute to the sequence of events. | **RI.3.2**—Determine the main idea of a text; recount the key details and explain how they support the main idea.<br><br>**RI.3.3**—Describe the relationship between a series of historical events, scientific ideas or concepts, or steps in technical procedures in a text, using language that pertains to time, sequence, and cause/effect. | **W.3.5**—With guidance and support from peers and adults develop and strengthen writing as needed by planning, revising, and editing. | **SL.3.40**—Report on a topic or text, tell a story, or recount an experience with appropriate facts and relevant, descriptive details, speaking clearly at an understandable pace. |

support mechanisms in place in White River that help drive the work of our teams and ensure that collective commitments are aligned with our organizational goals.

For many of these visitors, their day begins at White River High School, and it has been interesting to see how the feedback of this group has changed over the last few years. As you might imagine, there are plenty of questions during our debrief session, and most of them seek to understand how to guide and support a group of teachers from traditional and autonomous teaching practices performed in isolation to a collaborative and strategic approach to teaching and learning that is standards based and data driven. What is interesting is that over the course of the last few years, the team that visitors are most interested in and excited about is one that most folks might not expect. While everyone feels the pressure of raising scores in language arts, math, and science, the team many visitors want to talk about is our social studies team.

At first glance, the social studies team at White River looks much like teams in every other high school in the country. The team consists of mostly male veteran teachers who each coach at least one sport. I know the question you are about to ask, and the answer is yes, our head football coach is a history teacher. In other words, this is a very traditional social studies team, and four years ago, its approach to social studies education was very traditional as well. It had unit and course standards that were primarily based on content, and its assessments were made up of level-one questions that focused on historical knowledge and comprehension tasks. It had common pacing guides and common assessments, but the level of rigor and student engagement was lackluster. In a typical day of class visits, you would find several lectures with an accompanying PowerPoint presentation. Students would be taking notes dutifully in preparation for the upcoming assessment.

This is said in order to paint the picture and in no way should be taken as a commentary regarding the skills, abilities, and professionalism of each teacher on the team. They are all dedicated teachers who want the best for the students they serve. The reality is that their practices represented their best individual thinking and not the collective efforts of the team. The story of the White River High School social studies department is the story of a group of teachers who were making the shift to a team of professionals becoming a PLC. Their story is about the journey that teams embark on, and it is about the power of collaboration in the face of increasingly challenging mandates that teachers are inundated with today. To understand the power of the team, it is important to know what each individual, John, Jer, Joe, Nate, and Matt, brings to the table.

John has been the social studies team leader for several years at White River. To put it mildly, John *loves* history. He is the teacher you had in high school who spent three days on the Bretton Woods Conference and the making of the International Monetary Fund (IMF) and World Bank. He would give you insightful details about every participant including the room that John Maynard Keynes slept in and then talk with you about his trip to the Mount Washington Hotel, where he visited the site of the conference that made the United States dollar the international currency that it is today. John took his role as team leader seriously and did a great job managing the logistics of our distributive leadership and PLC model. With that said, John was a historian and kid magnet, but not an innovator. He was traditional in every sense of the word and uninterested in chasing trends.

Jer began his career as a mathematics teacher and then moved into social studies along the way. Jer is modest about his historical background knowledge and tends to disengage when in-depth conversations about the Bretton Woods Conference arise. However, he is perhaps the most talented high school teacher you will ever find when it comes to the strategic use of assessment data to guide instruction as well as working with students to use data to determine areas of growth and set learning goals. You can walk into his advanced placement (AP) government class at any time and by looking at the graphs and charts on the wall know exactly how his students are doing. Jer's students regularly outperform the national average on the AP exam, and his work in the assessment cycle led him to pilot and work with standards-based grading before anyone else even knew the term. Unfortunately, Jer was unwilling to share his work with the rest of the team. He was largely disengaged from the rest of the team and often took the opportunity to work with the other AP subjects' teachers.

Joe is the physical education major who also happens to be the head football coach at White River. Joe has also taught AVID (Advancement Via Individual Determination) and therefore has a tremendous amount of training when it comes to critical reading, study, organization, and testing strategies. He uses many of those in his lessons, but you would never hear him advocate for any of the skills development that he knows students need to be successful. He is comfortable taking a back seat and allowing his peers to lead the way in unit planning and lesson development. Moreover, as the only AVID teacher in the department, Joe knows the work that other teams are doing in our school as a result of the tutorials and knows the intervention plans he puts in place for his AVID students. Unfortunately, this was something not generally shared with the team.

Nate is an extremely talented teacher who often feels like a square peg in a round hole. He teaches history but isn't as passionate about the content as he is about the skills that students develop in his class. He is a baseball coach and therefore focuses on skills and technique as a lens for development. If you can develop your technique as a hitter, you can hit any pitch. As a student, if you develop your skills as a thinker, you can solve any problem. This approach simply didn't mesh with that of his colleagues, and he was unwilling or unsuccessful to move the team during PLC meetings. He instead continued to make a difference for the students he served and spent his time working on projects such as creating a digital platform for his course through the use of Edmodo or working on a flipped classroom using his own YouTube station.

Matt was a middle school teacher who was assigned to White River High School involuntarily during the times of difficult staff reductions in force. Matt is an experienced social studies teacher who doesn't do extremely well with change. Matt is not an innovator or early adopter when it comes to his teaching and instructional practices, but rather relies on his ability to build positive relationships with his students as the foundation for academic pursuits. With that said, Matt is someone you can always count on to teach the district-adopted curriculum with fidelity. He is a team player and will adhere to collective commitments regardless of his personal feelings. Moreover, Matt is perhaps one of the best high school teachers when it comes to communication with students, parents, and counselors about the academic progress of his students.

As you can see, each one of these teachers has important strengths, but their inability to come together as a team prevented them from turning these individual strengths into increased team effectiveness. In other words, they were "doing" PLC and not making the shift to becoming a PLC. This all changed in the fall of 2011 when the Washington State Board of Education increased the social studies graduation requirements. This was one of many changes that were occurring at the time, but this is the one that required immediate action. There was a small window of time and lots of work to do in order to change the course of study, add a new class, complete the curriculum adoption, and communicate with all stakeholders. This was also a perfect time for us to take a step back and look at our vertical alignment and course standards. Common Core had released the ELA History / Social Studies standards, and we knew that Washington State had not only adopted those standards but was also committed to making the transition to Smarter Balanced assessments. For the purposes of our work in White River, this meant that students would have to pass the new Smarter Balanced ELA as a graduation requirement. With 70 percent of that exam focusing on informational text, we all recognized the important role that our socials studies team would play in ensuring the success of our students.

One of the important things to remember when working toward becoming a PLC is to think like someone who is investing in the stock market. Anyone who has listened to their financial planner knows that you have to have patience, dedication, and be willing to think long-term in lieu of immediate short-term gains. The journey toward becoming a PLC is much like that, and while the social studies team was not considered to be a high-functioning PLC team in the fall of 2011, there had been an incredible amount of work done to lay the foundation for success and these folks were ready to see that work pay off. We often tell our visitors that culture trumps strategy, and one of the undeniable accomplishments of this team was that they had developed a culture of trust, appreciation for each other's strengths, and a shared commitment to ensuring higher levels of learning for all kids. It was time for this team to begin the transition into becoming a high-functioning PLC team.

With new standards and new graduation requirements, we started from scratch and went back to question number one: What is it that we want students to know, understand, and be able to do? We took a long time talking about skills versus content knowledge. This was a difficult shift for many, but for John most of all. He will openly say to our PLC visitors that he was the last one manning the ramparts on the wall of the Alamo when it comes to content, but he ultimately came to accept the fact that knowledge is no longer the commodity that it once was now that we are living in the information age and students have computers in their pocket and declarative knowledge at their fingertips. We came to a place where we have a shared vision for social studies at White River High School, where students use history as a way for us to develop important reading, writing, thinking, and listening skills. Moreover, we understood that we would have to address the depth-versus-breadth conversation and make important choices about what to cut and what to keep. This is tough for history folks because we love it all, but at the end of the day we decided to focus our instruction on four enduring understandings that we were committed to and that all students would be challenged with each year. They are the cornerstones of our unit planning and consist of the role of government, causes of conflict, economic impact, and human rights. We then had a lens to help us make some of those tough decisions and determine whether or not it helped us achieve our goals.

These conversations were tough, but they paved the way for the critically important conversation about Common Core State Standards and skills. This is where teachers often say things like, "I am a history teacher, not an English teacher. I don't know how to teach reading and writing." It is easy to get frustrated with a comment like that, but it comes from a place of uncertainty and not a disregard for the Common Core. The team struggled with this one, but this is where the strengths of Jer and Nate began to emerge. Both Jer and Nate understood this important shift instinctively and were steadfast in their commitment to helping the other team members get it as well. Their leadership during this fork in the road was instrumental to the ultimate success of the team. At the end of the day, we came to a shared understanding that we weren't teaching students how to read and write, but rather we were teaching them to read, write, and think like historians. These are important skills that each student will need as citizens in a democracy, and we all agreed that they were essential college- and career-ready skills that needed to be taught explicitly in our social studies classes.

Now that we were clear on our power standards and our enduring understandings, it was time to look at possible instructional materials that were aligned to the standards. The team took this work seriously and poured over every packaged curriculum that was available. The important part of this is that we started with question number one and our standards and then looked for instructional materials. Most teams do it the other way and start with a textbook. The result of this approach is that the textbook is driving the instruction instead of the standards. For anyone who knows the ELA History / Social Studies standards you can imagine where this is headed. For our purposes, it is enough to ask you to remember your high school American history textbook (they haven't changed all that much) and then consider just one eleventh-grade standard.

> *RH.11–12.7—Integrate and evaluate multiple sources of information presented in diverse formats and media (e.g., visually, quantitatively, as well as in words) in order to address a question or solve a problem. (NGA & CCSSO, 2010)*

This is just one standard, but highlights the dilemma that our teachers faced in their efforts to identify a curriculum that was truly aligned to standards. Once again, the strength of the team emerged, and Nate shared with the team the quality and quantity of open educational resources that are available for free on the Internet including several online textbooks. The team came to the conclusion that to truly align their practices, students would have to use computers to research, create, and share information and ideas. Thankfully, the superintendent and the board of directors were on board and approved the purchase of mobile labs for every social studies classroom. This is an incredible shift and one that our PLC visitors ask the most questions about. However, this is where the really heavy lifting begins, and it is where the strengths of each individual begin to emerge. The reason for that is because now our teachers weren't adopting a curriculum, they were writing a curriculum.

One of the challenges was to shift from a chronological approach to a thematic approach in an attempt to target the power standards strategically. This requires an in-depth knowledge of history and an understanding of how historical events are relevant today. This is John's undeniable strength, and it is evident when observing the team develop their units. He has the ability to see how Depression-era programs such as AFDC, the Great Society programs of the 1960s, and the Welfare Reform Act of the 1990s fit together as students are challenged with determining the appropriate role of government in response to domestic poverty. As a result of this important contribution, John's leadership voice has emerged and he is more committed than ever to helping his students develop the skills they need to become historians. However, he is the first to tell you that this required a shift in his practices that he was reluctant to make.

With our shift from teaching content to teaching skills, it is important to recognize that this is a much different approach to social studies education, and it was a significant shift for several of our teachers. The team needed to learn how to teach critical reading strategies and how to ensure that differentiation strategies and scaffolds were in place for students to analyze multiple sources in order to solve a problem. Moreover, they had to then develop the skills needed to share and communicate those ideas both verbally and in written form. The team recognized this area of growth, and the district responded with support in the form of professional development. We spent multiple days with Yolanda Westerberg, who crafted meaningful professional development that was targeted to the needs of our teachers. Most importantly, Joe became our resident expert when it came to critical reading strategies and not only provided amazing AVID resources, but then modeled the strategy and provided examples of what student work would look like and the feedback they would need to improve.

Another major hurdle that needed to be addressed is the fact that our teachers didn't have a tremendous amount of experience with the strategic integration of instructional technology. This is a significant shift for many educators, and we often see technology sitting in classrooms idly because it was purchased and fielded without the forethought to acknowledge the support that educators need in order to use the technology as a tool to improve student learning. While there was professional development provided in the beginning, it focused mainly on the nuts and bolts of the computer cart and the use of the classroom management software. The transition of the team's instructional practices was largely the result of Nate's leadership and expertise. Nate has always been an innovator and was essential as we began using technology as part of our daily practices. He shared his use of learning management system platforms such as Edmodo and how this tool can be used to share ideas, create a library of resources, and communicate with students. He then modeled examples of how he uses technology to increase student engagement and capitalize on the value of student talk. One example of how this works is by using the chat function in Edmodo as a platform for student discourse while watching brief video clips of the same news story. The news story in this case happened to be one from the West Bank and the juxtaposition of the story being told from the lens of the Palestinians and the Israeli. Keyboard courage can be a good thing, and you would be amazed at the thoughtful contributions students make when allowed to share ideas digitally.

Now that we spent the time identifying our power standards, building our unit plans and assessments, and aligning our instructional practices, we found ourselves in a position where we needed to address question number three and our response to students when they struggle. For Jer, this was a natural opportunity for him to take a leadership role and guide the team in the analysis of student achievement data and the building of targeted interventions for struggling learners. He has always been a data guy and now that we were focused on skills and not declarative knowledge of historical facts, he recognized the support that his team would need to identify the skill gaps and intervene appropriately. Part of this process is the importance of timely, specific, and meaningful feedback, and the team leaned heavily on Jer for his expertise when it came to standards-based feedback and grading. They also took this a step further and started to work collectively on differentiated instruction and alternative assessment opportunities for struggling learners. This is important work that many schools are engaged in throughout the country, but for this team, it was a byproduct of the work that they were doing as a PLC.

Throughout the process, we continued to build shared knowledge about our work and the direction we were headed. We read portions of *Overcoming Textbook Fatigue* by ReLeah Cossett Lent (2012) and *Creating Innovators* by Tony Wagner (2012) as well as watched numerous TED Talks. The purpose for this lies in the fact that this is tremendously difficult work and it is easy to forget why we are doing this. The time we spent building shared knowledge reinforced the importance of our task and revitalized our commitment to the work and each other. There is no shortage of amazing examples out there, and it is important to take the time to learn from others as we continue on our own journey.

We always say that we believe in two guiding philosophies, and those are that culture trumps strategy and that we should get started in order to get better. The visitors who come to White River High School see a social studies team that has a technology-rich curriculum that is aligned to Common Core standards in a way that creates rigorous, relevant, and highly engaging learning opportunities for their students. They also see student work that reflects the transferable skills that students will need regardless of their post–high school pathway, and they instinctively recognize the fact that these students will have a better opportunity for success on the Smarter Balanced assessments than their peers who are receiving traditional social studies instruction in other schools. They see this and instantly become fixated on the current reality and want to know how to make this happen. The easiest way to explain the journey is to have them focus on the work of becoming a PLC and remember that each teacher is a dedicated professional with unique and important strengths that they bring to the team. Only by working as a team can we see the results that we envision for our students.

For the building administrators reading this, it is important to note that we have celebrated each and every accomplishment in the journey and supported teachers both formally and informally throughout the process. Your role is to be a coach, guide, mentor, encourager, cheerleader, technical expert, and unwavering resource for the teachers you serve. The teachers highlighted in this story have worked extremely hard over the last four years (probably harder than they ever have in their career), and we are only now beginning to see the fruits of their labor. Each one of these teachers has grown professionally and recognizes the difference he is making for kids. John has taken on our AP U.S. history course and is more focused on data than ever before. He has taken a step back from coaching so that he can focus on his instruction. Jer has developed an amazing voice as an instructional leader and is beginning his first year as a full-time assistant principal at White River High School. Nate has become someone that the team relies on when it comes to innovative ideas and strategies, and he is an incredible resource as a mentor for our new teachers. He has taken on the task of developing the AP human geography program at White River and has just completed a very successful first year. We are excited to see the AP test results so that we can use that data to guide our work. Joe has taken a step back from AVID and is doing more to share ideas, particularly when it comes to critical reading strategies and writing strategies learned from his AVID training. He has the ability to be one of the best teachers in the school and has been challenged to see himself as a teacher leader first and a head football coach second. Matt is perhaps the most heartwarming of all the stories we share about teachers. He wasn't valued at all by the administration in his previous school and was sent to White River High School willingly. Matt's value to the team and his profession is that he is a team player at his core and simply refuses to go back on the collective commitments of the team. As a result, his practices have changed dramatically over the last three years and he, like many teachers, continues to struggle with the enormity of change associated with being a teacher today. However, he doesn't realize that he is making tremendous strides each year and that he has become an amazing teacher. He always had a heart for kids and now realizes that the relationships that he forges with his students put him in a unique position to challenge them academically because his students know that he will do whatever it takes to ensure their success. He has been challenged to develop his leadership voice in the PLC team and take on a new role as a teacher leader as we bring on new staff.

We have a story that we like to share when discussing the journey of the social studies team. This particular story is about a veteran socials studies teacher named Keith who attended a PLC conference in Seattle and was excited to bring the information back to his team and begin the work of a PLC. Unfortunately, Keith's story is one that we hear often: he soon became frustrated when he didn't get the support from his administrators or the buy-in from his team that was needed to move forward. We use the term *frustrated*, but that doesn't exactly convey his emotions appropriately. He was so incensed at the actions of his colleagues that he wrote to All Things PLC (allthingsplc.info) sharing his frustration and asked if the only way to change people's behavior was to report them to Child Protective Services and the office of the Superintendent of Public Instruction for child neglect, professional malpractice, and dereliction of duty. What makes this a White River story is the fact that his message was forwarded to Janel, and we reached out to Keith. He visited White River High School and spent time with the social studies team asking questions and learning more about the work that this team has been doing over the last few years. He was so impressed that he decided the best course of action for him was to abandon the school that he has taught in for over twenty years and come work in White River. Unfortunately, that approach robs him of the professional journey that these teachers have taken and the work that they have done together. And, as we like to say in White River, "The journey matters!"

One of the most rewarding footnotes about this journey is the difference you see when visiting social studies classrooms at White River High School. It is difficult to fully express in words, but the best way to describe it would include the phrase "actively engaged." From the very beginning, the impetus for our work together was always to ensure high levels of learning for our students, and our students continue to benefit from the work of this dedicated and talented team. Our students are wrestling with extremely complex and challenging issues each day and deploying a vast array of newly formed skills to analyze important issues and develop creative responses based on their research. Moreover, they are learning to express their ideas in both oral and written form and engage in civil discourse with their fellow citizens when their ideas are challenged.

This is just one example of a team of professionals working together to improve learning, and we are fortunate to have an amazing team of teachers in White River. The challenge for us as we continue our work is to develop a thoughtful approach to how we ensure the work of the team when hiring and mentoring new teachers. This has caused us to rethink many of our traditional hiring practices including interview questions, performance tasks, and new teacher training. There is much work to do, but the undeniable importance of involving teachers in the process is critical. Our teachers are more invested than ever before in the decision of who teaches down the hall from them, and their input is incredibly valuable to the process. An example of this can be seen in the types of questions that our social studies teachers ask applicants who are interested in joining their team.

- Tell us a bit about your understanding of professional learning communities and your experience in working with teams of professionals within this model.

- Social studies classes at White River High School are technology rich in both content and structure. How do you use technology to enrich the learning opportunities you provide for students?

- One powerful way we can improve learning is to provide meaningful, specific, and timely feedback to our students. How do you do that in your classroom within the context of your grading practices?

- Tell us about a typical unit or lesson you have created. What were the power standards that were addressed, and how did students demonstrate mastery of the standards?

- Each teacher has his or her own style when it comes to classroom environment and culture as it pertains to the development of a healthy learning environment for the students they serve. How do you create and monitor a healthy learning environment in your classroom?

- As you know, Washington is one of the states that joined the Common Core State Standards movement, and this has important implications for our work in social studies. Tell us about your understanding of the Common Core standards in social studies and how you target those standards in your instructional practices.

You can see the shift in the team's practices as well as their core values in the questions that they ask. More importantly, the number of "I don't know, but I am excited to learn" responses that we get only reaffirms the important work that this team has done.

## Types of Teams

Teacher teams are not the only teams that focus on learning. In this section, we'll take a quick look at a few other types of teams in a PLC.

### School Leadership Team

Teachers in a professional learning community benefit from regularly scheduled meetings of the team leaders. This grouping is often referred to as the school leadership team, and team leaders model the kind of work that is expected of teacher teams throughout the building; that is, they anticipate issues and questions, they share learning data, they practice and rehearse the work that is expected of teacher teams, and they engage in collaborative planning.

The collaborative sharing of learning data begins at the team level but is also viewed schoolwide in regularly scheduled leadership meetings composed of the principal and team leaders. A school that functions as a PLC has processes and procedures in place to keep track of student learning team by team, subject by subject, and course by course on a formative basis. Annual summative data reflecting student learning should come as no surprise to teachers who work in a PLC.

### Cross-District Teams

Like many districts, White River was challenged to truly ensure a guaranteed curriculum across the district. Essentially, we needed to ensure that third grade was third grade and a child's learning wasn't dependent on the school he or she went to or the assigned teacher and grade-level team. It just made sense that third grade across the district should have the same essential standards, generally the same pacing, and the same common formative preassessments and common formative summative assessments. It also made sense that if a student moved across town, he or she would slide into the same units of study. That's what we'd want for our own children. For example, if one school was working on narrative writing and a student moved to another school across town, that child would slide right into a unit on narrative writing. We could guarantee the parents that the standards and assessments would be the same. The difference would be in the unit design. The preassessment would determine the level of scaffolding and the extension opportunities that would need to be built into the unit. The school team would craft the common formative quick checks for understanding and the instructional strategies that best fit the unit based on research and the needs of their students. It was important that we allowed for the art of teaching on every team and in every classroom in the district. But at the end of the unit, the district would be able to see how many students met the standard on narrative writing. We didn't have to wait for the results of the state assessment to check on the learning of all third graders.

So how'd we do this? Let's use our cross-district English language arts team as an example. We selected one highly effective ELA teacher from every grade level from nearly every school across the district. We provided them time to meet, typically by providing a substitute teacher. This highly effective team brought their best thinking to the table to develop a scope, sequence, and pacing guide, and a basic unit that included a unit plan, preassessment, common formative summative assessment, and performance tasks. This team then took the work back to the grade-level team in their school. They asked for input and feedback, essentially giving each teacher in the district ownership to this important work. It actually looked like an accordion—from district team to building teams back to the district team to make the necessary changes. After each school taught the unit and analyzed the data in their building, the cross-district team came back together to analyze the data from their building, share effective instructional strategies, and highlight what worked regarding additional time, support, and extension opportunities. The work of this cross-grade-level team is making each grade-level team in each school better. No longer do we have a teacher or a teacher team working in isolation. You can find the work of this team on the district share drive.

## Teacher on Special Assignment Team (TOSA Team)

What do an elementary English language arts teacher on special assignment, middle school math teacher on special assignment, and K–12 technology teacher on special assignment have in common? Not much at first glance, but this is one of the PLC teams in the White River School District. Just like any other PLC team in the district, they meet weekly to have conversations that can improve student learning.

This diverse group of educators shares their varied backgrounds, knowledge, and skill sets to benefit colleagues and groups of students throughout the district. They have the opportunity to share successes and challenges relating to the groups of teachers they work with and talk through areas of concern in their daily jobs.

It would have been easy to let the tech specialist work in isolation with such a specialized role or have the math and ELA TOSAs work apart as they specialize in such different subjects. However, knowing the power of collaboration, we knew they would learn from each other and support one another's work. Their projects link technology to teachers' work in content areas, for example:

- Creating computer-based assessments
- Examining and implementing tools to improve student feedback and efficiency
- Developing online student portfolios
- Using instructional technology to engage students

This unlikely team found a way to focus on the four essential questions of a PLC in unconventional ways.

## Singleton Teams

In every state, there are small, isolated schools and school districts that have limited budgets for travel and staff development and virtually no up-to-date resources to support the teacher and the kids in the classrooms. The teachers in these schools are often the only teacher teaching their course/content area and seldom, if ever, have the opportunity to collaborate with colleagues about instructional strategies, assessment results, or innovative ideas that may enhance learning for their students. This can be used as an excuse to not implement the PLC process.

James Sims, a retired administrator from Hood River, Oregon, has worked in many rural schools as a leadership coach emphasizing the work of the PLC process. For more than a half dozen years, he talked with district leaders about developing an algebra 1 singleton team across several districts. Although many superintendents supported the idea, none would commit the time necessary to make the process happen with fidelity.

In the summer of 2013, James developed a professional working relationship with Dirk Dirksen, algebra 1 teacher for Elgin High School. Dirk was working with the middle-level staff, specifically with the eighth-grade math teacher, on aligning his instruction with the Common Core State Standards for algebra 1. After several days of working with the teacher and our consultant, Dirk was "strong-armed" into leading an algebra 1 singleton team.

He made contact with four other small districts (Echo, North Powder, Umatilla, and Wallowa). Each district committed to the process by allowing their algebra 1 teachers to attend a PLC 101 training at InterMountain Education Service District. The training was conducted by Liz Durant, staff development specialist. Following the training, Dirk led the teachers in developing a set of norms and a common calendar for future meetings. The ultimate goal was to create a scope and sequence, common lessons, common assessments, and a reasonable intervention process that would be implemented within the resources of their respective districts.

The geographical distance between the schools was somewhat problematic. Two of the schools were on the west side of the Blue Mountains, and three of the schools were on the east side of the Blue Mountains. (There was a total distance of about 100 miles between the schools.) The only things they had in common on both sides of the mountains were the Common Core State Standards and teachers who wanted what was best for their students.

The group agreed to set a time and meet monthly at a defined location with 100 percent of their time devoted to creating common assessments, discussing the scope and sequence of their work, and analyzing student data. Due to the fact that algebra 1 is now taught in many eighth-grade classrooms, both Umatilla and Elgin middle school teachers joined the collaborative team. In off weeks, the team used Google Hangouts to communicate with each other.

The singleton PLC process and meetings did not come without some frustrations. Teachers coming from different districts had never been held accountable to and with their colleagues. All teachers did not follow the guaranteed viable curriculum as decided, and some altered the assessment cycle. This did create great discussion during the face-to-face meetings. The first meetings were not always easy because strangers were sharing data that reflected their teaching. As time progressed, the teachers realized they were all trying to accomplish the same thing.

The singleton PLC process is growing. The same schools and districts started a biology team in the fall of 2014. English language arts is also testing the water to see if there is enough interest to create a functional group. The process has certainly helped individuals improve their instructional practices and student achievement. You must have a dream and support from a district-level administrator to sustain the work and efforts. The bottom line is: it is the right thing to do.

## The Continuous Improvement Cycle of a Team

The work of a professional learning community is not one and done. It is a process, always evolving, always improving. The following figures represent the work that visitors see when they come to White River School District: the repeating process (figure 3.11), a team narrative (figure 3.12, page 92), a unit plan for mathematics (figure 3.13, page 93), and a team analysis of a common assessment (figure 3.14, page 97).

---

**Teams Repeat This Process Unit by Unit or Chapter by Chapter**

1. Identify essential standards.
2. Write learning targets.
3. Create quick checks for understanding / responsive assessments.
4. Create the common formative end-of-unit assessment.
5. Give the assessment.
6. Analyze the assessment.
7. Look at data and student work.
8. Apply interventions and extensions along the way.
9. Repeat . . .

---

Figure 3.11: Repeating process.

*Source: White River School District. Used with permission.*

*By Tracy Nelson*

We looked at our TACA [team analysis of a common assessment] form from the previous school year and were reminded that problem solving was strong, but fluency wasn't as strong—79 percent meeting standard. This reminded us to increase focus on this for this school year. Our reflection from the previous year also reminded us that we wanted to beef up the work we did with kids on constructing an understanding of division and the relationship it has to multiplication.

We then looked at the CCSS, which were new to us last year, and knew we needed to not only work on the array model in multiplication and division but clearly connect this to area for kids.

It was then time to get going on revising and improving our unit plan from the year before—work in progress, continuous improvement, and fine tuning.

We set our new SMART goal for the unit based on the success and challenges kids had from the year before. You will see problem solving and conceptual work was set a bit higher than comprehension. We know this is a different group of kids we are working with, but we have seen improvement over time (multiple years) by goal setting this way.

We have districtwide common pre- and summative assessments, so we quickly review these and also look at our team-developed formative assessments to remind ourselves how we are asking kids to demonstrate what they are learning related to standards.

Next, our team looks at daily lessons, differentiation, homework, and intervention, and revises and plans what we think kids will need to be successful. Along the way, we might need to tweak and change our thinking because the data look different than what we expected, but proactively planning helps us save time during the unit. (You can see all of this preplanning on the unit plan, including predicted intervention needs.)

After the preassessment, when we look at kid-by-kid data, we sometimes find we need to change instructional focus—they either know more on a subject than we expected (great news!), or they are struggling with an area we will now need to spend more time on. There are often those kids who are really lacking even prerequisite skills they will need for the unit. These kids will need reteaching of skills or preteaching of skills to be more successful during CORE instruction. Our team plans this learning for our intervention block time, as well as time for classroom instruction, checks for understanding, differentiation, and monitoring and adjusting based on learner needs in each classroom.

Common formative data are brought to the table to help us make next-step decisions. Do our data tell us all/most kids need more work? If so, back to the classroom we go for more CORE instruction after talking about techniques we might try. Are many kids good to go? If so, let's plan "walk to math" intervention time that allows us to skill-group kids with the intensive group being really small with the most support. Teachers on our team work with groups they have had success with. For example, if we have a team member who has had great success moving kids forward in CORE, that teacher will most likely work with the more intense learners.

After intervention, whatever that might look like, including another check for understanding, our team reviews for the assessment with the kids and gives kids the summative assessment including an advanced section for kids that were at standard on the preassessment. All kids need the opportunity to see and demonstrate how their learning has grown.

Celebration time! Kids get a chance to celebrate growth throughout the unit, and the team brings data to the table to share and reflect on. What was the overall percentage of kids meeting standard? What did the class-by-class data tell us? If a team member had great success, what was he or she doing? What are our kid-by-kid celebrations? Who still needs support, and how will we provide this? (You can also see on the TACA, there is a list of kids with specific needs for continued instruction.) All of this thinking ends up on our new TACA form. We had 85 percent meet standard on the conceptual work and 84 percent meet standard on fluency, but our biggest celebration was connected to the number of learners who moved out of the intensive category— YEAH!!!! Our TACA and unit plan will be ready to revisit the following year to get us going once again.

Figure 3.12: A team narrative.

*Source: White River School District. Used with permission.*

# Unit 4 Math (Multiplication and Division)

Mountain Meadow 3rd Grade Team

**SMART GOAL**

3.2A and 3.2F—87% of grade 3 students will meet Unit 4 math standards as measured by Unit 4 assessment tools.

3.2E—85% of grade 3 students will meet Unit 4 math standards as measured by Unit 4 assessment tools.

**Power Standards**

3.2A—Represent multiplication as repeated addition, arrays, counting by multiples and equal jumps on a number line and connect each representation to the related equation.

3.2E—Quickly recall those multiplication facts for which one factor is 1, 2, 5, or 10 and the related division facts.

3.2F—Solve and create word problems that match multiplication or division equations.

**CCSS**

OA.3.A—Represent and solve problems involving multiplication and division.

OA.3.B—Understand properties of multiplication and the relationship between multiplication and division.

OA.3.C—Fluently multiply and divide within 100.

OA.3.D—Solve problems involving the four operations and identify and explain patterns in arithmetic.

MD.3.C—Geometric Measurement: Understand concepts of and relate area to multiplication and to addition.

| Instructional Timeline | Check for Understanding / Learning Targets | Assessment |
|---|---|---|
| **Common Pacing Guide** | **Check for Understanding** | **Common Formative / Preassessment** |
| Mid January–Mid March | • 3rd grade team or teachers analyze pre- and formative assessments. | Unit 3 preassessment and Multiplication Fluency #1 |
| **Assessment timeline:** Preassessment (day 1), common formative assessment (day 20), post-assessment (day 30). These are just approximate days. | • Teacher conferencing and observation. • Peer sharing and feedback. • Quick check skill grouping during workplaces | **Formative Assessment** Multiplication Fluency Checkup (Home Connection #14 revised with zero facts added) |
| **Intervention timeline:** Intervention will be after day 20; pull small groups for skills. (See power standards listed above; grouping will be done based on these skills.) | • Daily learning activities • Exit slips • Intervention learning activities | **Team-generated common formative assessment** **Review for Assessment** Go over preassessment and scoring criteria. |

Continued →

Figure 3.13: A unit plan for mathematics.

*Source: White River School District. Used with permission.*

| Differentiated Instruction / Daily Lessons / Learning Activities Emphasizing Essential Outcomes/Learning Targets | Learning Targets | Common Summative Assessment |
|---|---|---|
| • Lessons 1–24 (skipping lesson 17 and 18)<br><br>Adding:<br><br>• Independent practice from session 16; move to session 6 with equal jumps on a line instruction before practice sheet. We replaced practice sheet that is only times 2 with a number line blackline they can use to practice different equal jump amounts.<br>• Math story writing and solving after session 1 to replace session 2 and Animal Parts Multiplication and Multiplication Word problems from Super Teacher<br>• Move session 2 after session 8.<br>• Teach 10, 15, and 20 back to back.<br>• Fact Family practice A.2 at lessons 18 and 19, move to around 23.<br>• Around Session 19 some conceptual work with division will need to happen. Work will center around division problem solving (teacher generated).<br>• Differentiate through workplaces and challenge activities.<br>• Multistep problem solving warm-ups 2–3 times a week using Super Teacher.<br><br>Additional Array Lessons:<br><br>• Multiplication Array Table from Super Teacher with array tool and grid paper for kids to make and label arrays<br>• Array worksheets from Super Teacher | Note: Many of these targets aren't aligned with the power standard because Bridges is a spiraling curriculum.<br><br>We are learning to:<br><br>• Recognize common items that come in equal groups (lesson 1)<br>• Generate multiplication equations, models, and pictures to show we understand multiplication using repeat addition (lesson 2)<br>• Generate multiplication equations, models, and pictures to show we understand multiplication using equal groups and skip counting (lesson 3)<br>• Generate multiplication equations, models, and pictures to show we understand multiplication using arrays (lessons 4, 5, 7, 8, and 22)<br>• Recognize and communicate patterns in multiplication (lesson 6)<br>• Solve a multiplication or division problem using an efficient strategy (lessons 9, 12, 13, 14, and 23)<br>• Demonstrate computational fluency with multiplication facts 0,1, 2, 5, and 10 (lessons 10, 11, 15, 20, and 21)<br>• Write a multiplication/division story problem (session 13)<br>• Solve multiplication problems using a variety of dictated strategies (session 16)<br>• Predict, record, analyze, and draw conclusions from multiplication game (loops and groups) data (session 17)<br>• Compare and contrast multiples of different numbers (session 18) | Unit 4 post-assessment and team-generated advanced sheet |

- Identify all factors of products (session 19)
- Multiply 2 digit by 1 digit by using efficient strategies (session A2 activity 1 and 2)
- Write multiplication and division problems that are in the same fact family (session A2 worksheets 3 and 4)

Additional Area Lessons:
- *Balobbyland* TERC book—From Paces to Feet Investigation 4
- Scholastic printables on Area

Additional Division Lessons:
- Division, Making Equal Groups—Super Teacher
- Division Story Problems—Super Teacher

**Student Practice/Homework**
- Home Connections 13, 16, and 17
- Problem solving from Washington Supplement section F1
- Fact family homework from WA supplement (A2)
- Scholastic Printables: A Ray of Fun and Picture Perfect, front to back

**Differentiated Instruction / Instructional Strategies**

Additional Time and Support or Enrichment

Tier 2:
- Scaffolding steps
- Small group
- Support homework
- One-on-one teaching
- Peer teaching
- Differentiated workplaces

Tier 3:
- Tier 2 steps
- Intensive intervention skill grouping

Intervention skill grouping after lesson 20 including enrichment

Continued ↓

## Plans for Intervention

**Timeline for intervention:**

Intervention skill grouping after lesson 20 including enrichment

**Preventive Interventions:**

**Intense skill interventions:**

- The team will examine common assessment data to determine which kids need intensive support. The team will use the intensive part of the Strategic Support plan in next column.
- This will be done during our intervention block by one of the teachers from the team with strong assessment results on these skills.
- Redo or repeat activities can be used to check for new understanding.

**Strategic skill interventions:**

Preteach or reteach groups—Mixed operation problem solving during morning intervention block

Unit 4—After lesson 20 and unit 4 formative, kids will be skill grouped during PM math block.

Teacher 1 and support staff—Fact fluency, array model, and multiplication and division word problems

Teacher 2—Problem solving, recognizing add, subtract, multiply, or divide

Teacher 3—Enrichment, larger number multiplication, and multiple-step word problems plus IXL

**Enrichment opportunities:**

- The preassessment, classroom checks for understanding, and common formative assessment will all be indicators of mastery of skills and allow teachers and teams to plan for enrichment opportunities.
- We will have advanced-level skill opportunities both during math menus, intervention/enrichment block, and attached to some of the days kids are working on checks for understanding.
- The summative assessment has advanced-level section that kids who met standard on the preassessment have a chance to complete to measure growth in their learning.

**Intentional non-learner interventions:**

Kids will be identified by common assessments and classroom checks for understanding including daily work.

If the team has determined these are "won't" kids not "can't" kids, these kids will have the opportunity to complete learning with a teacher available each Friday at lunch recess. The team will rotate this responsibility so each teacher has this group every third Friday.

Kids that complete their learning activities will have the choice of heading out to recess or using the following computer websites for more practice:

- www.ixl.com
- www.coolmath.com
- www.xtramath.com

**Redo/repeat:**

- Solve two ways (team generated).
- Practice 7-1, 7-2, 7-3, 5-2, 5-3 from Scott Foresman.
- Washington Supplement A2 independent practice pages

## Math Assessment

School: Mountain Meadow                     Grade Level: 3rd

Subject Area: Math                          Name of Assessment: Unit 4 2013–2014

| 5 minutes | **Power Standards or Learning Targets Measured** |
|---|---|
| | SMART GOAL |
| | 3.2A and 3.2F—87% of grade 3 students will meet Unit 4 math standards as measured by Unit 4 assessment tools. |
| | 3.2E—85% of grade 3 students will meet Unit 4 math standards as measured by Unit 4 assessment tools. |
| | **POWER STANDARDS CCSS:** |
| | 3.OA.A—Represent and solve problems involving multiplication and division. |
| | 3.OA.B—Understand properties of multiplication and the relationship between multiplication and division. |
| | 3.OA.C—Fluently multiply and divide within 100. |
| | 3.OA.D—Solve problems involving the four operations and identify and explain patterns in arithmetic. |
| | 3.MD.C—Geometric Measurement: Understand concepts of area and relate area to multiplication and to addition. |
| 5 minutes | **In what areas did our students do well on this assessment?** |
| | Conceptual work: Pre—14% meeting and 53% intensive. Post—85% meeting and 0% intensive. |
| | Fact fluency: Pre—23% meeting and 55% intensive. Post—84% meeting and 5% intensive. |
| | Problem solving was strong overall. Kids did a great job labeling dimensions and computing accurately. |
| 5 minutes | **What instructional strategies helped our students do well?** |
| | (skip this question if you are using a preassessment) |
| | We did a lot more work with problem solving and concentrated heavily on the array model. Along with our normal walk to math intervention we also had Bari work with a group during morning intervention on problem solving. The team also added much more work with division supplementing with teacher-generated materials. Graph paper and manipulatives are a must. |
| 5 minutes | **What skill deficiencies do we see?** |
| | Multiplication factors—finding all three arrays for a given product. The kids that aren't at standard with fact fluency are accurate but just slow. |
| 5 minutes | **What patterns do we see in the mistakes, and what do they tell us?** |

Continued →

Figure 3.14: A team analysis of a common assessment.

*Source: White River School District. Used with permission.*

| 5 minutes | **Which students did not master essential standards and will need additional time and support?** |
| --- | --- |
| | Teacher/Class |
| | Student Name |
| | See Kid By Kid Spreadsheet in grade 3 math 2013–2014 on the share drive. Hannah, Katie, Reise, and Brian—number sense issues. Morgan, Jeff, and Kyle—need work with arrays. Carlos, Ryan, Jade, Katie, Reise, and Alexandra—problem solving. Maddie, Jade, Robert, Jeff, Morgan, Kyle, Brian—Fact fluency. |
| 20 minutes | **What intervention will be provided to address unlearned skills, and how will we check for success?** |
| | After formative intensive: fact fluency, array work, and problem solving—multiplication or division because we see the transfer of this skill to 4th and 5th the most. We not only solve equations, but provide problem-solving opportunities. Strategic: A problem-solving focus including addition, subtraction, multiplication, and division so the kids get practice breaking down the problem and analyzing it to pick best strategies from learned skills. Good to go: A variety of learning opportunities with larger multiplication problems and multiple-step word problems. After summative intervention: fact fluency work will continue in classrooms; number sense will be a reteach group with Bari concentrating on multiplication strategies like decade minus 1 using arrays for visuals. The array group will continue working with Martha, special education teacher, to practice the skill. |
| 5 minutes | **Do we need to tweak or improve this assessment?** |
| | We need to make sure that kids are given grid paper for arrays on every assessment opportunity just like daily work. The formative assessment needs the ice cream cone problem reworded to make distractor clear. |
| 10 minutes | **Which students mastered standards, and what is our plan for extra curriculum?** |
| | Kids who mastered skill continued on in fact fluency on the 4th grade standard. We have a number of kids who are at standard on the end of the year new CCSS standard. Kids were also provided advanced problem solving and math menu opportunities during CORE instruction. When had a big group in an enrichment block during intervention time. |

| Skill #1: 3.OA.A, 3.OA.D, 3.MD.D | | | | |
| --- | --- | --- | --- | --- |
| | **Class 1** | **Class 2** | **Class 3** | **Class 4** |
| Total Students | 26 | 26 | 23 | |
| Intensive | | | | |
| Strategic Standard | | | | |
| Approaching Standard | 2 | 3 | 6 | |
| Meeting Standard | 24 | 23 | 17 | |

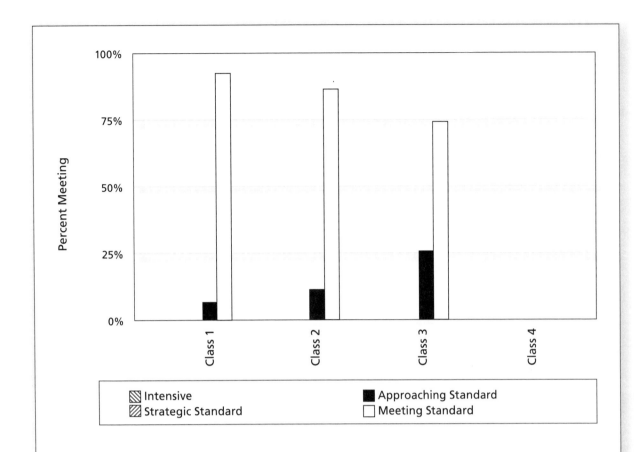

Skill #2: 3.OA.C Fact Fluency (0, 1, 2, 5, 10)

|  | Class 1 | Class 2 | Class 3 | Class 4 |
|---|---|---|---|---|
| Total Students | 26 | 26 | 23 | 0 |
| Intensive/Problematic |  |  | 2 |  |
| Strategic/Approaching Standard |  | 1 | 1 |  |
| Meeting Standard | 3 | 4 | 1 |  |
| Exceeding Standard | 23 | 21 | 19 |  |

Continued →

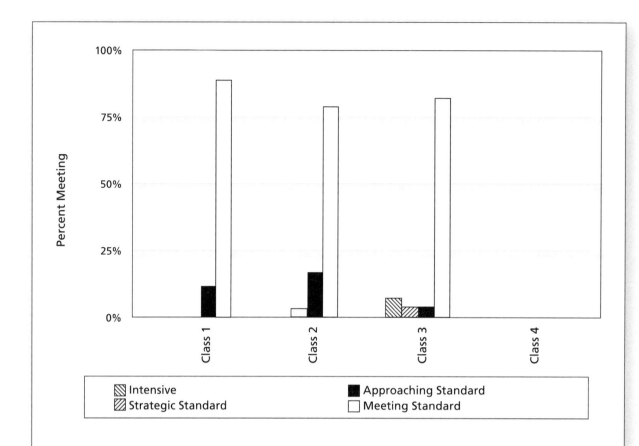

Skill #3:

|  | Class 1 | Class 2 | Class 3 | Class 4 |
|---|---|---|---|---|
| Total Students | 0 | 0 | 0 | 0 |
| Intensive/Problematic |  |  |  |  |
| Strategic/Approaching Standard |  |  |  |  |
| Meeting Standard |  |  |  |  |
| Exceeding Standard |  |  |  |  |

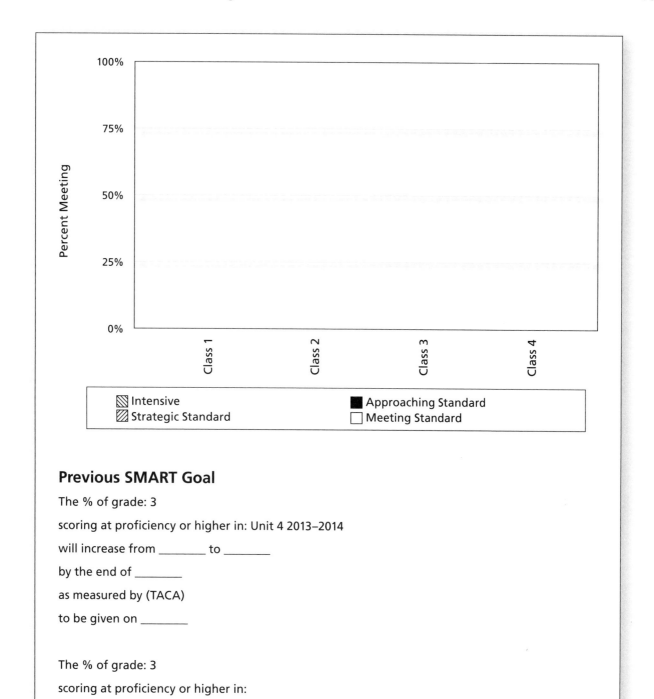

## Previous SMART Goal

The % of grade: 3

scoring at proficiency or higher in: Unit 4 2013–2014

will increase from _____ to _____

by the end of _____

as measured by (TACA)

to be given on _____


The % of grade: 3

scoring at proficiency or higher in:

will increase from _____ to _____

by the end of _____

as measured by _____

to be given on _____

# Chapter 4

# Using the Effective Teacher's Toolbox

*In the last decade of the 20th century, the picture of what constitutes an effective school became much clearer. Among elements such as a well-articulated curriculum and a safe and orderly environment, the one factor that surfaced as the single most influential component of an effective school is the individual teachers within that school.*

—Robert Marzano

Although the fundamental shift—the big idea—on which the concepts and practices of a professional learning community are based is a shift from a focus on teaching and the coverage of content to an intense and passionate focus on learning, in no way is this cultural shift meant to devalue the importance of effective teaching. The difference is that in traditional schools, effective teaching is often seen as an end unto itself, while in a PLC, teachers view teaching as a means to an end, which is to ensure student learning.

And there is another important difference. Teachers in traditional schools are increasingly subjected to observations and evaluations by administrators that are based on the assumption that there is one set of effective teaching methods that virtually all teachers should include in their lessons, while teachers in PLCs teach in schools in which the underlying assumption is that there is no one right way to teach. The teachers in PLCs understand the importance of context, the unique context of each lesson, and the characteristics of the students who comprise each particular class.

In PLCs, assumptions about effective teaching strategies are much more aligned with the thinking of Jerry Bellon, Elner Bellon, and Mary Ann Blank (1992), who write:

> It is impossible for effective teaching to be reduced to scripts and prescriptions. In order to be effective, teachers must view their work as being highly contextual, requiring them to make decisions in action, so that they can integrate their knowledge of content and the needs of their students with the most appropriate instructional processes. This is a difficult and complex task, but when successfully carried out the rewards for students and teachers are immeasurable. (p. 13)

Marzano (2007) is equally succinct, noting, "It is certainly true that research provides us with guidance as to the nature of effective teaching, and yet I strongly believe that there is not (nor will there ever be) a formula for effective teaching" (p. 4).

In PLCs, there is the recognition that the science of teaching can only take us so far in terms of impacting student learning. There is also the recognition and appreciation for the art of teaching—an artistic aspect that every teacher brings to the classroom. As Marzano (2007) observes, viewing teaching as part art and part science is not a new concept. He points out that researchers, such as Berliner (1986), characterized effective teaching as part art and part science decades ago.

Teachers' knowledge and enthusiasm regarding the subjects they teach are also critically important. How many students have pursued a career in a particular discipline simply because they were inspired by a teacher who was interesting and passionate about the subject he or she was teaching? Ultimately, highly effective teaching is interplay between the science of teaching, the art of teaching, and content knowledge and enthusiasm, and teachers in a PLC continually and collaboratively work to improve in each of these three domains (figure 4.1).

Like all professionals, teachers continually work to improve their repertoire of skills as new knowledge emerges. Whether they are skilled woodworkers or surgeons, professionals not only work to increase the number of tools available to them as they perform their craft, they also work to improve the skill with which they use them. But most important, they work to know which tools to use in each unique circumstance. The professional teacher ultimately relies on his or her experience and professional judgment regarding which tool to use under which conditions. While there is no definitive number of tools in an effective teacher's toolbox, the following sections represent an example of some of the basic tools that effective teachers in a PLC regularly utilize.

There are a number of important points that should be made when reviewing teacher tools or instructional skills. First, as we mentioned earlier, there is no definitive list; the following is a sample. Second, these skills are interconnected, affecting the effectiveness of each other. Third, all of these skills are enhanced by planning and working together in a highly effective collaborative team.

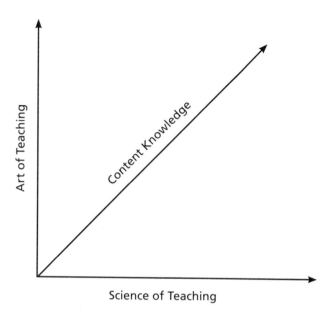

Figure 4.1: A three-dimensional model of effective teaching.

## Differentiation of Instruction

There are few aspects of education about which virtually all teachers agree, but one is that students learn in various ways and at various rates. Since this is true, knowledge and skills associated with differentiating classroom instruction are essential tools in the effective teacher's toolbox. If students learn at different rates and in different ways, and if classrooms are becoming increasingly diverse, it only makes sense that one size—one way of teaching—will not fit everyone. We all know we need to differentiate our instructional practices, but as with many things, the devil lies in the details—issues associated with the question, How do I do it?

> *If students learn at different rates and in different ways, and if classrooms are becoming increasingly diverse, it only makes sense that one size—one way of teaching—will not fit everyone.*

Effective teachers understand what differentiated instruction is and, importantly, what it isn't. Carol Ann Tomlinson and Susan Demirsky Allan (2000) define differentiated instruction as

> *a teacher's reacting responsively to a learner's needs. A teacher who is differentiating understands a student's needs to express humor, or work with a group, or have additional teaching on a particular skill, or delve more deeply into a particular topic, or have guided help with a reading passage—and the teacher responds actively and positively to that need. Differentiation is simply attending to the learning needs of a particular student or small group of students rather than the more typical pattern of teaching the class as though all individuals were basically alike. (p. 4)*

In other words, differentiated instruction begins with planning for differentiation. Differentiated instruction is not a program or initiative that is separate from what good teachers have been doing for years. It is simply one key element that is part of teachers' decision-making process as they plan for effective instruction in each unit of learning.

Tomlinson (2010) describes a framework, a context, for differentiated instruction that contains five elements. First is a positive or growth mindset—a mindset that is not fixed, based on ability, but rather is fluid, based on student effort. Second is teacher-student connection developed to support student learning. This involves building bridges of trust with students, since learning something new always involves an element of risk. Teachers plan to ask each student to learn a little beyond their reach. Because of this, scaffolding for support is essential. The third element is the development of community. Tomlinson (2010) notes that "in a differentiated classroom, a sense of community or team not only energizes learning, but also enables students to trust one another, support one another's growth, and celebrate one another's successes" (p. 254). Fourth, effective differentiation of instruction must be done in the context of a high-quality curriculum as the target for all students. Differentiation of instruction does not mean differentiation of curricula. Virtually all students are expected to learn the essential curriculum goals for which they will ultimately be held accountable. In other words, what students are expected to learn remains rather fixed; what is differentiated are the instructional strategies, time, and support. And the fifth element involves assessment to inform instruction.

*Formative assessment is a powerful tool that enables teachers to reflect on individual learners, skill by skill, as opposed to always thinking about the group or the class.*

Teachers who effectively differentiate their instruction rely heavily on common formative assessments. They use frequent and timely assessments of student learning to inform their practice and provide support for students. Formative assessment is a powerful tool that enables teachers to reflect on individual learners, skill by skill, as opposed to always thinking about the group or the class.

Within this context, Tomlinson (2010) observes that there are three key elements to effective differentiation of instruction, and effective teachers consider each of these elements when planning for differentiation.

1. Recognizing and understanding variances in student learning

2. Monitoring and adjusting of instructional strategies

3. Collaborative teaming

## Recognizing and Understanding Variances in Student Learning

The first key element is the recognition and understanding of the categories of variance in student learning. Student learning varies from student to student in a number of significant ways, and the more significant variances can be grouped into categories of:

- **Readiness**—A student's knowledge, understanding, and skill as he or she relates to specified content goals

- **Interest**—The recognition of individual student interests and connecting the content and instructional strategies to those interests, as well as developing new interests in learners

- **Learning profile**—Developing instructional strategies that connect to ways in which students learn most efficiently, recognizing that the way students learn most efficiently can be shaped by culture, gender, learning style, intelligence, preference, and so on

Teachers who seek to differentiate their instruction do so by responding to student readiness, interest, and mode of learning often and in effective ways when teaching specific content.

The ways that teachers differentiate their instruction differ from teacher to teacher, grade to grade, and subject to subject. What is important to remember is that the basis for planning for differentiation begins with the collaborative analysis of student work and the results of formative assessments—kid by kid, skill by skill. It is only by deep, rich analysis of formative assessment results and examination of student work that teachers can begin to share ideas about appropriate differentiation strategies for individual students as well as groups of students.

## Monitoring and Adjusting of Instructional Strategies

Second, while effective differentiation of instruction begins with collaborative team planning of units of instruction, teachers who are highly skilled at differentiation of instruction monitor and adjust their instructional strategies as they teach. Effective teachers are constantly reading their students and working to connect with each student in various ways. This is why the highly effective teacher has a significant number of teaching tools in his or her toolbox and, most important, has the professional judgment, wisdom, and experience to know which tool is needed at any particular moment with which student. This is also why checklists of specific instructional practices—even if the lists are grounded in solid research—are limited in their effectiveness. Most of these observational checklists remove the professional judgments that teachers make during the teaching process from the equation.

*Effective teachers are constantly reading their students and working to connect with each student in various ways.*

## Collaborative Teaming

Last, collaborative teaming greatly enhances teacher effectiveness regarding differentiation of instruction. Teachers who are left on their own to develop instructional approaches that will successfully impact an ever-growing range of learners often feel overwhelmed. They understand the need to differentiate their instructional practices, but they are left to their own devices when figuring out just how to do it. Compare these teachers with those in a professional learning community.

Teachers in a PLC have the benefit of the combined years of experience of their colleagues. As they collaboratively plan units of instruction, they share ideas and materials that aid in the differentiation of instructional practices. The group's collective ideas are powerful and greatly enhance teachers' feelings of self-efficacy. In addition, as teachers collaboratively analyze formative learning data on a frequent and timely basis, they can reflect on the effectiveness of various instructional approaches, both individually and as a team, and make notes about ways to enhance the effectiveness of their differentiation when the unit is next taught. In a PLC, the teacher team is continually engaged in a process of improving its effectiveness impacting the learning of *every* student.

## Organizing for Learning

It may seem obvious, but it is true: effective teachers organize their classrooms and their lessons, and they do this in such a way that being organized has a positive impact on student learning and student behavior. This section includes a number of important ways that teacher organization can have a positive effect on student learning.

### Collaborative Unit Planning

Collaboratively planning units of instruction is at the heart of what teacher teams do in a professional learning community. Unit planning begins with deep, rich discussions about what the standard means (and importantly, what it doesn't mean) and the standard's relative importance to other standards. This leads to the obvious discussion of how much time should be allotted to the unit. Such planning has been done earlier, as the team identified the power standards or the essential standards that each student must learn and sketched out the year in a rough pacing guide.

However, when organizing to teach to specific learning outcomes, the team also addresses other important questions. It asks, "What would this standard look like in student work if it is met?" This helps the team begin to address issues related to proficiency standards and common scoring, and the team collaboratively breaks the standard down into specific learning targets for each lesson.

### Formative Assessment

The team also organizes and plans for assessing student learning on a frequent and timely basis. The effective use of ongoing, frequent formative assessments—if used properly—is one of the most powerful tools in a teacher's toolbox. When teachers are constantly and collectively addressing the questions, Are the students learning, and how do we know?, the likelihood of student success is enhanced tremendously. How well teacher teams organize the work associated with developing and using the results from common formative assessments will have an impact on student learning.

The power of formative assessment lies in how it is used. An impact on student learning is ultimately the result of providing students with additional time and support when they struggle with their learning, as well as extending and expanding their learning when they demonstrate proficiency. The quality of the planning and organization for additional time and support at the classroom, team, and school levels is a major factor in the ultimate effectiveness of interventions. Effective intervention is much more than a haphazard recognition that struggling students need help. The organization of effective intervention is the result of collaborative planning that ensures that the plan is organized in such a way that it is systematic, timely, flexible, and directive (DuFour et al., 2008).

> *The effective use of ongoing, frequent formative assessments—if used properly—is one of the most powerful tools in a teacher's toolbox.*

## Common Assessments and Technology

At White River, there were a number of driving forces behind developing computer-based assessments. The common assessments had already been created by the various teams. Common formative assessments must be shared, and technology is an easy way to do that. In this format, assessments can easily be shared to all, including revisions and updates. Moving the assessments to a digital format for students to complete seemed logical. While today's generation of kids may be comfortable with tablets and computer for play, authentic experiences using technology for learning are critical to making them comfortable and more proficient with technology.

The technology teacher on special assignment (TOSA) and English language arts TOSA collaborated to examine the pros and cons of various computer-based assessment formats. This thinking was brought to the larger district ELA team to discuss and see in practice. A decision was made by that team on using a format that provided the students with the most thorough feedback while at the same time allowing the students to view the work they had submitted. With some great instruction from the technology TOSA, the ELA TOSA took on the responsibility of creating the computer-based version of the assessments to share digitally in Google Drive with the teachers using them throughout the district. The assessments were made available to students through a learning management system called Google Classroom. After students submitted their assignments, teachers wrote comments to the students digitally and also provided feedback using a digital rubric. The students signed back into Classroom to view the feedback from their teacher in context and also the scored rubric at the bottom of their assessment.

We learned that no format is perfect. Teachers need training on how to use the tools, from getting assessments out to students through the computer to learning how to score the assessments on the computer. We learned to celebrate successes and work to improve the tools used based on feedback. We learned that building the capacity of teachers over time instead of expecting everyone to embrace and implement the changes immediately was hugely beneficial. We also learned that the transition to this format was often more difficult for the teacher than the students. Finally, something like this would not have been possible if two people with two different perspectives and knowledge bases hadn't undertaken the work together.

### Variability of Instruction

As the team constructs the unit plan, it is at this point that the teachers share ideas about how to differentiate and ensure variability in instruction. If we know that students learn in different ways and at different rates, it only makes sense that teachers plan for variety in their instruction. And the quality of this variation, along with smooth transitions, relates to teacher effectiveness. Variability of instruction is a matter of context and judgment. Teachers can have too many activities or too few. The activities may be relevant to the standard being addressed or of little relevance. The issue is one of the quality and appropriateness rather than any specific number of activities. There is a strong correlation between student achievement and how well teachers vary their instructional strategies, and again, teacher effectiveness in this area is greatly enhanced by the collective power of teacher teams.

### Task-Oriented Culture That Focuses on Learning

Organizing for student learning has another positive benefit. When the work of individual teachers, teacher teams, and the school as a whole (and, of course, the school district) is highly organized, the collective result is a task-oriented culture, and students learn quickly that doing their work, behaving appropriately, and learning are important. This message is also true for teachers and staff—especially new teachers. It is difficult to convince both students and adults that learning is the fundamental purpose of the school if the school does not reflect a task-oriented culture, and a task-oriented culture is developed not so much by what is said, but rather by how teachers, especially teacher teams, organize for learning.

## Specific Learning Objectives

Effective teachers are experts at aligning their classroom instruction to specific learning objectives. Teaching to specific learning objectives is obviously affected by the quality of the overarching organization for learning that is done by administrators, teachers, and teams of teachers, but there are some specific teaching behaviors that have been shown to enhance student learning.

### Relating to the Students' Frame of Reference

When planning for activities, explanations, and examples, it is helpful if teachers consciously relate to the students' frame of reference, rather than relying on adult examples. They plan their lesson from the viewpoint of "If I were a student in this class, how could I learn this lesson? What would the teacher need to do to help me get it?"

For example, a major concept that is often taught in high school economics is inflation—a general rise in prices. When planning a unit of instruction on the topic of inflation, a teacher might plan to use the example of buying and selling a home. He or she may even use a personal example and say something like, "When we bought our first house, we paid $90,000 for it. That was what houses in the neighborhood were generally selling for at the time. Five years later, when we moved, we sold the house for $120,000. Again, this is what houses in the neighborhood were generally selling for at the time. This difference—this general rise in prices—is the result of what economists refer to as inflation." While this example is an accurate example of inflation, it is not a good one. From the students' perspective, buying and selling a home is something they will do someday way in the future when they are much older.

Another economics teacher might teach the inflation unit by pointing out that the way economists measure inflation is by regularly keeping close track of the prices of specific goods and services. The teacher might engage the class in the development of a list of products and services that teenagers typically purchase and then organize the class into teams that have the assignment of going shopping and recording the baseline prices of each item and then each week for the entire semester tracking the price. Or the teacher could also simply engage the class in developing a list of items teenagers typically use and then ask the class to identify products of which they believe the price has increased rather significantly. Whatever the examples or activities that are used, teachers should think about how to teach to specific learning objectives from a student frame of reference rather than automatically using adult examples and analogies.

> *Whatever the examples or activities that are used, teachers should think about how to teach to specific learning objectives from a student frame of reference rather than automatically using adult examples and analogies.*

## Making Essential Points Stand Out and Increasing Time on Task

Another important way teachers can emphasize specific learning objectives is by posting specific learning targets for each lesson and going over these learning targets with the students at the beginning of the lesson. During the lesson, teachers must make the essential points stand out in a number of different ways. They emphasize the essential points of the lesson at the beginning of the class, and when they get to a particular essential point, they slow down and point out to the class that it is important. At the end of the lesson, the teacher reviews the essential points that were taught, solicits questions, and checks for understanding. Making essential points stand out reinforces the importance of collaborative team unit planning, during which teachers share with each other ways to emphasize the essential points of each lesson.

The effective use of learning targets is one important way teachers make essential points stand out. The goal of learning targets is to make the focus of learning clear to those learning. This might happen by posting the target and going over it at the beginning of the lesson. It might occur as the lesson progresses and the class works together to build an understanding of what the target is through their common learning experiences. Of course, the teacher has a clear understanding of the target at the onset. It is just not revealed to the learners. The target is constructed, communicated, and importantly, *emphasized* as the lesson progresses.

Another strategy is having students take ownership in recording the target on their work samples, continually referring to it to check in on their progress as the lesson moves forward. The approaches are numerous, but the point of the target remains constant; if the student knows what is being learned and the purpose behind the learning, more engagement will occur.

The following are a few additional examples of ways teachers can make essential points stand out during a lesson.

- **Student-generated strong examples:** Put the student in the role of the teacher and use student work to reinforce strong examples of learning that are aligned to the target. If the teacher has spent time creating an environment of trust and risk taking, this has amazing power. Students are able to look at something they are working on right then, measure it against the standard and their own sample, and provide feedback for the sample being used.

- **Students self-assessing their progress with the target:** Students know the target for the lesson and have success criteria for what it looks like to meet the target. They are able to then look at the two and determine where they are in the continuum toward reaching the target.

- **Peer check-in:** This is a great way for students to engage in student talk to provide feedback to each other on how they are progressing toward understanding the target.

These examples, when built into the instruction, allow students to check in on essential points of the lesson, allow the teacher to collect immediate feedback on how learners are doing, and allow the teacher to adjust instruction as necessary to best meet the needs of the students.

## Student Practice

Ultimately, students are asked to do various things to demonstrate whether or not they have learned what was expected of them. They may have to answer essay questions or develop a product or give a performance. They may have to complete a multiple-choice test. Regardless of what students are asked to do in order to demonstrate proficiency, they will only get better if they practice the kinds of things that they will be asked to do on summative assessments. Planning for appropriate student practice is a critical tool in an effective teacher's toolbox involving consciously aligning student practice with both the formative and summative assessments.

Any discussion of student practice must involve the recognition that homework is one way teachers provide for extended practice. Since time at school is limited, teachers often assign students additional practice time at home. This makes the planning for appropriate homework assignments critically important.

Planning for homework is best accomplished as part of the team unit-planning process and is linked directly to the standards and learning targets that are the focus of instruction. In addition to the standards and learning targets, teacher teams consider other factors such as age, amount, and student readiness when planning for appropriate homework. Effective teacher teams will not assign homework practice to students who cannot do the required work. It makes little sense to assign multiple problems for students to do in their homework if they cannot complete one problem correctly in school. This is especially harmful if the homework is then graded and averaged in as part of the overall grade for the grading period. There is a strong connection between thoughtless, inappropriate use of homework and student failure. Collaborative planning for appropriate homework is one way to improve student learning by *appropriately extending* student practice time. Appropriate homework is tied directly to the standard and asks students to practice in ways that reflect what the standard, if met, would look like in student work. Appropriate homework is also age and subject appropriate. In short, teams of teachers collectively plan for homework that reinforces and extends learning time for students, depending on the subject and the age of the students.

## Feedback

Student practice, in and of itself, is not enough. To be effective, student practice must be coupled with effective feedback—feedback that is timely. Effective teachers do not wait until after the summative assessment to provide students with feedback. The best examples of focused and timely feedback can be found in athletics, band, art, and theater classes. These teachers intervene when students make a mistake, stop them and show the students where they made a mistake, and importantly, explain how to correct the mistake. They do not allow students to continually practice incorrectly. Think of how football or basketball coaches blow their whistle and stop a play to show a player what he or she is doing incorrectly and how to do it right. And there is the band director who will stop practice in the middle of a musical piece and point out to a particular student that the note is a flat or a sharp or that he or she is coming in a beat too early or too late. Think of the drama teacher who stops a student actor who says a line incorrectly or goes to the wrong place on the stage. What is common in each of these examples is that the teachers do not wait until after the game or the concert or the play to give students feedback.

Of course, feedback also involves appropriate, timely, focused, and meaningful praise. Praise is positively linked to enhanced student learning, and planning for recognition and praise is different from a more willy-nilly approach to praise. To be effective, praise must be linked directly to the desired behavior, whether it is for academic learning or behavior. And it must be tied to improvement toward a standard in addition to achieving a standard. It is difficult to convince students that improvement is valued if they are never praised when they do improve—even if the improvement is somewhat modest.

When Hattie (1992) completed his first synthesis of 134 meta-analyses of all possible influences on student achievement, he soon realized that feedback was among the most powerful influences. However, although feedback is widely recognized as a powerful tool for enhancing student learning, capturing the power of effective feedback is a complex endeavor and cannot be reduced to a simple recipe of "teachers should provide more feedback." Hattie (2009) warns:

> *Increasing the amount of feedback in order to have a positive effect on student achievement requires a change in conception of what it means to be a teacher; it is the feedback to the teacher about what students can and cannot do that is more powerful than feedback to the student, and it necessitates a different interpretation of the power of feedback if a teacher were to encourage students to provide more feedback . . . Simply applying a recipe (e.g. "providing more feedback") will not work in our busy, multifaceted, culturally invested, and changing classrooms. (p. 4)*

## Product and Process Feedback

There are two basic types of feedback: (1) product feedback and (2) process feedback. Typically, product feedback is feedback a teacher provides that informs students if their work is right or wrong. For example, if a teacher gives a short mathematics test consisting of ten problems, and a student missed numbers two and five, the teacher marks these two problems with an *X* and puts a grade of 80 on the paper. Or, a teacher calls on a student. The student answers the question, and the teacher responds by saying, "Right!" and then moves to another topic or question.

In contrast, process feedback is quite different. When teachers effectively use the tool of process feedback, specific elements are present. As in product feedback, there is information regarding whether the answer is correct or not. If the response is incorrect, the teacher also identifies where or how the response is incorrect and how to correct the response. For example, in the case of the student missing two mathematics problems, a teacher who provides process feedback identifies the two problems with incorrect answers, perhaps circling the part of the answer where the mistake is made, and on the side of the paper demonstrating the correct way the incorrect step in the problem should have been addressed.

The issue is one of intent. Product feedback simply informs. Product feedback, by itself, has little effect on the improvement of student learning. Process feedback, on the other hand, can assist students in their learning since students learn not only that they answered incorrectly, but also where their answer was incorrect and how it should have been answered. Teachers should remember, however, that the issue of feedback is far more complex than merely providing more process feedback in a more thoughtful way.

## Practice and the Immediacy of Feedback

Much of the power of formative assessments lies in the fact that they can enhance teachers' ability to provide feedback to students—and parents—on a frequent and timely basis. Feedback from summative assessments is rarely immediate. For example, in many graduate-level college courses, such as those offered in law school, it is not uncommon for the student to have only one assessment at the end of the course and for that assessment to be the sole determinant for the grade in the course. In some high schools, a course is structured around the one big project or one all-important writing or research paper, and there is little feedback to students along the way. In courses of this kind, students receive feedback after it is too late to use the feedback for improvement.

If students are to fully benefit from feedback, they should receive meaningful feedback on a frequent and timely basis and in multiple ways. Teachers who work in schools that function as high-performing PLCs plan with their collaborative team to develop the tools to use for quick checks for understanding throughout the lesson. Both the student and the teacher are able to keep their fingers on the pulse of learning during the lesson.

Teacher teams not only share ideas for effectively checking for understanding during the lesson, they also develop common formative assessments in order to periodically monitor the learning of the entire group, kid by kid, skill by skill. Collaborative analysis of the results from these assessments allows the teachers to reflect on the effectiveness of their instructional practices and plan for specific additional time, support, and extension of learning for their students.

> *To reap the full benefits of frequent, timely, and accurate feedback, the issue of feedback must be viewed in the larger context of learning.*

To reap the full benefits of frequent, timely, and accurate feedback, the issue of feedback must be viewed in the larger context of learning. This is especially helpful if viewed through the lens of common sense. Simply put, most often skill development results from appropriate focused practice. Students and adults improve their skills when they practice doing things correctly. This fact necessitates connecting feedback with practice. Practice without accurate feedback can actually hinder learning if the practice is being performed incorrectly. For example, improving one's golf score is unlikely to happen regardless of how much the golfer practices if the practice is performed incorrectly. To be truly effective, practice must be linked to frequent, timely, accurate, and specific feedback.

## Connection of Practice, Feedback, and Encouragement

Practice and feedback alone are not enough. If done poorly or thoughtlessly, feedback can be devastating. Great teachers—those teachers who truly make a difference in the lives of their students—follow a rather simple formula, a way of thinking about teaching and learning. They are very clear on not only what they want their students to learn, but equally important, what the particular standard, if met, would look like in student work. It would be difficult to overstate the importance of this point. Unless teachers know what student work would look like if a standard is met, it is almost impossible to know what students should practice. The secret, then, is to have students practicing the right things—those things they are going to be held accountable for doing in high-stakes summative assessments.

Next, as noted earlier, effective teachers plan with their collaborative team to provide students with timely, frequent, and accurate feedback in multiple ways. But great teachers will also connect encouragement with feedback. In multiple and sincere ways, these teachers frequently say and write things such as, "Very good!" "Much better!" "Way to go!" "You're getting there!" "I'm so proud of you!" "You can do this. It's going to take some work and time, but you can do this. I know you can!" Truly effective teachers mentally connect practice, feedback, and encouragement in ways that help students improve.

> *Truly effective teachers mentally connect practice, feedback, and encouragement in ways that help students improve.*

## Feedback From the Students

Hattie (2009) makes the following observation about feedback:

> *In Hong Kong, a questioner asked what was meant by feedback, and I have struggled to understand the concept of feedback ever since. I have spent many hours in classrooms (noting its absence, despite the claims of the best of teachers that they are constantly engaged in providing feedback), worked with students to increase self-helping (with little success), and have tried different methods of providing feedback. The mistake I was making was seeing feedback as something teachers provided to students— they typically did not, although they made claims that they did it all the time, and most of the feedback they did provide was social and behavioral. It was only when I discovered that feedback was most powerful when it is from the student to the teacher that I started to understand it better. When teachers seek, or at least are open to, feedback from students as to what students know, what they understand, where they make errors, when they have misconceptions, when they are not engaged— then teaching and learning can be synchronized and powerful.*
> *(p. 173)*

The true power and importance of feedback tools can only be fully understood when viewed through the lens of feedback to the teacher or team of teachers. Understanding this concept explains why common formative assessments are such an important tool for teachers in a PLC. It is from the feedback gained from a collaborative analysis of these assessments that teachers and teacher teams are able to focus on enhancing the learning of every kid, skill by skill.

## Group Alerting and Accountability

Effective teachers employ a number of skills to keep the students alert and focused on the lesson at hand—to hold the class accountable for paying attention and focusing on its work. Perhaps it goes without saying that keeping students focused on the lesson begins with teachers planning for lessons that are interesting and engaging, and of course, in a PLC, teachers enjoy the benefit of working in collaborative teams in order to plan lessons that are interesting, focused on significant learning outcomes, and actively involve students in the learning process. But beyond simply planning interesting lessons that engage the students, effective teachers utilize a number of tools that work to hold the class alert and accountable.

Many group alerting and accountability skills are related to teacher questioning. For example, there is much more accountability when a teacher first asks a question, then after a short pause calls on a particular student for an answer. Consider two examples.

In the first example, the teacher asks, "Robert, who was the secretary of state during the Second World War during the presidency of Franklin Roosevelt?" The entire class hears the question, but only one student, Robert, is accountable for thinking and responding. While other students may know the answer, Robert is the only student who must respond.

In the second example, the teacher asks, "Who was the secretary of state during the Second World War during the presidency of Franklin Roosevelt?" After a short pause and looking around the room, the teacher then calls on Robert. During that short pause, the entire class is thinking of a possible answer because everyone realizes they may be called on. By simply rearranging the way the question is asked, the teacher increases the level of accountability and group alertness throughout the classroom.

Calling on students in a particular order such as starting on one side of the classroom then proceeding down each row, student by student, lessens student accountability since students know when they will have to respond—and when they won't. On the other hand, when students are called randomly, they are much more likely to remain alert and attentive.

The conscious use of questioning can have a positive impact on group alerting and student accountability. We will discuss the different types of questioning and how to use them later in the chapter. Effectively redirecting questions can also assist in keeping students alert and creating a classroom culture of high accountability. For example, if the teacher calls on a student who is paying attention and is engaged in the class but at the same time notices that another student is not paying attention or seems to be disengaged, the teacher can redirect the question after responding to the initial student's response. For instance, he or she could say, "So, Fred, what do you think about what Jeff just said?"

Consciously phrasing questions, calling on more students, and redirecting questions and discussions to students who are not paying attention are important tools for teachers to have in their toolbox. Effective teachers not only work to become skilled at using questioning tools, but they also work to improve their judgment as to when to use different tools for different purposes.

Additionally, teachers who effectively utilize tools associated with group alerting and accountability consciously move around the room. If a student is drifting away from the lesson and becoming disengaged, the teacher simply moves to be near the student. Teachers' physical movement around the room may seem like a rather insignificant teaching tool, yet highly effective teachers are masters at using their physical presence to keep students on their toes and paying attention to the work at hand.

## Student Products and Performances

One of the most powerful tools in a teacher's toolbox involves planning for student products and performances. When students are engaged in a meaningful activity that results in a specific product or a performance, they become more interested in their work, and the quality of their learning is often enhanced. And like virtually all of the tools effective teachers employ, planning for student products and performances is greatly enhanced when done by a collaborative team.

The first point to be considered is that the products and performances must be tied directly to a specific standard or set of standards. Engaging students in an activity that results in a product or performance that isn't tied directly to a standard can actually have a negative impact on student achievement. Teachers and students have only a limited amount of time, so it is important that student activity be aligned with essential learning outcomes.

Second, teacher teams should collaboratively develop rubrics in order for products or performances to be assessed against a set of predetermined standards. Developing rubrics that reflect predetermined standards not only enhances the quality of common scoring, it also enhances the quality of student products and performances, since descriptions of high-quality work are clearly communicated to students.

Third, in order to reap the full benefit of planning student activities that result in student products and performances, teacher teams should plan for periodic internal and external audience review. Students become much more engaged and strive to do higher-quality work if they know an audience will see the product or performance. Sometimes the products or performances are displayed or performed within the classroom or within the larger school setting (internal review), and sometimes they are open to the public (external review). However, keep in mind that external reviews such as a science fair require more elaborate planning and can detract from the time teachers need for other important planning priorities.

## Teacher Clarity

Effective teachers utilize a number of tools and materials that collectively guide student thinking in deliberate ways along a structured route that leads to enhanced student thinking and learning. Robert Gagné (1985) identifies clarity as the variable that most clearly separates effective from ineffective teachers. Teacher clarity is about much more than teachers having organized lessons and speaking clearly. As Saphier and colleagues (2008) remind us, "clarity means to cause mental acts within students' heads that will result in their understanding or being able to do something. It's what happens inside the students' heads that matters, not what the teacher is doing" (p. 162). However, there are things that teachers can do to teach lessons in a clear and cogent manner that are likely to enhance student understanding.

Bellon, Bellon, and Blank (1992) group teacher behaviors that impact clarity into three categories.

1. **Substantive:** Factors related to content to be learned

2. **Semantic:** Factors related to the way teachers use language

3. **Strategic:** Deliberate use of strategies to improve learning

They remind us that teachers who communicate with clarity pay careful attention to each of the three areas.

Saphier and colleagues (2008) organize teacher behaviors that impact clarity into five categories.

1. Framing the learning

2. Presenting information

3. Creating mental engagement

4. Getting inside students' heads (cognitive empathy)

5. Consolidating and anchoring the learning

Regardless of how the topic of teacher clarity is framed, there are specific teacher behaviors that effective teachers regularly employ in an effort to make sure their students understand what they are being taught. And, importantly, it is the interplay of a number of behaviors, such as those listed, that has a positive impact on clarity. Let's take a look at what Bellon et al. (1992) and Saphier and colleagues (2008) tell us are factors of clarity.

Effective teachers are clear in the directions they give students, being careful not to give too many directions at one time. They give simple cues, emphasize important points, utilize a variety of instructional methods including technology (remember, technology is a means to an end—not an end unto itself!), and use graphic organizers in their instruction. Effective teachers also use language that students can understand—and relate to. They effectively use analogies, metaphors, and examples in their teaching. They ask students to compare and contrast important ideas, concepts, and events. The language that teachers use helps students develop a mental image of important concepts and ideas. Of course, other aspects of language, such as questioning and explaining concepts, affect clarity.

By using quick checks for understanding during the lesson, teachers can continually assess whether their students are getting it and, if not, clear up any confusion. Teachers enhance clarity when they effectively summarize the lesson by re-emphasizing the essential learning objectives that were to be learned. Clarity is also enhanced when there is a seamless flow and connection to homework assignments that extends student learning beyond the classroom in a meaningful way.

One last point about teacher clarity: As with other aspects of effective teaching, the instructional tools and materials that impact teacher clarity are greatly enhanced when a teacher is a member of a high-performing collaborative team that plans together, shares with each other, collaboratively analyzes the results of formative assessments and student work, and uses these analyses to reflect and improve their instructional practices. It is this persistent and passionate focus on student learning by collaborative teacher teams that is the heart and soul of a school that functions as a PLC. The constant focus on the questions, Are the students learning, and how do we know?, coupled with a culture of continuous improvement, helps make teachers' lessons more purposeful, clear, and cogent.

## Meaningfulness

Effective teachers make their lessons meaningful, as viewed through the lens of a student. They move from the act of simply covering material to teaching lessons that students find interesting and meaningful in various ways and at various levels. Robert Marzano, Debra Pickering, and Ronald Brandt (1990) write, "Something is meaningful to a person only if it fits with his or her goals. Effective teaching involves finding ways for students to relate school knowledge to their personal goals" (p. 21).

Making lessons meaningful for students involves a synthesis of many other aspects of instructional effectiveness—putting it all together. For example, if lessons are to be meaningful, they must be planned from the students' frame of reference. Meaningfulness is closely related to and affected by instructional clarity. It is not difficult to make lessons meaningful if students are clear about what should be learned and why the main ideas or concepts of the lesson are important. Effective teachers work to clearly communicate, in multiple ways, the connection between the content being taught and the real world. And, meaningfulness is enhanced when the products and performances that are required of students have some connection to the day-to-day world of students.

Making lessons meaningful requires a great deal of creativity, energy, enthusiasm, and imagination on the part of the teacher, and again, developing lessons that are meaningful to students is greatly enhanced when teachers plan together in a collaborative team structure, sharing ideas and learning from each other.

> *Meaningfulness is enhanced when the products and performances that are required of students have some connection to the day-to-day world of students.*

## Enthusiasm

Speaking of enthusiasm . . . It is unreasonable to think that students will be more enthusiastic about their learning than their teacher. While the concept of teacher enthusiasm may be difficult to define, the importance of lessons being taught by an enthusiastic and energetic teacher would be difficult to overestimate.

What would one see in an enthusiastic teacher? Vocal delivery that is strong and confident would be one thing. The delivery would be at a good pace, and the teacher would use his or her voice to emphasize important points and to keep the class alert. Effective teachers avoid dwelling too long and go to great lengths to keep their classes from being boring.

When it comes to demonstrating energy, excitement, and enthusiasm within a classroom, a teacher's nonverbal expressions are also important, especially facial expressions. Something as simple as smiling communicates that the teacher is happy to be in the class, teaching this particular lesson, on this particular day. Energy and enthusiasm are also communicated by how a teacher moves around the room, where he or she stands, and what he or she does with his or her physical body.

The words teachers use—and do not use—affect a climate of enthusiasm within a classroom. Effective teachers avoid beginning a lesson or unit with aversive statements. For example, they would not begin a lesson by saying, "I realize this unit isn't very interesting, but . . ." or, "This concept is probably going to be difficult for some of you, but . . ." Instead, they say things that introduce the lesson or unit in a way that communicates a sense of excitement, interest, relevance, and enthusiasm.

A culture of contagious enthusiasm is enhanced when teachers interact with their students—especially when they accept students' ideas and feelings. Of course, this idea goes hand in hand with the importance of student engagement. Accepting students' ideas and feelings goes much beyond enhancing student involvement. If teachers know their students, listen deeply, and value what students are saying, students are much more likely to look forward to coming to class and engaging with the content being taught.

## Tools for Questioning

It would be difficult to overestimate the importance of questioning skills in regards to teacher effectiveness simply because teachers spend so much instructional time asking questions. Kathleen Cotton (1988) finds that teacher questioning is the second most frequent strategy teachers employ, surpassed only by teacher talk. Researchers such as Michael Long and Charlene Sato (1983) report that teachers spend between 35 and 50 percent of classroom time asking questions. Kathleen Mohr (1998) reports that teachers ask as many as one hundred questions per hour, and Amy Brualdi (1998) reports that teachers ask between three hundred and four hundred questions per day (Hattie, 2009). Because questioning is such a frequently used teacher tool, there is a danger that questioning can become a thoughtless behavior on the teacher's part.

Questioning is not important simply because it is used so frequently by teachers. Questioning is one of the primary ways that teachers check for understanding and hold students accountable during the lesson, and responding to student answers is one way teachers provide feedback to students.

Effective questioning also facilitates meaningful student classroom engagement. Rather than allowing a student to stop participating with a simple "I don't know," effective teachers will provide hints, clues, and a reasonable amount of wait time in order to keep the student engaged.

This type of effective questioning creates a culture in which each student is valued as part of day-to-day classroom life. In such classrooms, students learn to be engaged speakers and questioners as they work through lessons. Discussion and questioning become a natural part of the classroom dialogue.

*Effective teachers are deliberate in their questioning strategies and use multiple tools when questioning students.*

## Types of Questioning

Effective teachers are deliberate in their questioning strategies and use multiple tools when questioning students. The three most common approaches are convergent questioning, divergent questioning, and choral questioning.

### Convergent Questioning

Convergent questions are those questions that seek a specific, correct response. For example, "Who was the first president of the United States?" is a convergent question. Convergent questions essentially serve two purposes. First, since the teacher is seeking a specific correct answer, convergent questions can inform the teacher if a student knows a particular fact or can explain a particular concept. By asking a number of different students convergent questions, the teacher can get a sense of how the entire class is progressing with its learning.

Second, convergent questions can decrease the amount of student talk and inter-action. Since the teacher is seeking a correct answer from a specific student, the entire class must wait until the student answers. If the answer is correct, the teacher simply goes on to the next question. If the answer is incorrect, the teacher then generally goes to another student with the same question. If the discussion tends to be getting out of hand, the teacher can bring the class back by asking a few convergent questions.

### Divergent Questioning

Divergent questions are the opposite of convergent questions. With divergent questions, the teacher is not seeking a specific, correct answer. Divergent questions are open-ended. For example, a teacher may ask, "Mary, do you think the idea of term limits for the office of the president of the United States is a good one?" For this question, Mary cannot give an incorrect answer. The teacher can then follow up Mary's answer with, "Why do you think that?" or ask another student or ask the entire class, "Does anyone else have an opinion?"

Open-ended questions serve to enhance discussion and student involvement in the lesson. And since the questions are not designed to solicit a correct answer, students who may be unlikely to answer or participate in the lesson can do so knowing they will not be embarrassed by their answer. Divergent questions, then, are an excellent way to draw particular students into the lesson and help them learn to feel comfortable participating in the class.

### Choral Questioning

Questions that call for a choral response from the entire class are used less frequently than convergent or divergent questions and are used primarily in the elementary grades. Choral responses are especially helpful to focus the entire class on a particular point that is being made. When used this way, choral questioning is an effective tool to emphasize a main idea.

Choral questioning is also helpful in refocusing the class after it has engaged in whole-group class discussion. It is not unusual for some discussions to get a little too noisy, so effective teachers will often ask for a response from the entire class that summarizes a main point.

## Managing a Lesson With Questions

Highly effective teachers use all three of these questioning tools to conduct a lesson. By purposefully choosing the kind of questions they are asking, teachers can manage a class much like a conductor manages an orchestra. If the teacher wants to start the lesson in a more deliberate way, he or she will sprinkle in a few convergent questions. As noted earlier, this limits participation and discussion. But, as the lesson progresses, the teacher might want the class to become more involved, perhaps noticing that some students seem to be mentally dropping out of the class. The teacher will ask a divergent question and, after the student answers, ask another student what he or she thinks. The teacher may ask the entire class, "Does anyone have anything to add?" or "Do you agree with that?" And as an orchestra conductor might do, teachers can call for a resounding crescendo from the students by asking for a choral response, then following with a few convergent questions to quiet the class.

Questioning is such a normal part of classroom instruction that it is not unusual for teachers to ask questions without giving much thought to the kinds of questions they are asking. On the other hand, effective teachers understand the power of questioning to do more than merely seek an answer from students and will use multiple questioning tools for specific purposes.

## Levels of Questioning

Teachers should not only be deliberate in the kinds of questions they ask and why they are asking them, they should also be deliberate and purposeful in the level of questions they are asking. Some questions seek a low-level, factual response, while questions at the higher levels seek more thoughtful and analytical responses from students. Although a number of classification categories exist, by far the one most frequently utilized is based on the *Taxonomy of Educational Objectives* (Bloom, 1956).

The level of questions should be tied directly to the learning objectives for a particular lesson or portion of a lesson. Bellon et al. (1992) write:

> *The key to preparing an effective questioning strategy is developing clearly defined learning objectives. The level and sequence of questions to be asked depends entirely on the knowledge that is acquired and the cognitive processes necessary to respond to the strategy. (p. 320)*

In this way, the level of questioning is designed to fulfill a specific purpose by eliciting a particular kind of response from the students. For example, the question, "On which side was Italy during the Second World War?" elicits a much lower-level memory response than the question, "Why was Italy initially allied with Germany during the Second World War?" This latter question requires thinking that involves both analysis and evaluation of facts.

Figure 4.2 (pages 125–126) provides a fourth-grade example of how to move from standard to question stems that can be used during daily instruction in the classroom and on common formative assessments.

## Wait Time, Hints, Clues, and Restating

Highly effective teachers are deliberate in how they behave after they have asked a question, especially if the student does not immediately know the correct answer. They are thoughtful and deliberate in how much wait time they give students after asking a question. This may seem like a simple and relatively unimportant thing, but the amount of wait time varies greatly from teacher to teacher and, most importantly, from student to student.

**ELA Test Item Specifications**

| CCSS | RI.4.1—Refer to details and examples in a text when explaining what the text says explicitly and when drawing inferences from the text.<br><br>RI.4.7—Interpret information presented visually, orally, or quantitatively (e.g., in charts, graphs, diagrams, time lines, animations, or interactive elements on web pages) and explain how the information contributes to an understanding of the text in which it appears. |
|---|---|
| Claim 1 | Students can read closely and analytically to comprehend a range of increasingly complex literary and informational texts. |
| Target 8 | Key Details: Given an inference or conclusion, use explicit details and implicit information from the text to support the inference or conclusion provided. |
| DOK | DOK 1, DOK 2 |
| Stimuli/ Passages | Three basic categories for informational text include:<br>• Literary nonfiction<br>• Historical / social studies<br>• Scientific/technical texts<br><br>Informational text include biographies and autobiographies; books about history, social studies, science, and the arts; technical texts, including directions, forms, and information displayed in graphs, charts, or maps; and digital sources on a range of topics. |

**Stems**

MC (multiple choice, 1 correct answer)

Appropriate stems:

- Which detail/sentence from the passage supports the idea/conclusion/inference that shows that [inference or conclusion based on the passage]?

- [Inference or conclusion based on the passage.] Which detail/sentence from the passage best supports this idea/statement/conclusion/inference OR best shows that [idea in the inference or conclusion]?

- Read this sentence/statement and the directions that follow. [Inference or conclusion based on the passage.] Which detail from the passage best supports this sentence/statement/conclusion/ inference OR best shows that [idea in the inference or conclusion]?

Appropriate stems for dual-text stimuli only:

- Which [detail/sentence] from [text #1 name] best shows that [inference or conclusion based on the two passages] is true of both passages? Note: This stem can only be used with two informational passages.

- Based on the information in [text #2 name OR literary text name], [inference or conclusion based on text #1]. Which detail/sentence from [text #1 name] best supports that [idea in the inference or conclusion]?

Figure 4.2: Question stems.

Continued →

MC (multiple choice, multiple correct answers; 5–8 choices, 2–4 correct)

Appropriate stems:

- Pick the [number] details/sentences from the passage that best support the idea/conclusion/ inference that best shows that [inference or conclusion based on the passage].
- [Inference or conclusion based on the passage.] Pick the [number] details/sentences from the passage that best support this idea/statement/conclusion/inference OR best show that [idea in the inference or conclusion].
- Read this sentence/statement and the directions that follow. [Inference or conclusion based on the passage.] Pick the [number] details from the passage that best support this sentence/ statement/conclusion/inference OR best show that [idea in the inference or conclusion].

Appropriate stems for dual-text stimuli only:

- Which [details/sentences] from [text #1 name] best show that [inference or conclusion based on the two passages] is true of both passages? Pick [two/three] choices OR pick all that are correct. Note: This stem can only be used with two informational passages.
- Based on the information in [text #2 name OR literary text name], [inference or conclusion based on text #1]. Which detail/sentence from [text #1 name] best supports that [idea in the inference or conclusion]? Pick [two/three] choices OR pick all that are correct.

HT (hot text—whole section taken directly from text, click on one or more than one)

Appropriate stems:

- Click the [number] details/sentences/paragraphs/etc. that best support the idea/conclusion/ inference that best shows that [inference or conclusion based on the passage].
- [Inference or conclusion based on the passage.] Click the [number] details/sentences/ paragraphs/etc. that best support this idea/statement/conclusion/inference OR best show that [idea in the inference or conclusion].
- Read this sentence/statement and the directions that follow. [Inference or conclusion based on the passage.] Click the [number] details/etc. that best support this sentence/statement/ conclusion/inference OR best show that [idea in the inference or conclusion].

Appropriate stem for dual-text stimuli only:

- Both [text #1 name] and [text #2 name] show [inference or conclusion based on both passages]. First, click the sentence in the paragraph from [text #1 name] that best supports [inference or conclusion]. Next, click on the sentence in the paragraph from [text #2 name] that supports [inference or conclusion]. Note: This stem can only be used with two informational passages.

How much wait time is appropriate? Generally speaking, teachers should wait between three and five seconds after asking a question. Obviously, the amount of wait time varies depending on the difficulty and cognitive level of the question. Teachers can wait too long if it is unlikely that the student will respond correctly. Also, waiting too long can disrupt the flow, the continuity, and momentum of the lesson (Brophy & Evertson, 1976).

Mary Budd Rowe (1969) finds a number of benefits occur when teachers are made aware of the importance of wait time and train to increase their wait time to five seconds or more:

- *Longer student responses*
- *More speculative thinking and arguments based on evidence*

- *More child-to-child comparing of differences and fewer teacher-centered interactions*

- *More student questions*

- *Opportunities for teachers to hear and think, thus a wider variety of questions asked*

- *Changed teacher expectations for some students because they contributed more (as quoted in Bellon et al., 1992, p. 19)*

Other researchers have identified additional benefits that occur when teachers are thoughtful and deliberate in increasing the amount of wait time. For example, studies find that slower students make more contributions and disciplinary issues are often reduced (Lehr, 1984). Teachers interrupt students less often (Tobin, 1984). Additionally, Kenneth Tobin (1984) reports that extended wait time gives students time to think about prior answers, formulate their own reaction, and generate an oral answer if called on. Rowe (1986) reports that increasing wait time improves the quality of student answers. Students provide more complex answers, provide more logical arguments, and are more willing to speculate. She also finds that the communications and interaction patterns in class are less teacher centered when wait time is increased, and competition among students to respond is reduced. Increased wait time reduces nonresponses and decreases the number of students rated as poor (Bellon et al., 1992).

Not only do teachers differ in the amount of wait time that is provided, they also differ in the quantity and quality of hints and clues they provide as students are attempting to formulate a response. Importantly, some teachers—particularly teachers with low expectations for student success—will provide hints and clues for some students and not for others. It should surprise no one that students who receive additional wait time, coupled with appropriate hints and clues, successfully answer more questions than those who don't.

Although there have been literally hundreds of research studies, articles, and books focusing on questioning, the primary point for teachers is that they become aware of various questioning tools and make conscious decisions regarding the questioning techniques they will use for a specific instructional purpose.

## Time on Task

Time is a precious resource for teachers, and teachers in a PLC work with their colleagues to create lessons that utilize time effectively and efficiently. They also work hard to create classroom cultures in which student behavior is managed in such a way as to capture the full use of the instructional time that is allocated each day. Effective teachers are aware of the importance of the relationship between student learning and the amount of time students are actively engaged in their learning. Saphier et al. (2008) summarize, "School effectiveness researchers over the past three decades have ranked time—and time related instructional variables—either number one or number two on a list of eight to ten factors that are important to student achievement" (p. 50).

In thinking of the tools teachers need to employ in order to use the time that is allocated to them effectively, it is important for teachers to understand the concept of academic engaged time, or what is commonly referred to as *time on task*. This is the amount of time that students actually spend actively engaged in the lesson. There are numerous studies focusing on time on task. Berliner (1984) reports that students are engaged only about 40 percent of the time. Of course, the amount of academic engaged time differs from teacher to teacher.

It is also important to remember that as important as time on task is, the more significant factor is what students are actually doing when they are engaged. Gettinger (1989) writes, "How much time a learner needs to spend in learning . . . depends largely on what goes on during the learning time" (p. 74). Since increased learning is associated with the amount of time students are actively engaged in effective and meaningful lessons, it is important for teachers to develop the tools to take full use of the instructional time in each day in ways that enhance student learning.

High-quality academic engaged time begins with teacher teams collaboratively planning lessons that are meaningful, engaging, tied directly to the standard, and make full use of the allotted instructional time. And because collaborative teams use the results of their common formative assessments, they are able to collaboratively analyze their instructional effectiveness and seek ways to continually improve.

One of the many tools in a teacher's toolbox that can enhance the amount of student academic engaged time is the simple awareness of the issue. For example, teachers can simply make sure that they are not wasting time during transitions between activities. Teachers should examine how their class is organized for simple tasks. This is especially true for teachers at the elementary level, where the teacher has to think about efficient and time-saving ways to have students complete such mundane tasks as sharpening pencils, going to the restroom, and moving from group to group. And while the use of instructional technology can enhance student learning, media and instructional technology can have a detrimental effect on academic engaged time when used inappropriately or when the technology is faulty.

*When students are constantly moving from class to class or to a special program or teacher, they are not engaged in learning.*

Some things that affect student time on task are beyond an individual teacher's control, but in a PLC, when the principal is highly engaged with teacher teams, issues such as interruptions, the daily schedule, and the overall school organization can be addressed. For example, the school should be organized in such a way as to protect core instruction. When students are constantly moving from class to class or to a special program or teacher, they are not engaged in learning.

## In-Class Instructional Groups

A collaborative team addresses a number of issues when planning for instruction, one being effective ways to group students at various times in the lesson or unit in order to maximize their learning. In-class grouping should not be confused with ability grouping or tracking of students. The effects of ability grouping or tracking are marginal, at best. Hattie (2009) reports the summary of more than three hundred studies of tracking and concludes, "The results show that tracking has minimal effects on learning outcomes and profound negative equity effects" (p. 90). On the other hand, in-class grouping in which teachers use multiple grouping patterns, especially when used for small-group instruction, can have a modest effect on student learning.

Small-group instruction is especially useful after core instruction and a collaborative analysis of common formative assessments. As the team reviews the results of a common formative assessment, it can develop strategies for providing small groups of students with additional time, support, or extension of its learning. For example, one teacher might agree to take one particular small group of students to work on a specific unlearned skill, while the other teachers are working with students who have been grouped for other purposes, such as extending student learning.

In short, teachers in a PLC develop the tools to effectively group students within the lesson or unit either spontaneously during the lesson or, more likely, as part of the predetermined unit plan. Whole-group instruction is utilized for core instruction, and a variety of grouping patterns, such as cooperative learning groups, are used for more specific follow-up.

## Teacher Physical Movement

Teachers can use physical movement within the classroom to enhance their instructional effectiveness. And, as with most instructional tools, effective use of teacher physical movement simply begins with awareness—realizing that physical movement patterns can often become so ingrained that they become a way of life without consideration of effectiveness.

For example, some teachers fall into the habit of standing in the center front of the room throughout most of their lessons. Teachers who teach primarily from this position often pay more attention to the students who are sitting in the first few rows across the front of the classroom and a few rows down the middle. (This is often referred to as the pattern of *teaching to the T*). These students get not only more attention during the lesson, but they receive more wait time, cues, and hints when asked a question. In this physical pattern, teachers tend to teach to the T and correct the rear corners. Students sitting in the back of the classroom, in the corners, receive less attention, wait time, clues, and hints. The nonverbal message that is often sent is that students who are sitting in the T are expected to learn, while students sitting in the back corners are expected to behave. It's important to remember that teachers who constantly teach to the T rarely do so as the result of a conscious instructional decision. Like many aspects of teaching, a teacher's physical movement during a lesson is more or less the result of a habit he or she developed over time.

Moving around the classroom in a conscious, deliberate manner sends another powerful message to students, and that is, "I'm aware. I'm moving around the room to keep everyone's attention and to see if you are on task and learning." Teachers can use their movement around the room to manage behavior and receive feedback from students by observing their work.

There is no one right way for teachers to move around the room. Much depends on the lesson that is being taught and the students' ages. Of course, the discipline itself has a huge impact on a teacher's physical movement. For example, physical education teachers, art teachers, music teachers, and career and technical education teachers are examples of teachers whose physical movement is dictated, to a great degree, by the subject they teach. The overriding message for teachers is this: Be conscious of your physical movement around the room and the effects it is having on both students and the teacher, and make deliberate decisions about your physical movement.

## Affective Tools

Effective teachers employ much more than instructional tools to enhance the learning of their students. They also use affective tools—a way of viewing and interacting with students—that, together with effective instructional methodologies can have a huge impact on creating a positive and effective classroom culture. And, of course, teachers in a professional learning community enhance the effectiveness of their affective toolbox by learning and planning as a member of a collaborative team.

*Students pick up quickly whether or not their teacher likes them, cares for them, and will encourage them and help them succeed.*

Students pick up quickly whether or not their teacher likes them, cares for them, and will encourage them and help them succeed. It is difficult to imagine that someone would choose to be a teacher who does not like students, but unfortunately, this happens. Fortunately, such instances are the exception. Most teachers want to create a warm, caring, encouraging, and supportive classroom environment, and they begin by making sure students know they are excited to have them in their classroom, and that it is going to be a great year for each and every one of them. Other affective behaviors will have little or no impact if students perceive the teacher does not like students.

It is important to remember that affective communications and behaviors should not be viewed individually. They are interconnected, intertwined, and the quality of one behavior can have a huge impact on—and even cancel out—the positive effects of the others. While there is no definitive list of the affective behaviors teachers should employ, the following provides examples of the affective lens through which teachers can enhance their effectiveness.

## Task-Oriented Culture

Effective teachers constantly send signals, both verbal and nonverbal, that the primary purpose of the class is for students to learn. Developing an effective task-oriented culture begins with collaborative team planning. Units of instruction are tied directly to the standards, broken down into lesson learning targets, and clearly communicated in various ways to the students.

In a task-oriented culture, a message is constantly communicated: "This is what we are going to learn. This is important, and here's why. You must do your work, and you must behave." Of course, teachers communicate much more than this, but the overarching message is that the classroom is primarily a place for student learning.

## Quality of Student-Teacher Communication

The quality of affective classroom interactions is influenced, to a great degree, by the quality of communication between teachers and their students. One specific example of a communications-related behavior that is influenced by teachers' affective skills and attitudes involves listening to students in deep and meaningful ways.

It is natural to think that the quality of communication between teachers and their students should be viewed through the lens of what they verbalize to each other and the quality of those interactions. Of course, this is important. But, affectively, listening to students individually and deeply at all levels is a powerful tool. There is a huge difference between *hearing* a student and *listening* to a student.

Listening deeply to what students are saying is one important way that teachers let students know they care about them, not simply as a student, but as a person. Listening deeply communicates to students that they are valued and that what they think, their experiences, and their views are valued. A culture of caring is one of the most powerful motivators in a teacher's affective arsenal.

## Caring

For decades the primary technique for motivating students has been the threat of a low grade—the threat of failure. While grades are powerful motivators for high-achieving students, there is no evidence that the threat of a low grade is effective for students who struggle to succeed in school. A much more powerful motivator, and one that effective teachers use with all students, is the consistent and genuine message that "I care."

Communicating a sense of caring gets played out in multiple ways. Teachers demonstrate they care for their students when they take a personal interest in each student. They pay attention to student interests, problems, and accomplishments both within and outside of the classroom.

Insisting that students do their work and learn at a high level is another way teachers communicate that they care for their students. If teachers tell students that a particular concept or skill is essential, it is important that they insist students do their work. Likewise, teachers should insist that students behave properly, not simply to avoid punishment, but because teachers care enough to correct students when they misbehave. Few things destroy a teacher's relationship with his or her students faster than an unwillingness to confront an obvious problem and to do so by communicating the message, "I care so much for you I will not let you leave my class without learning this!" Or "I care so much about you I will not let you behave this way. If you continue to behave like this, it is going to cause you problems for the rest of your life, and I care too much to allow that to happen!"

## Empathy

Caring and empathy go hand in hand. Teachers in a professional learning community work to view their lessons and schooling, in general, through the lens of their students. For many students, their time at school is the best part of their day. It is naïve to think that student learning and behavior are not affected by the larger environment in which students live outside of school.

*Much is gained when teacher teams discuss and share knowledge and information about individual students.*

Much is gained when teacher teams discuss and share knowledge and information about individual students. One member of the team may know something about a particular student that is not known by another teacher. This kind of team discussion about individual students can offer teachers powerful insights into the world of their students outside of school.

However, a word of caution is in order. Empathy is not the same as feeling sorry for a student or group of students. Feeling sorry for a student or group of students can easily lead to low expectations. Empathy's power lies in its impact on both student and teacher to move forward together, overcoming often seemingly overwhelming odds.

## Specificity and Concreteness

Positive and effective connections are enhanced when the teachers' verbal interactions are specific and concrete. More effective teachers shy away from using vague phrases such as, "You've got to do better!" or "Johnny, I need you to behave." Instead, they are specific in their verbal directions to students. For example, they might say, "Johnny, I need you to get your homework in on time," or "Johnny, you must not interrupt other students when they are answering questions."

Specificity and concreteness are also powerful tools for reinforcing desired behaviors. For example, rather than simply saying, "You were very good today, Johnny," teachers should point out specific behaviors, saying something such as, "Johnny, you did a very good job staying focused on your work today. I am so pleased!" or the teacher might say, "Your manners are so much better. I love the way you are remembering to say please and thank you!"

Teachers engage in hundreds of quick interactions with students each day. Often a simple awareness of the need to be specific and concrete in shaping student behavior can be a powerful tool and can go a long way to strengthening relationships with students.

## Immediacy of Relationships

Closely associated with specificity and concreteness are the teacher tools associated with focusing on the present—the immediacy of the relationships with students. Effective teachers focus their attention on the present and dwell less on issues in the past or the distant future.

Teachers who place too much attention on events in students' pasts run the risk of losing objectivity about particular students. For example, while it makes perfect sense for teachers to review students' cumulative record, if they are not careful they may use information about the past to explain why a student is unlikely to learn in the present.

Occasionally, a teacher might know a student's sibling who previously attended school. Perhaps he wasn't a very good student, or perhaps he had behavioral problems. Teachers must be careful to not dwell on the past behavior of the sibling and conclude that the student currently in their class will have the same problem or issues.

Some teachers focus too far in the future. Especially with elementary-age students, it is necessary to focus on the here and now. Phrases such as "stay in school and get a good job" have no meaning to a student of this age. Even placing too much emphasis on making good grades in order to get into a good college or university has little meaning. It is much better for teachers to realize that each student holds great potential and then focus on each day and the day after, and then the next day—lesson by lesson, unit by unit, kid by kid, skill by skill.

## Sensitivity and Respect

Tied directly to caring and empathy are sensitivity and respect. Teachers in a PLC operate within a norm, a commitment, to be sensitive to students' feelings and demonstrate respect for each and every student—even those who are struggling with their learning or behavior or both. Students of all ages are very sensitive about all manner of things—their looks, their clothes, their background, how they speak, to name just a few.

Teachers who create a positive affective culture in their classroom and with their students do not make a little joke about a particular student just to get a chuckle from the other students. Thoughtlessness of this kind can have a devastating effect on students. One of the most important norms for teaching in a professional learning community

*One of the most important norms for teaching in a professional learning community is always being respectful and courteous to students, even to students who do not reciprocate.*

is always being respectful and courteous to students, even to students who do not reciprocate. Being courteous and respectful is more than a matter of modeling the behavior expected of others, it is the basis for the culture that everyone expects within the school family—administrators, faculty, staff, and students.

## Genuineness and Personal Self-Disclosure

An important part of connecting with students relates to how the students view their teachers as people, rather than simply as teachers. This is often a result of how teachers project themselves to students and how much they share about themselves. In some cases, students find it difficult to imagine that their teacher has a personal life, or that she was once young, or that she has hobbies, or that she found certain subjects in school very difficult, or that she struggled with certain aspects of schooling. Communicating a sense of genuineness and a sensible amount of personal self-disclosure contributes to building a healthy connection with students.

And, personal self-disclosure can be used in the learning process. For example, when teachers are teaching students aspects of effective writing, they often emphasize how writers can draw from their own personal experience. Teachers can share with students an example in their personal life and how that example can become a major theme for a story. In this way, teachers are modeling self-disclosure, not only in a positive way, but also as a part of the teaching and learning process.

Of course, common sense, moderation, and good judgment play a huge role when it comes to teachers sharing personal aspects of their lives with students. For example, if a student is having difficultly learning a particular concept or if a student is struggling with a particular problem in school, the teacher might relate to the student how he or she had to deal with a similar issue when he or she was a student and how he or she dealt with the problem. On the other hand, teachers should avoid sharing with students aspects of their personal life that are irrelevant to the students or the class. For example, it would be inappropriate for a teacher to use valuable instructional time to share stories about a vacation trip he or she took during the summer, if the experiences had no relevance to particular learning expectations.

A good place to start is with the entire teacher team discussing this topic and sharing and learning together. This is especially helpful to new teachers. New teachers do not necessarily have a sense of proportion, so learning from their more experienced team members can prove to be invaluable.

*Any teacher who complains that his or her students are apathetic or that they are not enthusiastic should first look inside.*

## Enthusiasm, Warmth, and Humor

Any teacher who complains that his or her students are apathetic or that they are not enthusiastic should first look inside. Teachers' behavior, word selection, voice, tone, and examples communicate much more than content to be learned; these things also communicate how the teacher feels about the content at hand.

The same holds true for creating a warm and caring classroom environment. Such classrooms do not happen by accident. They are the direct result of teacher behavior. Smiling, asking how students are doing, or inquiring about a student's personal life such as his or her family, pet, or car can draw students in and make them feel that you are interested in them. Expressing concern for students' academic, social, and family life can contribute to this sense of warmth. Listening deeply to students with a genuine attempt to understand is critically important. And, when behaviors such as these are demonstrated frequently, consistently, and genuinely, they will go a long way in creating a warm and caring classroom environment.

It is essential that teachers demonstrate a healthy sense of humor. This involves tremendous professional judgment. For example, at times it may prove helpful not to take something too seriously and perhaps make a humorous remark. At other times, things must be taken seriously, and the use of humor could be totally inappropriate. Teachers must be especially careful of telling jokes. Telling jokes in classrooms can be fraught with danger—especially if there is the slightest connotation of race, ethnicity, religion, sex, or politics—which means that most jokes are off limits in classrooms.

Another serious aspect of humor involves the usually unconscious teacher behavior of making fun of a student in front of the entire class in thinking it might lead to a sense of levity. It can have a devastating effect on the student. Effective teachers know that humor can be a powerful tool in creating a healthy classroom culture, yet, if not used in an appropriate and positive way can have equally negative consequences. Humor can have a positive effect when used in moderation, especially if it has some relevance to the lesson. For example, when studying the presidency of Abraham Lincoln, it is a good thing to include examples of Lincoln's keen sense of humor or quote examples of what others said or wrote about Lincoln that were humorous. On the other hand, making fun of a particular student in order to get a laugh out of the class can be extremely hurtful to a student. And, it goes without saying, that racial or ethnic jokes, or jokes that reinforce negative stereotypes (for example, humorous stories about blond women) should be avoided at all cost.

## Model Emotional Intelligence

Perhaps the greatest importance of excelling in the use of affective tools rests in the fact that teachers who effectively utilize these tools, collectively and genuinely, day in and day out *model* for students healthy and productive ways to interact with those around them—other students and adults alike. And, in the long term, developing these emotional tools can prove to be as beneficial for students as the content knowledge they learn in school.

While there is not a definitive list of proven affective behaviors of teachers, connecting with students involves a genuine caring and a helpful attitude toward students. A positive, successful classroom culture depends on how students perceive their teachers feel about them. A positive regard for students positively impacts student attitude, behavior, learning, and importantly, the development of student self-regard and confidence. A negative attitude impacts students negatively.

Teachers in a professional learning community are not expected to thoughtlessly utilize a predetermined set of instructional methodologies regardless of the particular subject, lesson, students, or context. It is important to remember that the focus is on the learning of each kid, skill by skill. The questions that drive a PLC are, Are our students learning, and how do we know? It is not, What instructional methods are you using? In a PLC, instructional methods are viewed as a means to an end (student learning), and not as an end unto themselves.

*A positive regard for students positively impacts student attitude, behavior, learning, and importantly, the development of student self-regard and confidence.*

# Chapter 5

# Managing Classroom Behavior

*Even the best program requires good management techniques to get children started and moving. Your destination won't be reached if you can't get the car started and keep it moving (or stopped when necessary). And educational objectives won't be achieved if a teacher can't get children involved in the work and keep them from disturbing others.*

—Jacob Kounin

Most educators recognize the impact student behavior can have on learning. Teachers spend a great deal of time dealing with behavior issues—in some cases, a disproportionate amount of time. In fact, the issue of student discipline and the amount of time spent dealing with student behavior looms so large in the minds of some teachers it causes them to give up on the teaching profession entirely because they feel they rarely deal with anything else (Saphier et al., 2008).

The terms *discipline* and *classroom management* are often used interchangeably. One way to differentiate between these terms is to view *discipline* as those tools teachers employ *after* a student misbehaves. *Classroom management*, on the other hand, refers to the tools teachers utilize to manage their classrooms, preventing discipline problems from occurring in the first place. Teachers need to be skilled in both kinds of tools, and teachers in a PLC place a great deal of emphasis on gaining the knowledge and skills that can help them effectively manage their classrooms.

## Collective Inquiry Into Best Practice

Whatever the issue being addressed, the first step for educators in a professional learning community is to gain shared knowledge—to seek "best practices." Certainly there is no shortage of research, programs, or methods related to managing student behavior. Even a cursory review of the research on effective management techniques and procedures can provide a broad framework for organizing schools and classrooms.

Bellon et al. (1992) propose that, although specific guidelines may vary, effective school and classroom management contains four collaboratively developed, distinct elements: expectations, rules, procedures, and consequences. *Expectations* are defined as the assumptions teachers make about future student behavior. *Rules* are statements that communicate general expectations and standards of behavior. *Procedures* refer to routines for specific activities. And, *consequences* are rewards and penalties for appropriate or inappropriate behavior. Thinking about and collaboratively planning around each of these four areas is an excellent way of developing ways to enhance the management of student behavior, within both schools and classrooms.

## Classroom Management That Works

An excellent place to begin a look into best practices for managing student behavior is Robert Marzano, Jana Marzano, and Debra Pickering's (2003) *Classroom Management That Works: Research-Based Strategies for Every Teacher*. The power of this review is that the findings are based on a meta-analysis of over one hundred research studies and reports.

The authors group their findings into major areas, with supporting research and effective programs, as well as suggested research-based action steps included in each area. Importantly, included in the discussion of each action step are examples for specific, research-based behaviors and activities that apply to both students and teachers. The major areas and the action steps for each include the following (as found in Marzano et al., 2003).

### *Rules and Procedures*

Action Step 1: Identify specific rules and procedures for your classroom (p. 18).

Action Step 2: Involve students in the design of rules and procedures (p. 26).

### *Disciplinary Interventions*

Action Step 1: Employ specific techniques that acknowledge and reinforce acceptable behavior and acknowledge and provide negative consequences for unacceptable behavior (p. 35).

Action Step 2: Establish clear limits for unacceptable behavior and an effective system to record these behaviors (p. 40).

### *Teacher-Student Relationships*

Action Step 1: Use specific techniques to establish an appropriate level of dominance in the classroom (p. 49).

Action Step 2: Use specific behaviors that communicate an appropriate level of cooperation (p. 52).

Action Step 3: Be aware of the needs of different types of students (p. 64).

### Mental Set

Action Step 1: Employ specific techniques to maintain or heighten your awareness of the actions of students in your classes (withitness) (p. 69).

Action Step 2: Employ specific techniques to maintain a healthy emotional objectivity with students (p. 73).

### The Student's Responsibility for Management

Action Step 1: Employ general classroom procedures that enhance student responsibility (p. 80).

Action Step 2: Provide students with self-monitoring and control strategies (p. 85).

Action Step 3: Provide students with cognitive-based strategies (p. 89).

### Getting Off to a Good Start

Action Step 1: Arrange and decorate your room in a manner that supports effective classroom management (p. 94).

Action Step 2: Begin with a strong first day of class (p. 98).

Action Step 3: Emphasize classroom management for the first few days (p. 102).

### Management at the School Level

Action Step 1: Establish rules and procedures for behavioral problems that might be caused by the school's physical characteristics for the school's routines (p. 106).

Action Step 2: Establish clear schoolwide rules and procedures regarding specific types of misbehavior (p. 108).

Action Step 3: Establish and enforce appropriate consequences for specific types of misbehavior (p. 110).

Action Step 4: Establish a system that allows for the early detection of students who have high potential for violence and extreme behaviors (p. 113).

## Discipline With Dignity

Since 1988, one of the more popular approaches to preventing and dealing with misbehavior when it occurs is based on the book *Discipline With Dignity* by Richard Curwin and Allen Mendler. In *Discipline With Dignity, 3rd edition: New Challenges, New Solutions*, Curwin, Mendler, and Mendler (2008) propose a number of core beliefs that are "central to all effective behavior-based programs and define a healthy classroom that uses discipline as a learning process rather than a system of retribution" (p. 29). They also offer specific ideas for managing student behavior that are based on the following core beliefs:

*Dealing with student behavior is part of the job.*

*Always treat students with dignity.*

*Discipline works best when integrated with effective practices.*

*Adults see it as their professional responsibility to make positive, consistent connections with students.*

*Acting out is sometimes an act of sanity.*

*Fair is not always equal. (pp. 29–31)*

*Discipline With Dignity* is based on a three-pronged approach to discipline problems:

**Prevention**—*What can be done to prevent problems from occurring?*

**Action**—*What can be done when misbehavior occurs to solve the problem without making it worse?*

**Resolution**—*What can be done for students who are chronically challenging? (p. 20)*

The specific actions recommended in each of these three areas are based on a twelve-step plan. Each step includes specific things administrators and teachers can do to better manage student behavior and enhance student success. The twelve foundational steps presented in *Discipline With Dignity, Third Edition* (Curwin et al., 2008), are:

1. Let students know what you need, and ask them what they need from you.

2. Differentiate instruction based on each student's strengths.

3. Listen to what students are thinking and feeling.

4. Use humor.

5. Vary your style of presentation.

6. Offer choices.

7. Refuse to accept excuses, and stop making them yourself.

8. Legitimize misbehavior that you cannot stop.

9. Use a variety of ways to communicate with children.

10. Be responsible for yourself, and allow children to take responsibility for themselves.

11. Realize that you will not reach every child, but act as if you can.

12. Start fresh every day. (pp. 21–24)

The *Discipline With Dignity* approach for managing student behavior both before and after misbehavior occurs is but one of a number of resources available to educators. And again, the first step educators—particularly teacher teams—under-take when seeking to develop effective student behavior management plans and strategies is to gain shared knowledge by seeking out best practices such as those proposed by Curwin et al. (2008).

## Specific Teacher Behaviors for Limiting Student Misbehavior: The Kounin Research

Once a student misbehaves, the options available to teachers are rather limited. Most programs or initiatives that focus on discipline strategies—what teachers do following student misbehavior—contain similar components, such as having rules for behavior, setting specific consequences for students when misbehavior occurs, and reinforcing, recognizing, and rewarding appropriate behavior. On the other hand, managing classroom behavior—preventing, or reducing, misbehavior before it occurs—is much more complicated, but if done well, it is much more effective.

Although the research is somewhat dated, the work of Jacob Kounin (1970) is the gold standard for focusing on what effective teachers do during their teaching that reduces student misbehavior.

Kounin's research on discipline and classroom management began somewhat accidently. As he was teaching a class, he stopped and reprimanded a student for reading a newspaper. He noticed that the fact that he had reprimanded one par-ticular student had affected the rest of the class. He began to wonder about this phenomenon: "Why were students who weren't targets of the reprimand affected by it? Do differences in the qualities of the reprimand produce different effects, if any, on non-target students?" (Kounin, 1970, p. iii). Such questions led Kounin to five years of research on the subject of discipline, how a teacher handles misbehavior. More specifically, the studies focused on how the correction of misbehavior of one student affects the behavior of others in the classroom. He referred to this as the "ripple effect" of different discipline approaches (p. 5).

Kounin sought to learn if some discipline techniques are more effective than others when it comes to influencing the behavior of the entire class. Do teachers who are perceived as having good discipline in their classrooms—teachers who seem to manage their classes well—utilize different discipline tools when a student misbehaves than teachers who are perceived as weak disciplinarians?

After five years of study, Kounin did not find much, if any, difference in the effects of different disciplinary techniques on the larger classroom environment. He concludes, "We found that the manner in which teachers handled misbehavior made no difference in how audience students reacted. It was not possible to predict any ripple effect from any quality of a disciplinary event" (Kounin, 1970, p. 70). However, he does find that "desist techniques are not significant determinants of managerial success in classrooms" (Kounin, 1970, p. 71).

Why then are some teachers generally viewed as better disciplinarians than others? What differentiates good disciplinarians from weak disciplinarians? These questions led Kounin to pursue another research project. In the second study, Kounin and his colleagues collected data from videotapes of eighty elementary school classrooms. The use of videotapes allowed for the analysis not only of the effectiveness of various desist techniques, but also the effects of larger issues such as managing a classroom.

In this second study, Kounin (1970) hit pay dirt! He found there "are different dimensions of group management that far outweigh disciplinary techniques in their power to influence the behavior of children in classrooms" (p. vii). In short, Kounin found that what teachers do *after* a student misbehaves is not nearly as powerful as what teachers are doing *prior* to the misbehaving, and effective classroom managers employ different tools than teachers who are less effective in managing their classrooms. Interestingly, the teacher tools that led to more effective classroom management were not a part of huge initiatives, classroom management programs, or even teaching methods. Rather, they were the cumulative effect of dozens of small teacher behaviors that collectively led to well-managed classrooms. Kounin grouped these behaviors into five categories:

1. Withitness and overlapping

2. Smoothness and momentum

3. Group alerting and accountability

4. Valence and challenge arousal

5. Seatwork, variety, and challenge

It is important to note that the behaviors often influence one another and are interrelated. One behavior or group of behaviors, in isolation, is unlikely to have a significant impact on the management of an entire classroom. Hence, they should be viewed as a whole.

### Withitness and Overlapping

Most students can recall a teacher whom they felt was out of it—just not aware of what was going on in the class. Most students can also recall teachers who seemed to have eyes in the back of their head—teachers who demonstrated through their behavior what Kounin (1970) would refer to as "withitness." Importantly, teachers who demonstrate withitness experience fewer student behavior problems in their classrooms. Conversely, teachers who lack withitness spend a significant amount of time dealing with student misbehavior.

Kounin (1970) defines *teacher withitness* as "a teacher's communicating by her actual behavior (rather than by simple verbal announcing: 'I know what's going on.') that she knows what the children are doing, or has the proverbial 'eyes in the back of her head'" (p. 82). He found that teachers who fail to communicate with students an awareness of what's going on within the classroom make a number of mistakes. For example, they may correct the wrong student for misbehavior. The other students know who was actually misbehaving, but the teacher intervenes with someone else. Or, a teacher might intervene with a student who is misbehaving in a rather minor way and not notice that another student was engaged in more serious misbehavior. Some teachers communicate a lack of withitness with the timing of their intervening. Kounin found two common mistakes: either the teacher was too late when intervening, allowing the misbehavior to spread to other students, or the teacher was too late and allowed the misbehavior to increase in seriousness.

Teachers who benefit from being part of a collaborative team can learn from each other about ways to reduce student misbehavior by communicating that they are with it. They can also learn of rather simple tools effective teachers use to let students know they are aware of what is going on minute by minute. For example, effective teachers have learned how the physical position of the teacher affects teacher awareness. Teachers who constantly stand or sit in one place may miss student misbehavior at its earliest stages. Even things as simple as knowing students' names and something about the students outside of the classroom communicate an awareness and support an aura of withitness.

Closely associated with withitness is the issue of overlap. Kounin (1970) defines *overlap* as "what the teacher does when she has two matters to deal with at the same time. Does she somehow attend to both issues simultaneously or does she remain or become immersed in one issue only, to the neglect of the other?" (p. 85).

One of the most common forms of overlap is when an in-class intrusion occurs. For example, if a teacher is working with a reading group and a student approaches the teacher and asks a question, does the teacher turn attention away from the reading group and focus on the student? Also, the intrusion might come from outside the classroom. If a teacher is teaching a lesson and there is a knock on the door, how does the teacher respond? Does the teacher stop the lesson, walk to the door, open it, and interact with whoever is at the door? Or does the teacher have a student answer the door, see who it is, motion the person in, and let the person deliver the message, all while never losing eye contact with the students? In other words, teachers must learn to handle intrusions by dealing with one task at a time. Effective teachers do not drop one group of students in order to address an intrusion.

The issue of overlapping also has ramifications for how teachers plan for multiple groups. If a teacher is going to be working with a reading group, for example, what is the quality of the work that the teacher has planned for the other students? If teachers do not plan effectively for multiple groups, they may find themselves working with one group but constantly having to deal with the behavior of other students.

While there is no list of correct ways to better deal with in-class and outside intrusions, or ways to effectively work with multiple groups, teachers in collaborative teams learn tricks of the trade from their colleagues and work to continually improve the ways in which they communicate they are with it and can handle multiple classroom events (overlap situations) simultaneously.

### Smoothness and Momentum

As any teacher knows, a lot of activity occurs in classrooms—some planned and some unplanned. Kounin and his colleagues studied how teachers' management of movement affected student behavior. They found that effectively managing instructional and noninstructional transitions and movement reduced student misbehavior. They divided their findings into two categories: (1) factors that affected the smoothness of lessons in a negative way, and (2) teacher behavior that adversely affected instructional momentum.

The concept of smoothness is especially important for teachers in self-contained classrooms. Kounin (1970) explains,

> *A teacher in a self-contained classroom, then, must manage considerable activity* movement: *she must initiate, sustain, and terminate many activities. Some of this involves having children move physically from one point of the room to another, as when a group must move from their own desks to the reading circle. At other times it involves some psychological movement, or some change in props, as when children change from doing arithmetic problems at their desks to studying spelling words at the same desks. (p. 92)*

Kounin discovered that a number of teacher behaviors affect smoothness. One of these behaviors is referred to as *stimulus-boundedness*—an event in which the teacher "behaves as though she has no will of her own and reacts to some unplanned and irrelevant stimulus as an iron filing reacts to some magnet: she gets magnetized and lured into reacting to some minutia that pulls her out of the main activity stream" (p. 98).

For example, a teacher might be teaching a lesson and suddenly notice that it has begun to snow. The teacher abruptly stops and says, "Look, it's beginning to snow. I don't remember the weather forecast calling for snow today." As a result of the teacher's comment, students might look out the window and begin making comments about the snow, the weather forecast they heard, or whether or not they will get to go home early.

Another example is a teacher who is teaching a lesson and notices that students are not sitting with good posture at their desks. The teacher stops the lesson and shifts to a short lecture about the importance of sitting up straight.

Kounin (1970) referred to another behavior that affects smoothness and momentum as *dangles*. He found that dangles occurred when "a teacher started, or was in, some activity and then left it 'hanging in midair' by going off to some other activity. Following such a 'fade away' she would then resume the activity" (p. 100). For example, a teacher might announce that the next activity is going to be working in reading groups. The teacher instructs the students to get their reading books out. However, as the teacher moves to the area of the classroom where the reading circle is formed, the teacher notices the fish tank, pauses, and wonders aloud, "How long has it been since the fish have been fed?" Then the teacher checks who is responsible for feeding the fish each day and reminds the students they must remember to feed the fish. After this dangle, the teacher then begins the move into the reading lesson. Kounin observed that sometimes teachers never returned to the original activity. He referred to these teacher behaviors as *truncations*.

In some cases, during transition points, *flip-flops*—when a teacher stops one activity, starts another, and then returns to the original activity—occurred. Kounin (1970) provides an example:

> The teacher says, "All right, let's everybody put away your spelling papers and take out your arithmetic books." The children put away their spelling papers in their desks, and after most of the children had their arithmetic books out on their desk, the teacher asked, "Let's see the hands of the ones who got all their spelling words right." (p. 101)

Classroom momentum is affected by such slowdowns. Kounin notes:

> Slowdowns refer to movement properties that may or may not be both smooth and unidirectional but which clearly impede or produce friction in the forward momentum of an activity. Their effect is to hold back and produce dragginess in the progress of an activity. (p. 102)

Instructional smoothness is affected when teachers are suddenly distracted and change their focus and the focus of the students. The two most significant factors affecting momentum are overdwelling and fragmentation. *Overdwelling* occurs in a number of ways. For example, the teacher might go on and on about a certain event that has occurred such as student misbehavior. In such cases, the teacher is seen as nagging or preaching. Or, the teacher might focus more on a minor point of a lesson while paying scant attention to the major point. Another type of overdwelling occurs when teachers are dealing with props such as pencils, books, paper, and such. Kounin provides this example of prop overdwelling: "A teacher may overemphasize props by passing out sheets of paper one sheet at a time to one child at a time, clearly dragging out this procedure and producing significant waiting to the point of focusing more of the children's attention upon the props than upon the task for which they are to be used" (p. 104).

Another type of slowdown is fragmentation. Kounin (1970) defines *fragmentation* as "a slowdown produced by a teacher's breaking down an activity into subparts when the activity could be performed as a single unit" (p. 105). For example, the teacher might have individuals of a group doing something that could have been more easily done, and with fewer "waits," with the whole group. Fragmentation also occurs when teachers fragment a behavior into smaller components and focus on the smaller components when the tasks could have been performed as a single, uninterrupted sequence. For example:

> *The teacher was making a transition from spelling to arithmetic
> as follows: "All right everybody, I want you to close your spell-
> ing books. Put away your red pencils. Now close your spelling
> books. Put your spelling books in your desks. Keep them out of
> the way." Wait. "All right now. Take out your arithmetic books
> and put them on your desks in front of you. That's right, let's
> keep everything off your desks except your arithmetic book. And
> let's sit up straight. We don't want any lazy-bones do we? That's
> fine. Now, get your black pencils and open your books to page
> sixteen." (Kounin, 1970, p. 106)*

In short, teachers who avoid jerkiness during their lessons and ensure their behavior is not preventing the class from running smoothly have few student behavior
problems. And there is the additional benefit of keeping students more involved in
their work.

### Group Alerting and Accountability

By its very definition, a class consists of more than one student. How do effective
teachers maintain the focus of the entire group, and what teacher behaviors can
have a negative effect on group focus? Kounin found that teachers who have fewer
student behavior problems are able to keep the class focused on the lesson by a skill
he refers to as *group alerting*—the degree to which a teacher attempts to involve
nonreciting students in the recitation task, maintaining their attention, and keeping
them on their toes or alerted.

As discussed earlier, keeping the class or the group alert is negatively affected
when the teacher calls on a particular student first and then asks a question. Once
the teacher singles out a student who is accountable for answering the question, the
rest of the class doesn't need to pay attention. However, if the question is asked of
everyone first, everyone is accountable until a particular student is asked to respond.

Kounin (1970) articulated another dimension of maintaining group focus as *for-
matting*—what other students are required to do when one person or a small group
is being called on to perform or recite. He provides these examples of a simple
addition lesson:

> *During Miss Fulton's arithmetic lesson each child has each of
> the ten digits on his desk along with a cardboard with slots.
> The teacher calls out an addition problem, such as "eight and
> four." Each child then attempts to place an answer in the slots
> with a "one" in one slot and a "two" next to it to his right to
> make the sum of "12." The teacher then says, "All show!" Each
> child then raises his cardboard in the air to expose his answer
> to the teacher. This continues for all the addition problems in
> the lesson. (p. 112)*

In the second example, the teacher uses a different format.

*Mrs. Carter calls on Richard to go to the board. Richard goes to the board and the teacher says, "All right, Richard, show us how to add eight plus four." Richard writes eight and four with the sum of twelve. The teacher says, "That's fine. Now Mabel, will you go to the board?" Mabel goes to the board and does the next problem assigned by the teacher. (p. 112)*

Notice that in the first example, all students are held accountable, while in the second example only the students who are selected to go to the board are held accountable for staying focused on the task at hand.

Kounin's research points to three group alerting cues that have a negative effect on maintaining group focus, alertness, and accountability.

1. *The teacher moves the focus of his or her attention away from the group and becomes completely immersed in the performance of the student who is reciting; or, he or she directs a new question and subsequent attention to a single new student only, without an overt sign of awareness that there is a group.*

2. *The teacher picks a student to answer or perform before the question is asked.*

3. *The teacher has those who are reciting perform in a predetermined order. Thus, students know beforehand when they will have to answer or perform. This is in contrast to calling on students at random. (pp. 118–120)*

Positive teacher accountability cues are:

1. *The teacher asks the students to hold up their work exposing their work or answers in such a way as to be readily visible to the teacher.*

2. *The teacher requires students to recite in unison while the teacher shows signs of actively paying attention.*

3. *The teacher brings other students into the performance of a student who is reciting.*

4. *The teacher asks students who are prepared to perform or answer to raise their hands, and then calls on some of them (at random).*

5. *The teacher circulates around the classroom checking products of non-reciters during the performance or answering of a student performance. (pp. 118–120)*

### Valence and Challenge Arousal

Student misbehavior is decreased when students are motivated to engage in lessons and feel appropriately challenged by classroom activities. Kounin (1970) grouped these findings into the category of "valence and challenge arousal"—the ways that effective teachers enhance the attraction or challenge of classroom activities. Of course, the grade level also greatly influences the way teachers motivate and challenge students.

Teachers motivate and challenge students to engage in particular lessons in a number of effective ways. Kounin (1970) provides these examples:

> (1) showing genuine zest and enthusiasm; (2) making a statement pointing out that the activity possesses special valence such as, "This next one is going to be fun; I know you will enjoy it," or (3) making a statement pointing out that the activity possesses some special intellectual challenge. Example: "You're going to need your thinking caps for the next one, it's tricky." (p. 130)

Less effective classroom managers do the opposite. For example, they may start a lesson with an aversive statement such as, "You probably won't enjoy this particular lesson, but it's a state requirement that we cover it," or "Some of you may find this too difficult or confusing, so just pay attention and do the best you can."

### Seatwork, Variety, and Challenge

Closely associated to techniques teachers use to motivate and challenge students is the issue of variety. Simply put, variety is one element of keeping students from becoming bored. The issue of variety is difficult to nail down simply because there are no definitive answers as to how much variety is appropriate, especially in regard to grade level, subject, and classroom context of a particular day or lesson. On the other hand, teachers who plan variability in their lessons have fewer classroom management problems than teachers who have a very limited repertoire of instructional techniques and rely on the same approaches in their lessons practically every day.

## Planning for the Management of Student Behavior in a PLC

Generally speaking, teachers in a professional learning community develop plans to manage student behavior much the same way that they collaboratively plan to enhance student learning. After gaining shared knowledge about best practices related to managing student behavior, educators at the district, building, team, and classroom levels collaboratively develop broad foundational guidelines for both student behavior and positive dispositions.

The approach for collaboratively developing this framework mirrors the approach to enhancing student learning in a number of ways. First, the collaborative process addresses four critical questions, much like the four critical questions associated with learning. One, what dispositions do we want our students to acquire, and how should they behave? Two, how will we monitor the acquisition of the desired dispositions, and the behavior of students? Three, how will we respond when students are not acquiring expected dispositions or behaving appropriately? And four, how will we recognize, reinforce, and celebrate when students attain desired dispositions and appropriate practice?

The second way that managing student behavior in a PLC mirrors the approach to improved learning is through the development of a pyramid of interventions to address students who are struggling with their behavior or failing to attain appropriate dispositions. A helpful way to think of this is to envision a pyramid of interventions with a vertical line down the middle. One side contains the sequential steps for addressing learning issues, and the other side focuses on behavioral / social emotional issues. Importantly, teachers recognize that each side of the pyramid affects the other and ultimately the student's learning and the climate in the classroom.

Another way of managing student behavior in a PLC mirrors the way educators approach enhancing student learning through the collaborative analysis of student behavior data by teacher teams and reflection regarding the effectiveness of current practices. Such a collaborative analysis leads to identifying strengths in the management of student behavior as well as areas that need to be enhanced. Teams will then collaboratively seek best practices—proven, research-based approaches to classroom management and discipline. In this way, improving the management of student behavior mirrors the continuous improvement process for improving student learning levels.

The next section highlights the strategies and thinking the White River School District used to operationalize the positive behavioral interventions and supports (PBIS) / multitiered system of support (MTSS) work in every school across the district. District leaders started by using the discipline, tardy, attendance, and dropout data as the vehicle to communicate "why" this work was critical and a districtwide priority. Principals spent time building shared knowledge with their teams surrounding the PBIS/MTSS concepts and practices. Hugh Flint highlights the importance of and the implications tied to tackling this work on behalf of the kids. Janel and Hugh highlight point by point what the district learned when implementing these concepts and practices. Adam Uhler and Nick Hedman share what this important work looks like day to day in an elementary and a middle school.

## Multitiered Systems of Support

*By Hugh Flint, White River Director of Student Support Services and Northwest PBIS Board Member*

In an *Educational Leadership* article in 1982, *academic press* was defined as:

> *The degree to which environmental forces press for student achievement on a school-wide basis. The concept, however, is broader than high staff expectations; it pulls together various forces—school policies, practices, expectations, norms, and rewards—generated by both staff and students. Together, these forces constitute the academic "environment" experienced by students and press them to respond in particular ways, specifically, to work hard in school and to do well academically. (Murphy, Weil, Hallinger, & Mitman, 1982, p. 22)*

This vision of schooling as "a distinctive core of academic values which convey the universal importance of intellectual training" is often juxtaposed with a vision of schools increasing "their influence by responding to a diverse range of students' social needs and interests" (Shouse, 1996, pp. 47–48). In today's high-stakes, high-accountability environment, schools struggle with these two visions, sometimes seeming to treat them as mutually exclusive. Although educators recognize the importance of both, their actions indicate that academic rigor and achievement are far more important, and given the current pressure of accountability, it is no surprise. Results are what matters.

Much of that attitude is attributable to the immediate, daily pressure to achieve those academic results. A minute can't be wasted on the frivolous, the unnecessary, or the nonacademic. In order to truly get those academic outcomes for every student, however, school systems need to step back and consider what a report from the Council of State Governments Justice Center refers to as "conditions for learning" and defines as

> *the extent to which students are safe, connected, engaged, and supported in their classrooms and schools—collectively known as the 'conditions for learning'—is critical to their academic and personal success. Schools that create welcoming and secure learning environments reduce the likelihood that students will misbehave, and improve educators' ability to manage student behavior. (Morgan, Salomon, Plotkin, & Cohen, 2014)*

This is where the two visions of "academic press" and "responsive schools" come together, since the ideal conditions for learning are also, in fact, the ideal conditions for teaching.

The question then becomes, How do you establish those conditions for learning which will get us to those academic outcomes? The way we do it is to establish within our districts and schools a multitiered system of support (MTSS) framework that provides both academic support (RTI) and social and emotional support (positive behavioral interventions and supports [PBIS]). These two approaches are often seen as distinct, which reflect the tendency of schools to focus on the academics as the primary concern. Schools adopt RTI frameworks readily because of the direct academic support that fits with the focus on academic press. Although an RTI academic framework is essential, it is not sufficient since it does not establish by itself the conditions for learning. Braided and embedded with PBIS as an equally critical feature, however, schools can both provide academic press while at the same time provide the social and emotional support that "create welcoming and secure learning environments" that are necessary to academic success.

The good news for public schools is that from a resource perspective, schools have everything needed to implement PBIS at Tier 1. There may be a need to build shared knowledge through professional development, but in terms of fiscal and personnel resources, schools have everything they need. The classroom teachers, principal, counselors, specialists, and other existing school staff work together to establish buildingwide expectations, explicitly teach those expectations, determine a systematic way of recognizing when those expectations are being met, and develop a consistent response when they are not met. A representative team meets at least monthly to review discipline data and problem solve. The other good news is that if Tier 1 is fully implemented, it will prevent many students from needing Tier 2 services, which require more time and intensity of service. With the prevention framework in mind, however, we can devote the time and intensity those students require because we have reduced the number who need it. The same follows at Tier 3; effective Tier 2 interventions and practices reduce the number of students who require even greater time and intensity at Tier 3, but since there are fewer of them, we can provide the necessary level of support. The focus here is on PBIS, but of course the same prevention approach applies to tiered support in academics.

The core features of an MTSS for behavior are well established and are summarized in table 5.1.

Table 5.1: Core Elements of MTSS for Behavior

| Prevention Tier | Core Elements |
|---|---|
| Primary | Behavioral expectations defined<br><br>Behavioral expectations taught<br><br>Reward system for appropriate behavior<br><br>Continuum of consequences for problem behavior<br><br>Continuous collection and use of data for decision making |
| Secondary | Universal screening<br><br>Progress monitoring for at-risk students<br><br>System for increasing structure and predictability<br><br>System for increasing contingent adult feedback<br><br>System for linking academic and behavioral performance<br><br>System for increasing school-home communication<br><br>Collection and use of data for decision making |
| Tertiary | Functional behavioral assessment<br><br>Team-based comprehensive assessment<br><br>Linking of academic and behavior supports<br><br>Individualized intervention based on assessment information focusing on (a) prevention of problem contexts, (b) instruction on functionally equivalent skills, and instruction on desired performance skills, (c) strategies for placing problem behavior on extinction, (d) strategies for enhancing contingence reward of desired behavior, and (e) use of negative or safety consequences if needed.<br><br>Collection and use of data for decision making |

At each level, prevention is always the driver. At Tier 1, we want to prevent undesirable behavior from occurring and, if it does, prevent it from happening again. At Tier 2, when a student begins to exhibit any consistent pattern of not meeting behavioral expectations, we want to immediately put supports into place and prevent the problem behavior from escalating, at the same time correcting the behavior. Once data indicate that Tier 2 supports are not sufficient, Tier 3 supports are put into place to prevent the behavior from escalating while we individualize supports to correct the behavior. It is critical to recognize that Tier 2 supports continue at Tier 3, and that Tier 1 supports continue throughout the tiers.

The other core concept in an MTSS is that when we say "all" students we truly mean "each and every" student. One of the unfortunate outcomes of the total commitment to academic press without the accompanying system of supports in place to create the conditions for learning is that not all students are going to reach those high academic outcomes. The priority is to get the greatest number of students possible to standard, but not to get each and every student to standard. Administrators say "all," but their actions and practice often do not reflect that. This is not a condemnation of them. It is rather the reality of not having systems in place that they can implement and rely on to provide the support for students when it is needed and at the intensity it is needed. Nor is it just the school system that has failed. Failure to provide supportive systems necessary to support all students happens at multiple levels, many beyond the ability of school systems to directly affect. For students and families needing the highest levels of support, it takes collaboration and coordination among many systems including the schools, mental health services, medical services, social services, and drug and alcohol treatment services. This involves multiple levels of state, county, city, and regional service providers and administrative structures. The MTSS framework can be used as an effective means of structuring and coordinating those relationships. The prevention framework of MTSS is grounded in public health, and, though relatively new to schools, it is very familiar to many of the systems we need to interact with to provide those high intensity supports and services. This common vision can then be used not just as a model for the school system but also be used as a model for the larger system that schools are a part of.

The implications are clear: schools must make climate and culture a priority, even as they create and build academic press. There is no question that quality instruction is required for students to learn, but the conditions that allow for that quality instruction to occur and be effective must be established or, regardless of the talent, dedication, or proficiency of the teacher, learning will not occur for every student and learning will not be maximized for *any* student.

## What Have the District Leaders and the PBIS Team Learned?

- **Need for a core resource for social emotional learning just like a core resource for math and reading.** Just like we need a guaranteed and viable curriculum in math or reading, we need to provide a core support at Tier 1 for social and emotional learning. This is the resource that will get most kids (80–90 percent) to grade-level standards for social emotional growth and interaction. Having that core resource also gives adults the ability to identify students who need additional support because they can identify students who are not responding to that level of support rather than just identifying kids who never received that support and instruction but learn it once it is taught.

- **Need to stop changing up the language on the kids. All adults in the system need to respond in a systemic way.** Students do best with routine and structure and when they know what the expectations are. Having adults on the same page, with the same expectations, creates consistency and constancy. The rules are the same with everyone, which is interpreted by students as fair and positive. When expectations are not met, it is not the teacher giving arbitrary correction based on their approach, but reinforcing expectations agreed to by everyone in the building and explicitly taught to every student.

- **We have what we need to implement—the teacher.** At Tier 1, just like core academics, the main player in implementation is the classroom teacher. Teaching *all* students the behavioral expectations and reinforcing those is in the same vein as delivering core math or reading instruction. Just like RTI, if students need more support than what we have at Tier 1, we assign more targeted support time in Tier 2 and Tier 3. Plus social emotional instruction is completed tied to our CEL 5D Instructional Framework.

- **Need a data collection tool.** Just like with RTI, teams need to make data-based decisions. We can't provide an appropriate solution or meet a need if we do not know what the problem is or what the need is. Without data we do spray and pray instead of plan and implement. In White River, we use SWIS (School-wide Information System developed by the University of Oregon) as our data collection tool. Data are reviewed at monthly PBIS meetings.

- **Need a PBIS leadership team.** Systems, systems, systems! District, building, and classroom systems. The environments we exist in are complex, and without systems, they are overwhelming. People are not tired of solving problems; they are tired of solving the same problem over and over. Leadership teams are the vehicle for planning and implementing systems.

- **Need for a monthly PBIS meeting with an appropriate protocol.** The PBIS team meets monthly. The team includes the principal, counselor, and educational assistant from the lunchroom and playground, a classroom teacher, and a specialist from PE or music or library and technology. Use the TIPS (Team Initiated Problem Solving) protocol. Roles identified, starts and ends on time, data centered, reviewed last meeting's action plan and goal. Did everyone do what they agreed to do? Did it work? What do we need to change? Who, what, and when? Next meeting scheduled.

- **Importance of recognition.** Basic reinforcement. You get more of what you pay attention to. If a student is seeking attention and the quickest, easiest way of getting attention is to act out, then he or she will do so. And every other student in the class wonders why that kid gets so much of the teacher's time. Most kids are doing what they should be doing most of the time, providing outstanding models for the expectations. By recognizing that behavior publicly (and genuinely) they are reinforcing the behavior in that student *and* every other student in the class. Remember public positive recognition and private corrective feedback.

## Building PBIS Facilitator

Figure 5.1 is a position description for a school PBIS facilitator in White River.

**Job Summary:** The Building PBIS Coordinator works with the principal and the director of student support services to help develop, implement, and monitor the PBIS framework and processes within the building and to assist with districtwide implementation of PBIS. Open to current White River certificated employees only.

**Responsible to:** Building principal or assistant principal

**Qualifications:** The building PBIS coordinator must possess a valid Washington State teaching certificate. Prefer applicant with at least three years' experience in teaching. Recognition of leadership abilities and strong interpersonal communication skills by other teachers is essential.

**Essential Responsibilities:**

- Work with the director of student support services and building administrator to develop and support the PBIS processes and framework within the building
- Work with the director of student support services and building administrator to determine professional development needs related to PBIS in the building
- Implement all policies and procedures established for PBIS
- Collect and maintain the PBIS data for the school
- Monitor the fidelity of implementation of the PBIS system in the building
- Attend training/professional development sessions identified through needs assessments
- Monitor delivery of interventions for students
- Meet regularly with building PBIS teams to evaluate implementation of PBIS
- Provide training and coaching to building staff on PBIS
- Work collaboratively with other building PBIS coordinators and attend regularly scheduled meetings that may occur beyond the regular school day
- Coordinate PBIS assessments and surveys at the building

**Figure 5.1: Building PBIS facilitator position description.**

*Source: White River School District. Used with permission.*

# Examples From the White River School District

Let's take a look at a few examples of student behavior and classroom management in action.

## Glacier Middle School

*By Adam Uhler*

The 2014–2015 school year brought great opportunities for the Glacier Middle School (GMS) team to build a clear and shared vision. In addition to a number of new teachers, the entire leadership team was new. While GMS had a positive behavioral interventions and supports (PBIS) team in the past, the leadership and membership of the team were heavily weighted with intervention staff. With the change in staff, we recruited new teacher leaders for the PBIS team who consistently built great rapport with students while maintaining high expectations, taught core content, and were seen as credible by the staff. These teacher leaders, along with a counselor and administrative team, began by building shared knowledge and vision together through Tier 1 team training in the summer and applying this to our work with our colleagues throughout the year.

We began the year with a discussion about creating the school that we want for our own kids. The previous year, the staff created collective commitments to build respectful relationships in which students feel safe and valued. Individually, each staff member (teachers, educational assistants, paraeducators, and administrators) reflected on PBIS. What do you know? What do you want to know? What are you excited about? What are your fears and reservations? Then the entire staff joined in mixed grade-level teams surfacing current beliefs about the environmental factors that support effective learning for our students. What does this look like? What do we do? The staff shared characteristics of honesty, acceptance, patience, compassion, understanding, and having a "spotter" to support someone taking risks.

### Building Shared Knowledge

We then focused on building shared knowledge of PBIS by tying it to the idea of a guaranteed and viable curriculum. If we wanted to have a school that supported the learning of all students, all adults needed to have a common understanding. We shared that a traditional school focuses on students' problem behavior and relies on punishment to stop unwanted behavior. We also shared research of traditional school practices that illustrates that "punishing problem behaviors is associated with an increase in aggression, vandalism, truancy, and dropping out" (Mayer, 1995). We also shared our prior year's behavior data. In 2013–2014, staff wrote over 1,600 office referrals for a school of 800, and over 60 percent of those referrals were from the classroom. Even if an administrator spent only fifteen minutes with each student regarding each office referral, it was costing sixty-three days—one-third of the school year—in human resources, not to mention the loss of learning time. We had to ask ourselves if that was how we want to use our collective resources. While no one wants more aggression, more vandalism, more truancy, and more dropouts, we seemed stuck in a traditional, punishment-focused response. So, what were we to do?

We had to gain a new perspective. We shared with our teammates that school-wide positive behavioral interventions and supports (SWPBIS) is a solution-focused framework. It views behavior as a key component of learning. This meant we needed to collaboratively teach, recognize, and reinforce behaviors we expected. It meant we focused on replacing unwanted behaviors with new behaviors or skills. We altered environments so that they were learner centered. We sought to understand the motive behind the behavior. As we worked to these ends, we made sure that the school environment was predictable by using common language, common understanding, and common experience of expectations. There were no hidden expectations. Just like we were clear with our learning targets. We worked each day to build a positive environment by recognizing students demonstrating expected behavior. We ensured safety—violent behavior was not tolerated. We ensured the school environment was consistent—all adults in every setting used similar expectations.

We also had to recognize that educators cannot make students learn or behave. We could, however, create the environment that would increase the likelihood students would learn and behave. In fact, we already knew how. We just needed to apply the four critical questions we used to ensure academic learning to behavioral learning: What do we want all students to know and be able to do? How will we know they know it? What will we do if they do not learn it? What will we do if they already know it?

Through this discussion, our PBIS team leaders discussed that creating this environment starts with adult behavior. If we wanted a positive learning environment for all kids, what were we willing to do to create it? What were our universal expectations for each other? What did it mean for the adult members of the Glacier community to be safe, responsible, and respectful? Our colleagues blew us away as they collectively set the bar for themselves in the classroom, halls, and cafeteria. You can see the staff Grizzly Way for the classroom in figure 5.2.

Once we identified universal expectations for adults, we revisited the universal expectations the staff had previously defined for students. While the prior draft was a good start, the staff realized that some of the expectations did not clearly define the positive expected behavior that was clear to all members of our learning community, nor did it cover all areas of the school. For example, the prior Grizzly Way often stated the same description for each setting or used vague language, for example, "using your inside voice." We realized we needed to clearly define what respectful, responsible, and safe behavior looked like and sounded like in each setting: classrooms, hallways, cafeteria, assemblies, and restrooms. We built a five-point voice-level chart (for example, level 2 = small group) and refined matrix (see figure 5.3), which became our universal expectations.

| | Be Safe: Contain Yourself | Be Responsible: Participate Positively | Be Respectful: Respond Appropriately |
|---|---|---|---|
| In the Classroom | Physically Safe: Routines are taught for common class movements.<br><br>Emotionally Safe: Greet students at the door by name.<br><br>Recognize students meeting expectation.<br><br>Maintain clear access to materials.<br><br>Teach and practice building-wide emergency response procedures. | Be prepared with all teaching materials before each class.<br><br>Communicate clear learning targets and purpose.<br><br>Give timely learning feedback.<br><br>Give 4:1 positive feedback.<br><br>Take attendance in the first ten minutes of class. | Actively listen to students and colleagues.<br><br>Start and end on time.<br><br>Dress professionally. |

Figure 5.2: The Grizzly Way—staff.

| | Be Safe: Contain Yourself | Be Responsible: Participate Positively | Be Respectful: Respond Appropriately |
|---|---|---|---|
| In the Classroom | Sit appropriately.<br><br>Keep aisles clear and materials stored properly.<br><br>Keep hands, feet, objects to yourself. | Speak when appropriate.<br><br>Follow directions the first time.<br><br>Come prepared to learn.<br><br>Do your job as a learner. | Listen to the speaker.<br><br>Treat others how you want to be treated.<br><br>Use positive language.<br><br>Always give your best effort.<br><br>Follow classroom rules. |
| In the Hallway | Walk to the right—share the road.<br><br>Keep hands, feet, objects to yourself.<br><br>Use right-hand door. | Be in the proper place at the proper time.<br><br>Carry a hall pass.<br><br>Walk with purpose. | Use voice level 2 during passing.<br><br>Use school-appropriate language.<br><br>Honor personal space.<br><br>Compliment peers and adults.<br><br>Remove head covering. |

Figure 5.3: The Grizzly Way—students.

### Implementation

Once the adults were all on the same page, we had to get our partners in learning, our students, on the same page with us. Our grade-level teams collaboratively planned and taught lessons for expected behavior in each setting the first day of school. The staff developed a fun catchphrase, KAHFAOOTY, to redirect students who needed to "keep all hands, feet, and other objects to yourself." It is not uncommon to hear a student respond to an unwanted touch with "KAHFAOOTY." Staff also taught students an acrostic about respect, THINK: truthful, helpful, inspiring, necessary, or kind.

We also realized we needed a plan to recognize students when they demonstrated expected behavior and a plan for adult behavior when students demonstrated unexpected behavior. We created a behavior flowchart that clearly outlined what adults are expected to do when a student demonstrates unexpected behavior (see figure 5.4).

Perhaps more importantly, we created a universal system to recognize expected behavior. We recognize expected behavior through clear verbal and tangible feedback. We thank students for walking on the right side of the hall. We give students Grizzly Bucks, school currency that they can use at the student store or to purchase classroom privileges like using the teacher's chair or a special job. We also recognize students with Grizzly Tracks when they demonstrate great examples of expected behavior. Students who earn a track are publicly celebrated each Friday during lunch. We do not leave the recognition to chance. Once a month at a staff meeting, we make time to share the number of Grizzly Tracks written at each grade level and dedicate a few minutes for staff to share with a partner how he or she is currently using Tracks and Bucks to recognize positive behaviors.

We also recognize staff. We regularly take time at staff meetings for colleagues to share staff Grizzly Tracks celebrating colleagues that have demonstrated the Grizzly Way.

In addition, the SWPBIS team, led by teacher leaders, meets monthly to review our schoolwide behavior data and, based on that data, plan the next adult learning that will take place at a staff meeting. The staff learning is aimed at deepening our understanding of PBIS, practicing implementation, and monitoring our commitments. For example, based on our staff discussions early in the year, it was clear that not all of our staff agreed that a positive behavior approach was valid. Rather than argue, our team brought in short, research-based articles that articulated the impact of effective positive feedback and how punishment can reinforce unwanted behaviors. We also practiced our response to behavior using scenarios and our behavior flowchart. In addition, we consistently shared data. We celebrated that 90 percent of students are consistently demonstrating the Grizzly Way—that is, 90 percent of students have not received a major or minor office discipline referral. We also monitored the fidelity of our implementation with self-assessments. We checked again every six weeks and recognized the growth.

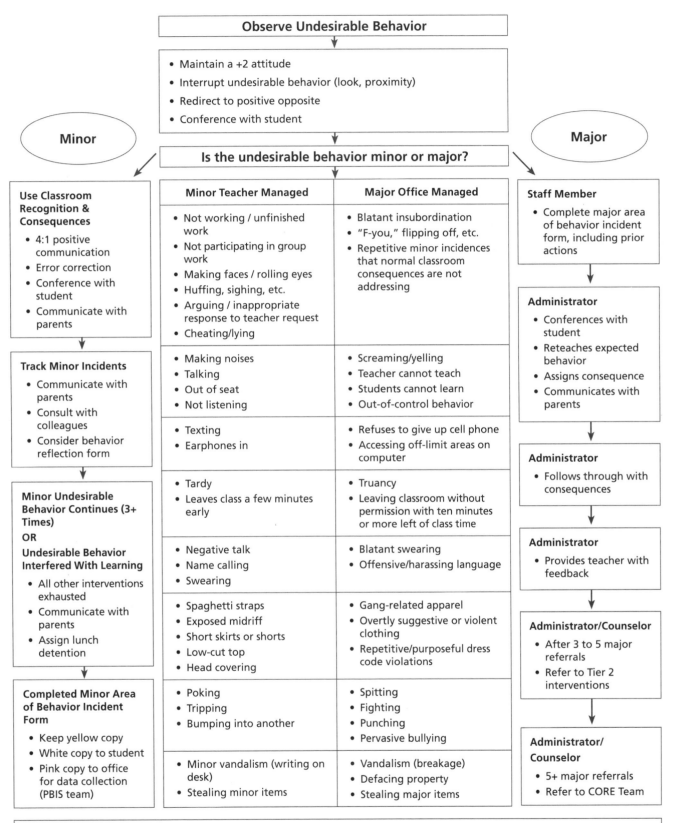

**Observe Undesirable Behavior**

- Maintain a +2 attitude
- Interrupt undesirable behavior (look, proximity)
- Redirect to positive opposite
- Conference with student

**Minor**

**Major**

**Is the undesirable behavior minor or major?**

**Use Classroom Recognition & Consequences**
- 4:1 positive communication
- Error correction
- Conference with student
- Communicate with parents

**Track Minor Incidents**
- Communicate with parents
- Consult with colleagues
- Consider behavior reflection form

**Minor Undesirable Behavior Continues (3+ Times)**
**OR**
**Undesirable Behavior Interfered With Learning**
- All other interventions exhausted
- Communicate with parents
- Assign lunch detention

**Completed Minor Area of Behavior Incident Form**
- Keep yellow copy
- White copy to student
- Pink copy to office for data collection (PBIS team)

| Minor Teacher Managed | Major Office Managed |
|---|---|
| • Not working / unfinished work<br>• Not participating in group work<br>• Making faces / rolling eyes<br>• Huffing, sighing, etc.<br>• Arguing / inappropriate response to teacher request<br>• Cheating/lying | • Blatant insubordination<br>• "F-you," flipping off, etc.<br>• Repetitive minor incidences that normal classroom consequences are not addressing |
| • Making noises<br>• Talking<br>• Out of seat<br>• Not listening | • Screaming/yelling<br>• Teacher cannot teach<br>• Students cannot learn<br>• Out-of-control behavior |
| • Texting<br>• Earphones in | • Refuses to give up cell phone<br>• Accessing off-limit areas on computer |
| • Tardy<br>• Leaves class a few minutes early | • Truancy<br>• Leaving classroom without permission with ten minutes or more left of class time |
| • Negative talk<br>• Name calling<br>• Swearing | • Blatant swearing<br>• Offensive/harassing language |
| • Spaghetti straps<br>• Exposed midriff<br>• Short skirts or shorts<br>• Low-cut top<br>• Head covering | • Gang-related apparel<br>• Overtly suggestive or violent clothing<br>• Repetitive/purposeful dress code violations |
| • Poking<br>• Tripping<br>• Bumping into another | • Spitting<br>• Fighting<br>• Punching<br>• Pervasive bullying |
| • Minor vandalism (writing on desk)<br>• Stealing minor items | • Vandalism (breakage)<br>• Defacing property<br>• Stealing major items |

**Staff Member**
- Complete major area of behavior incident form, including prior actions

**Administrator**
- Conferences with student
- Reteaches expected behavior
- Assigns consequence
- Communicates with parents

**Administrator**
- Follows through with consequences

**Administrator**
- Provides teacher with feedback

**Administrator/Counselor**
- After 3 to 5 major referrals
- Refer to Tier 2 interventions

**Administrator/ Counselor**
- 5+ major referrals
- Refer to CORE Team

In order to better manage data and behavior tracking, please keep records on your students who you deal with on a regular basis for minor incidents. ALL major incidents that are referred to the office must include a referral form. This will help us to determine if we have widespread, specific behavioral issues that we need to address.

Figure 5.4: Behavior flowchart.

As this year progresses, we are continuing to deepen our team's use of data. At the meeting in March, we noted that the majority of behavior incident documentations continue to be from minor disruption or disrespect in the classroom with the perceived motivation of garnering peer attention. At the next PBIS-focused staff meeting, the team plans to share this information with the staff as well as to set specific goals, which include challenging teams to recognize students demonstrating respect in the classroom in a way that garners positive peer attention.

### So What About the Kids Who Need Extra Time and Support?

As we answer critical question one (What do we want students to learn?) with the Grizzly Way and monitor their learning, answering critical question two (How will we know they learned it?) by tracking behavior incident forms, Grizzly Tracks, and staff feedback, we also must address critical question three (What are we going to do if they do not learn it?). Like the academic side answer to this question, our response must be systematic.

While most students (80 percent plus) respond to universal expectations and support, 10–15 percent of students will need Tier 2 additional time and support. Students who need ongoing additional time and support need to be provided with daily time to review expectations and multiple opportunities to practice expected behaviors with specific positive feedback. We support these learners through check-in/check-out (CICO). Each morning, the student checks in with the school counselor and reviews what he or she is going to do to demonstrate the Grizzly Way throughout the day. The key is for the student to articulate what he or she will do to show the expected behavior. Then, throughout the day, the student receives and records feedback from each teacher regarding his or her behavior. The feedback is stated in the positive and on a three-point scale. At the end of the day, the student checks out with the counselor and celebrates how he or she met the goal. If the student does not meet the goal, the conversation focuses on what the student needs to do to meet the expectations the next day. The counselor coaches the student to identify specific behaviors. Parents are a key component of this support. We teach our parents to, like the counselor, focus on the positive and what the student can do to meet the goals. For students who need more targeted support, we narrow CICO to specific behaviors in specific settings.

We also recognize that some students, approximately 5 percent, need intense support in order to positively engage in learning. Like the intense side of the academic support, we need a focused and skilled team to support these students. At GMS, this is our Core Team. Core was initiated in 2013–2014. The team-based, solution-oriented meetings focus on delivering intense behavior supports for our students in the most need of support. Like our schoolwide efforts, shared leadership and data-driven decision making are key. The Core Team includes the attendance secretary, the district social worker, the GMS counselors and a high school counselor, school psychologist, school nurse, and administrators. The team has clear guidelines and roles. In order to receive the support of the Core Team, students have earned multiple suspensions, demonstrate a pattern of truancy, are failing multiple classes, or are a danger to themselves or others. In short, these are kids on learning life support. Prior to bringing a student to Core, the team member must ensure that multiple lower-level interventions have been implemented. The Core Team meets weekly and focuses the conversation on monitoring the progress and implementation of support. Prior to each meeting, team members input data (attendance, behavior, meeting follow up, counseling reports, and so on). During the meeting, team members share progress and plan next steps. While student growth is often uneven, several students have exited the support this year.

### They Are All Our Kids

A piece of the culture in the White River School District is collective responsibility. The high school principal sees the kindergartners as her kids, just as an elementary school principal sees the students at GMS as his kids. One clear growth area for GMS was effectively transitioning students that need extra time and support from the four elementary schools to the middle school. We would see a student who on paper looked relatively successful or challenged but we did not know what the elementary school did to ensure the student's learning. Starting in the spring of 2014, we began systematically soliciting information on all students, especially those who needed extra support. Our elementary school administrators and counselors shared specific student's strengths, concerns, and interventions that worked. Thanks to this focused effort, the GMS team proactively formed plans of support for students who struggle to demonstrate expected behavior.

One example is a boy who often would say threatening or disturbing comments to peers to gain attention, lived with a grandmother in ill health, and had parents who struggled to agree on how to parent. In fifth grade, the boy received five major referrals for harassment, physical aggression, and verbal aggression. The elementary principal and counselor shared with us the boy's story and how he craved positive attention. The GMS counselor met with the grandmother, parents, and student during the summer. She focused on surfacing the student's strengths and what support he felt he needed. They collaboratively created an individualized CICO process, customized his schedule to include band and extensions for math, and set up a plan to collaborate frequently. The student has not had a documented discipline incident, major or minor, all year. He consistently meets his CICO goal 80 percent of the time. And, while the student continues to need consistent positive feedback, he is graduating to self-monitoring of his goals. He has also earned a B or better in all his classes and was chosen to be the sixth-grade representative when our counselors visited his former elementary school for registration this spring.

## Wilkeson Elementary School

*By Nick Hedman*

It has been my experience as a building principal and assistant principal that leading change in how to address student behaviors in a school setting can lead down a long road of frustration. A wide-eyed administrator could unwittingly walk into school where the staff and parents believe the burden for "fixing" student behavior falls squarely on the administrator's shoulders. Questions I have had to face include things like: What are the progressive discipline steps for behavior? We need a chart for discipline. How long do I allow one student to disrupt the class before I call the office? How are we going to hold parents responsible for their child's behavior? Why do some teachers allow students to talk in the halls? What is the rule?

We have learned at Wilkeson to address behavior like we would look at any other academic subject and ask the critical PLC questions of ourselves as a staff: What do we want our students to learn? How will we know if they have learned it? What will we do if they didn't learn it? And what will we do if they already know it? Addressing behavior through this framework has built shared knowledge and a collective commitment to positive behavior systems thinking.

### Common Expectations for Behavior

In our four-year journey at Wilkeson, we have used these critical questions to help shape a more positive behavior system that has led to increases in academic learning. In order to clearly articulate to students, parents, and staff what the behavior expectations were, all staff helped create and define common areas of expectation according to our STAR student frame. The STAR acronym stands for Safe choices, Trust, Achievement, and Respect. Staff who supervise lunch and recess helped determine what positive safe choices, trustworthiness, achievement, and respect looked and sounded like. Staff who helped supervise students during arrival, dismissal, and in the hallways did the same. We posted the expectations and explicitly taught them (see figure 5.5). The following year, we moved into the classroom and PLC teams collaborated to do the same work and clearly articulate and post the classroom behavior expectations. We regularly review and communicate these expectations.

The staff, in addition, needed to develop and agree upon a problem-solving strategy that could be taught to students and empower them to help solve the challenges they would face in interacting with others at school. This strategy started out very simple and has changed every year as we helped students become more sophisticated in their ability to solve problems. It became clear at the end of the third year (this was based on behavior data, which is discussed in the next section) that we as a school needed a core instructional program that addressed more than behavior expectations and common problem-solving strategies. A core program was needed to help build a common vocabulary and understanding on listening strategies, empathy, positive self-talk, and other critical social/emotional skills. It was difficult to expect that teachers at every grade level could create and deliver a comprehensive set of lessons on all the necessary social/emotional skills without some program to guide this. Moreover, there was no way to design and build the necessary interventions for students who would need additional time and support unless we had a guaranteed Tier 1 program in place. The district adopted the Second Step social/emotional program in kindergarten through fifth grade, and a common pacing guide was developed

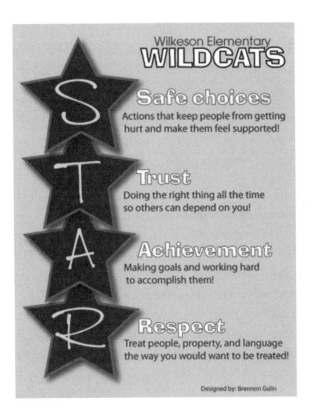

Figure 5.5: STAR student frame.

*Source: White River School District. Used with permission.*

at the beginning of the 2014 school year. Many other districts use this program, and there are numerous examples of common pacing guides available.

### Data Systems and Monitoring

In order to accurately assess our students' understanding and the active practice of these expectations, we agreed upon a behavior incident form that aligned with the School-Wide Information System (SWIS) behavior data tool. This went through several revisions. This data tool helps us by monitoring the types of misbehavior incidents that are happening in the building according to location, grade, time/date, and motivating factor(s). SWIS has become absolutely essential because regular reports can be generated to identify areas of success and concern. The PBIS team whose members are representative of various grade levels, a designated team leader, the building principal, the counselor, and classified staff regularly look at the data and use the TIPS (team initiated problem solving) protocol to guide the ongoing improvement cycle. What often happens over the course of the year is that the building staff raise concerns over certain student behaviors. It is very common that a staff can be quick to jump to conclusions and generalizations and spend most of the time planning solutions. The data tool helps the PBIS team and the staff by informing those conclusions and provides greater specificity around the problem that helps the staff identify possible solutions. For example, in the early fall of 2014, the incidents for playground behavior were seemingly excessive. As the team began to drill down into the data, the chart shows that the number of incidents were much greater for the students in kindergarten and first grade than all other grades (figure 5.6).

In fact, when the team looked back over the previous year, this kindergarten and first-grade pattern emerged when the district moved to full-time kindergarten. Students in kindergarten and first grade were more likely to be engaged in minor physical contact and physical aggression at recess. The data identified that the perceived motivation was to obtain peer attention. The PBIS team was able to identify a precise problem and set a SMART goal for the next month using the TIPS protocol. Behavior incident referrals for recess in these grade levels were reduced by more than half. One of the ways the team met the goal was by instituting a peer mediation team of older students who played with students during recess and helped solve conflicts using the new problem solving strategies that were being taught to all the kids through Second Step. The data, the precise problems, and the solutions are regularly shared at staff meetings, and input is collected from teachers. Often staff raise a question of inquiry, and this is where the data can be so helpful in informing the observation and helping keep the school on course with a systematic approach, which leads to: What do we do if they didn't learn it?

### Intervention and Support

The tiered instructional support for behavior has been an ongoing challenge. Once the social and emotional core program was in place and we had the data systems in place to inform the areas of concern, it was easier to identify the groups of students or individuals who would need further instruction.

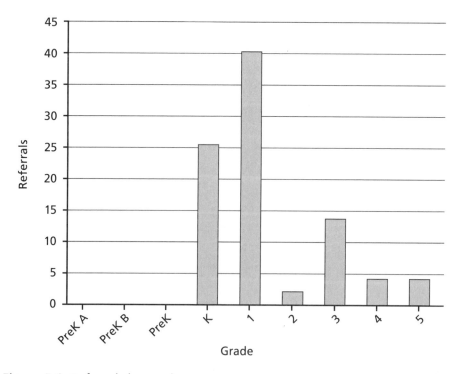

Figure 5.6: Referrals by grade.

*Source: White River School District. Used with permission.*

We have had to work hard and learn together to address misbehavior much the same way we look at academic misunderstandings. A student who adds a math problem incorrectly needs to have the skill (re)taught. If this does not work, then the teacher needs to teach the skill in a different way. This is very similar to the common misbehaviors we see at our school. We don't take it for granted that every student knows how to act properly in all situations or has the skill to do so. So we provide the initial instruction and then we provide the additional supports and time for students with recurring social errors. Tier 2 strategies that we have been learning to use include CICO, small-group social skill instruction, and small friendship groups. CICO is monitored using SWIS as well, and all students receiving Tier 2 services are discussed at the monthly RTI meetings. The behaviors for students and academics are both discussed at RTI meetings. Whereas the PBIS team is charged with stewarding the behavior system as a whole (implementation of Tier 1 instruction, provide professional development, monitor the system data, design solutions to precise problems), the RTI team is responsible for identifying the small group and individual supports for students based on their individual behavior and academic needs.

### Recognition

On our journey to create a positive behavior system, it was clear that we needed to regularly recognize students and classrooms that have been following the schoolwide STAR behavior expectations. Any and all staff are regularly encouraged to pass out STAR tickets when students are caught doing things correctly. Students who have more misbehaviors need more recognition than those who regularly follow the expectations. The PBIS team identified through a needs survey in the third year that the staff chose professional development in the area of positive recognition. The research was very clear that in order to change student behavior the student needed to receive a minimum of four positives for every negative. In some cases, students with more frequent misbehavior need many more positives. This is an ongoing effort to increase the positives, and we need to frequently remind ourselves to do this and share strategies that are working.

We also regularly conduct all school assemblies where teachers highlight students who have demonstrated a certain STAR expectation, and we invite family and friends to recognize the student together. We also recognize classrooms that have shown STAR behavior in common areas and in specialist classes. This is a fun and celebratory way to bring the community together. In addition, it is a way to communicate to our families and greater community the common STAR expectations.

# Chapter 6

# Teaching in a Results-Oriented Culture

*Effective use of formative assessment, developed through teacher learning communities, promises not only the largest potential gains in student achievement but also a process for affordable teacher professional development.*

—Dylan Wiliam and Marnie Thompson

Teachers in a professional learning community are passionate about results. They have a relentless focus on the learning of each student. They realize that even if a lesson is taught very well, some students may struggle with their learning. This shift from a primary focus on teaching (covering material) to the learning of each kid, skill by skill, is one of the major cultural shifts that occur when a school begins to function as a PLC.

For decades, the quality of schools has been measured by the quality of input variables that go into operating a school. Accreditation agencies have examined such factors as teacher credentials, class size, number of library books, and number of assistant principals, secretaries, and guidance counselors. The issue of the degree to which students were learning was rarely addressed.

While recognizing that resources, training, and credentials are important, teachers in a PLC experience an entirely different culture, a culture in which administrators, teachers, and support staff all work together to fulfill the fundamental purpose of all schools—to ensure high levels of learning for all students. DuFour et al. (2010) emphasize, "A results orientation is a focus on outcomes rather than inputs or intentions. In professional learning communities, members are committed to achieving desired results and are hungry for evidence that their efforts are producing the intended outcomes" (p. 183). Because of this passionate focus on the learning of each student, there is a laser-like focus on the questions, Are the kids learning, and how do we know?

## A Results-Oriented Culture

School culture can be defined in many ways, but one of the most easily understood is simply "how we do things around here." How are things done in a results-oriented culture? The foundation reflects an appropriate balance and use of both formative and summative assessments throughout the district. Notice the emphasis on the words *appropriate balance*. Since the 1980s, there has been a huge increase in the use (and misuse) of high-stakes summative assessments—assessments that measure the degree to which students have learned. While summative assessments serve an important purpose, they do little to improve student learning. In fact, the emphasis placed on the use of summative assessments has increased to the point that many are calling for a re-examination of the role high-stakes summative tests play in our system of public education.

Researchers tout the power of formative assessments—assessments *for* learning. Dylan Wiliam (2011) provides this definition of formative assessments:

> *An assessment functions formatively to the extent that evidence about student achievement is elicited, interpreted, and used by teachers, learners, or their peers to make decisions about the next steps in instruction that are likely to be better, or better founded, than the decisions they would have made in the absence of that evidence. (p. 43)*

Teachers in PLCs benefit from the power of common formative assessments—assessments developed by collaborative teams that allow teachers to check along the way to see if students are learning and use the results to make decisions for providing students with appropriate and focused additional time, support, and extension of learning. Additionally, the results of common formative assessments are a powerful tool that enables teachers, both individually and as a team, to reflect on and improve their instructional effectiveness.

This shift in emphasis from the overuse of summative assessments to an increased reliance on assessments that are formative is no small matter. Reeves (2000) uses the example of a checkup versus an autopsy to explain the difference between summative assessments and formative assessments. The power of formative assessments lies in the fact that the results can be used as part of an ongoing process to monitor each student's learning, skill by skill, on a continuous basis (DuFour et al., 2010). This allows teachers to employ ways to help students improve *prior* to the summative assessments. Researchers recognize formative assessments as some of the most powerful tools in a teacher's toolbox. Consider the following:

> *Formative assessment is a potentially transformative instructional tool that, if clearly understood and adroitly employed,*

*can benefit both educators and their students . . . formative assessment constitutes the key cornerstone of clearheaded instructional thinking. Formative assessment represents evidence-based instructional decision-making. If you want to become instructionally effective, and if you want your students to achieve more, then formative assessments should be for you. (Popham, 2008, pp. 3, 15)*

*There is strong and rigorous evidence that improving formative assessment can raise standards of pupils' performance. There have been few initiatives in education with such a strong body of evidence to support a claim to raise standards. (Black & Wiliam, 1998, p. 20)*

*Assessment for learning . . . when done well, this is one of the most powerful, high-leverage strategies for improving student learning that we know of. (Fullan, 2005, p. 71)*

*Studies have demonstrated assessment for learning rivals one-on-one tutoring in effectiveness and that the use of assessment particularly benefits low-achieving students. (Stiggins, 2004, p. 27)*

This is not to say that assessment *of* learning is not important. Both formative and summative assessments serve important, but different, purposes. Schools that function as professional learning communities strive to find the appropriate balance between the two.

## A Culture of Formative Assessments

The use of formative assessments—checking student learning along the way—isn't limited to teacher teams. PLCs reflect a culture of formative assessment, from individual students monitoring their own learning to districtwide data meetings. Teachers who utilize the full power of formative assessment understand that formative assessment begins with individual students taking responsibility for and monitoring their own individual learning.

*Teachers who utilize the full power of formative assessment understand that formative assessment begins with individual students taking responsibility for and monitoring their own individual learning.*

### Individual Students Monitoring Their Own Learning

Most teachers would say they want students to learn to take responsibility for their own learning. Yet, in many classrooms, there is little evidence of assessment strategies that lead to greater student responsibility. In PLCs, teachers employ strategies for students to monitor their own learning and thus develop an enhanced sense of ownership.

The role of assessment that monitors student learning along the way is much different than assessment in more traditional schools. This is especially true in the role of students in the assessment process. Stiggins (2005) highlights this difference by noting:

> *The student's role in assessment OF learning is as it always has been: study hard and strive for the highest score. But in assessment FOR learning contexts, that role changes. The student's role is not necessarily to strive to get a high score or grade. Rather it is to strive to understand what success looks like and to use each assessment to try to understand how to do better [with the] student as a key player in the ongoing assessment and record-keeping process. (p. 77)*

While there is no one right way to involve students in developing and monitoring their own learning, Stiggins (2005) emphasizes three elements are usually present: (1) student self-assessment, (2) student-involved record keeping, and (3) student-involved communication about their achievement success.

There are a number of strategies teachers use to create a classroom culture in which students learn to monitor and take responsibility of their own learning. Wiliam (2011) highlights five key strategies:

- *Clarifying, sharing, and understanding learning intentions and criteria for success.*

- *Engineering effective classroom discussions, activities, and learning tasks that elicit evidence of learning.*

- *Providing feedback that moves learning forward.*

- *Activating learners as instructional resources for one another.*

- *Activating learners as the owners of their own learning. (p. 47)*

Teachers—especially teams of teachers—develop and share a number of tools to implement these strategies. For example, in the elementary schools in the White River School District, mathematics students (and parents) are provided with pamphlets containing a number of "I can" statements that are tied directly to the learning targets for each mathematics standard. Teacher teams work together to create the "I can" statements for each ELA unit (example in figure 6.1).

Other tools teachers can use include student portfolios, or learning journals, that include learning targets, class notes, homework assignments, and results from simple formative checkups. Other teachers find the use of learning logs, in which students are asked to reflect on their learning at the end of each lesson, to be helpful.

Teachers employ many of the same tools to help cooperative groups of students monitor their learning. Group formative assessments can be an effective tool to support enhanced student monitoring and cooperative learning. When Janel asked her daughter about the fact that she missed a number of problems on a short quiz, Taylor responded by saying, "Don't worry, Mom; it's formative. My teacher will show me how to do it tomorrow."

**RL.4.1**

- I can use the details and examples in the text to explain or infer meaning.

**W.4.1**

- I can introduce my reader to the topic by clearly identifying the characters, setting, plot, narrator, sensory details, and sequence of events.
- I can describe experiences and events through character dialogue, which helps my reader to better understand.
- I can use a variety of transitional words and phrases to organize the sequence of events.
- I can use specific words or phrases and sensory details to describe experiences and events in narrative writing.
- I can write a clear conclusion when writing a narrative piece.

**SL.4.1**

- I can quote accurately from the text to explain or infer meaning.
- I can use the details and examples in the text to explain or infer meaning.
- I can use the details and examples in the text from what I read to explain the meaning of the text.
- I can use details from the text to explain what I read.

Figure 6.1: Example of "I Can" statements for an ELA unit.

*Source: Adapted from NGA & CCSSO, 2010.*

The key is one of balance and effectiveness, and in a PLC, the effectiveness of student self-assessment lies in team planning. Effective teacher teams make instructional decisions about the appropriate balance between individual student self-assessment and group self-monitoring.

Regardless of the method or frequency of student self-assessment, the power lies in how the information is used. Students or groups of students are not left to simply monitor their own learning, but rather teachers use the evidence of student learning to make instructional decisions in order to better meet student needs.

Most teachers who are constantly searching for ways to motivate their learning communities have learned that student self-assessment, if used appropriately, can be a powerful motivator for students. Such assessment practices can enhance students' sense of responsibility and pride in their accomplishments, forming a strong emotional foundation for success (Stiggins, 2005).

## Teachers Monitoring Learning

Effective teachers are constantly assessing student learning in multiple ways. Throughout the lesson, they check for student understanding and engage students in reflecting on their own learning and comprehension (DuFour et al., 2010). Perhaps the most frequently utilized tool individual teachers employ is quick checks for understanding.

We are often asked, "What assessment is the most important?" The assessment that's the most important is the one closest to the student—the kind of assessment good teachers do daily to check on the learning from the lesson that day or that week. They can very quickly answer the questions, Are the kids learning, and how do we know? We refer to these as responsive assessments. The teacher can respond by adjusting instruction strategies and support or extensions the very next day.

For example, teachers can hand out a sticky note to each student. The teacher then asks one question. On the way out the door, the students hand the teacher their sticky note. The teacher puts the sticky notes in three groups on the whiteboard: (1) the group that correctly responds to the question, (2) the group with a general understanding but that needs a little more help in the opening activity the next day, and (3) the group that doesn't even seem like they had been in class. These quick checks for understanding can take any number of forms.

## Common Formative Assessments

While there is a formidable body of research regarding the efficacy of individual teachers utilizing formative assessments as part of their regular classroom practices, the power of formative assessments is enhanced when they are collaboratively developed and utilized by teacher teams. Reeves (2004) refers to common formative assessments that teacher teams collaboratively develop as the "gold standard in educational accountability" and the "best practice in assessment" (pp. 71, 114).

This is not to say that individual teachers should not use a variety of formative assessments that they have developed individually. However, team common formative assessments are an integral part of a teacher's toolbox if he or she teaches in a high-performing professional learning community.

Team-developed common formative assessments are powerful for a number of reasons (DuFour et al., 2010):

- *Common assessments promote efficiency for teachers.*
- *Common assessments promote equity for students.*
- *Common assessments represent a powerful strategy for determining whether the guaranteed curriculum is being taught and, more importantly, learned.*
- *Common assessments inform the practice of individual teachers.*
- *Common assessments build a team's capacity to improve its program.*
- *Common assessments facilitate a systematic, collective response to students who are experiencing difficulty.*
- *Common formative assessments are one of the most powerful tools for changing the professional practice of educators. (pp. 76–81)*

The power of common formative assessment lies in its ability to inform individual teachers and teams of teachers. Because they inform, practiced, well-developed common formative assessments enable teams to make better decisions about the quality and specificity regarding additional time, support, and extension of learning for students. They also enable teachers, both individually and as a team, to reflect on the effectiveness of their own instructional practices.

The number of common formative assessments that are given depends on the unit that is being taught and the information that is being solicited. Generally speaking, it is best to have more frequent but less extensive assessments. These shorter, more frequent assessments allow teacher teams to monitor the learning of specific skills, kid by kid on a frequent and timely basis. See chapter 3 and the appendix for examples of common assessments.

## Collaborative Analysis of Results

Of course, simply developing common formative assessments does little to improve student learning. The key to capturing common formative assessment's power lies in what teachers do with the results, and the first step is a collaborative analysis of the results, kid by kid, skill by skill.

It is helpful when teachers develop protocols for reviewing the results of common formative assessments. Without these protocols, even well-intentioned teams tend to get bogged down in their discussions. Following is a team analysis of a common assessment form that teacher teams in the White River School District use (figure 6.2).

Date _____          School _____

Team _____          Unit/Assessment _____

5 min.    Power Standards or Learning Targets Measured

5 min.    In what areas did our student do well on this assessment?

5 min.    What instructional strategies helped our students do well?

Continued →

Figure 6.2: Team analysis of a common assessment form.

*Source: White River School District. Used with permission.*

| 5 min. | What skill deficiencies do we see? |
| --- | --- |
| | |

| 5 min. | What patterns do we see in the mistakes, and what do they tell us? |
| --- | --- |
| | |

| 5 min. | Which students did not master essential standards and will need additional time and support? |
| --- | --- |
| | |

| 20 min. | What intervention will be provided to address unlearned skills, and how will we check for understanding? |
| --- | --- |
| | |

| 5 min. | Do we need to tweak or improve this assessment? |
| --- | --- |
| | |

| 10 min. | Which students mastered standards, and what is our plan for extra curricula? |
| --- | --- |
| | |

Standard: 

| | Class 1 | | Class 2 | | Class 3 | | Class 4 | | Class 5 |
| --- | --- | --- | --- | --- | --- | --- | --- | --- | --- |
| | Unit Pre | Unit Post | Unit Pre | Unit Post | Unit Pre | Unit Post | Unit Pre | Unit Post | Unit Pre |
| Total Students | | | | | | | | | |
| Not Meeting Grade Level | | | | | | | | | |
| Working Toward Grade Level | | | | | | | | | |
| Meets Grade Level | | | | | | | | | |
| Exceeds Grade Level | | | | | | | | | |

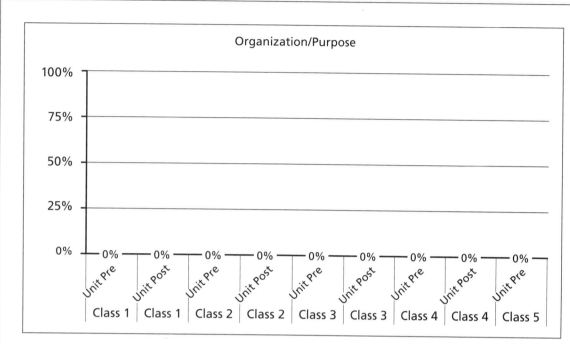

Standard:

| | Class 1 | | Class 2 | | Class 3 | | Class 4 | | Class 5 |
|---|---|---|---|---|---|---|---|---|---|
| | Unit Pre | Unit Post | Unit Pre | Unit Post | Unit Pre | Unit Post | Unit Pre | Unit Post | Unit Pre |
| Total Students | | | | | | | | | |
| Not Meeting Grade Level | | | | | | | | | |
| Working Toward Grade Level | | | | | | | | | |
| Meets Grade Level | | | | | | | | | |
| Exceeds Grade Level | | | | | | | | | |

Continued →

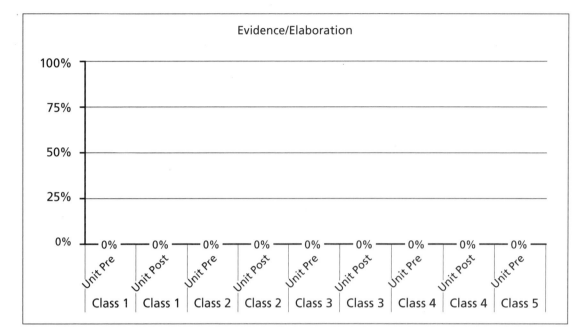

Standard: _____

|  | Class 1 | | Class 2 | | Class 3 | | Class 4 | | Class 5 |
|  | Unit Pre | Unit Post | Unit Pre | Unit Post | Unit Pre | Unit Post | Unit Pre | Unit Post | Unit Pre |
|---|---|---|---|---|---|---|---|---|---|
| Total Students | | | | | | | | | |
| Not Meeting Grade Level | | | | | | | | | |
| Working Toward Grade Level | | | | | | | | | |
| Meets Grade Level | | | | | | | | | |
| Exceeds Grade Level | | | | | | | | | |

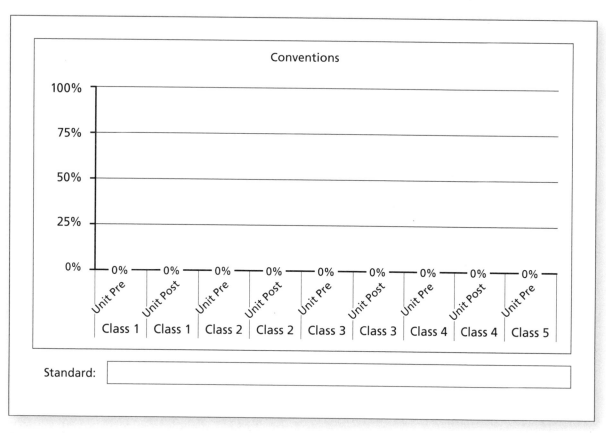

*Visit* **go.solution-tree.com/PLCbooks** *for a reproducible version of this figure.*

Team effectiveness is enhanced when teachers bring along the actual student work when analyzing the results of common formative assessments. Students may miss the same problems on a common formative assessment but miss very different skills within the problems. Having student work along with the assessment results helps teams focus on the learning of each student *skill by skill.*

Of course, even if teacher teams do a great job of analyzing student assessment data, little if any improvement in learning will occur unless something is done with the data. This is the critical decision point in a results-oriented culture—how do teachers, individually and as a team, respond when students experience difficulty in their learning? Additionally, how is student learning extended when students demonstrate proficiency? The answers to these questions are the true test of teachers in a professional learning community.

## Teacher Response to the Data

The power of student learning data, particularly data from commonly developed formative assessments, lies in how they are used. In a PLC, teachers use the results from a collaborative analysis of data to drive decision making primarily in two areas.

First, teachers use collaborative data analysis to plan for additional time and support for students who are struggling with specific skills or concepts or to extend the learning of students who demonstrate proficiency. Teacher teams are very specific in these decisions, focusing on the learning of each kid, skill by skill.

Second, teacher teams use a collaborative analysis of student learning data to reflect on their own instructional decision making—both individually and as a team. For example, as a team, they may decide to spend more time on a particular topic or concept. After comparing the performance of their students with that of students in other teams, they may meet with the high-performing team in order to learn new strategies. The same is true for individual teachers. Much of the power of collaborative teaming lies in the fact that collaborative teams provide a structural vehicle for teachers to learn from each other—sharing ideas and materials. When teachers search for best practice, the first place they should turn is to their fellow team members.

## Data Meetings

In more traditional schools, teachers are responsible for the learning of the students who are assigned to them. The culture is quite different for teachers in a PLC. In PLC schools—and, importantly, PLC districts—*all* the teachers, administrators, and support staff are responsible for *all* of the students. The attitude is, "These are all our kids!"

> *In PLC schools—and, importantly, PLC districts—all the teachers, administrators, and support staff are responsible for all of the students.*

Because these are our kids, schools frequently hold data meetings in which team leaders, accompanied by teachers, present learning data to the entire school leadership team (the principal, assistant principals, team leaders, guidance counselors, and perhaps others). Typically, in these periodic data meetings, learning data from a particular subject, grade, or course are presented, analyzed, and discussed.

The most important aspect of these data meetings is that everyone has the responsibility of making suggestions as to how strong growth data can be strengthened and how weaker learning data can be positively addressed. The idea is to model the work of collaborative teacher teams by collaboratively analyzing data, seeking and sharing best practices, and taking collective responsibility for improvement.

Typically, data are presented in a graphic format showing comparisons. It is important to remember that data are simply that—data. In order to have meaning, data must be viewed in comparison to other data. Teachers in a PLC frequently examine learning data in relation to previous points in time—by month, semester, or year. The point is to graphically demonstrate learning growth. Figure 6.3 is an example of a graphic data display from an elementary school in the White River School District displaying learning growth from the fall to the winter semester.

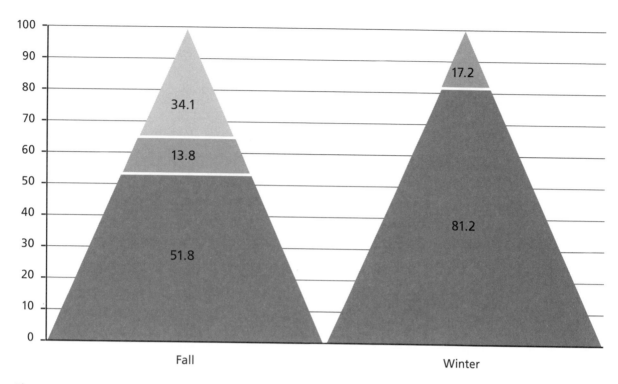

Figure 6.3: Visual depiction of improvement in student learning.

*Source: White River School District. Used with permission.*

Depending on district size, districtwide data meetings may be periodically conducted. For example, in the White River School District, principals and key teachers might be asked to bring their latest third-grade reading data to a districtwide data meeting. At the meeting, every school presents its third-grade reading scores, highlighting particular strengths and areas of concern. Most important, everyone is responsible for participating in ways to improve the reading data, even if it is only in one school, or one team, or one classroom. This is how PLCs reflect a culture of mutual accountability for student learning.

> *Everyone is responsible for participating in ways to improve the data, even if it is only in one school, or one team, or one classroom.*

The purpose and format of the districtwide data meetings are the same as those for the schoolwide data meetings. However, districtwide data meetings might be greeted with reluctance or a degree of anxiety. Janel realized this and began the process by clearly communicating with everyone the purpose of the districtwide data meetings and the protocol to follow.

Districtwide data meetings help principals and teachers improve student learning. It's a common understanding that to improve learning, we must hold students accountable for their work. And we hold students accountable by analyzing their work, providing feedback, providing focused interventions and additional time and support, and insisting students redo their work when it is not to standard. So too must adults—specifically teacher teams, principals, and district office leaders—be held accountable for the work connected to improving student learning.

A number of districts require principals to bring student learning data to a monthly data meeting. These districts hold the principals accountable for data—that they are accurate, that they are informing instruction, and that they are being used to guide and design student interventions. For example, one district recently reviewed the districtwide data from a third-grade unit 5 math assessment. Each principal shared his or her student data on the following standards:

- Fluently and accurately add and subtract whole numbers (up to four digits) using the standard regrouping algorithms.

- Estimate sums and differences to approximate solutions to problems to determine reasonable answers.

- Solve single and multistep word problems involving addition and subtraction of whole numbers.

In the data meeting, the principals were asked to share the areas/standards where students did well on the assessment. They were also to note the instructional strategies that helped their students do well and identified skill deficiencies. But here's the most important piece of the meeting: each principal shared in detail what his or her third-grade team did to provide those students who were not meeting the standard with additional time and support. The principals had the opportunity to learn from each other and were able to take that information back to their third-grade team. One principal commented, "I only have two third-grade teachers collaborating to meet the needs of our students. After this meeting, I can go back and share with my teachers the specific instructional strategies and intervention ideas from four buildings and fourteen teachers who teach third grade! The strength of these meetings is we learn from each other to help get more kids to learn more across the district." At a glance, principals and district leaders can see how all third-grade students are performing on the essential standards in unit 5.

In short, districtwide data meetings are helpful to principals for a number of reasons.

- To ensure schools and teams across the district are crystal clear about what is essential for the students to learn

- To collaboratively address the question, "Are the students *learning*, and what are their areas of strength and weakness?"

- To work as a system to increase specificity and precision regarding providing additional time, support, and enrichment

- To reflect, share, and learn from each other regarding professional practices—especially instructional practices

Because the principals are held accountable, they also hold the teams accountable for that data. The important thing about this though is to remember that data are not about filling out a spreadsheet and making graphs. Data are about understanding exactly where a student has lost his or her way and making a plan for how to get him or her back on track. Data are about improving student learning, in each classroom, on every team, in every school across the district.

Initially, educators may be reluctant to openly share data at these data meetings. They should be reassured that the purpose is solely for the improvement of student learning, *not* for an evaluative purpose. Once the data are used for evaluation of administrators, teachers, or support staff, the culture of formative assessment will be destroyed, and it will be almost impossible to recover. In addition, to use the data for decision making related to improving student learning, reluctance to share data is reduced when administrators and teachers see that everyone is responsible for all of the data. Individuals are not singled out for weak learning data. Likewise, it is recognized that others, rather than a single individual, played a role—even if it was a supporting role—when students succeed.

## Benchmark Assessments

Should individual teacher teams develop and use common formative assessments, or should representatives from each school develop them and the same assessment be used districtwide? The answer is yes to both. Teachers who teach in high-performing PLCs engage in the development and use of common formative assessments at their team level, but periodically throughout the year, they participate in districtwide benchmark assessments. Just as with team-developed common formative assessments, the frequency and complexity of the districtwide benchmark assessments depend on the standards and learning targets that are being assessed.

The purpose of both types of assessments is to improve student learning. While team assessments deeply examine student learning kid by kid, skill by skill, the districtwide benchmark assessments provide districtwide data subject by subject, standard by standard.

## Annual School Reviews

Increasingly, teachers in PLCs participate in schoolwide and districtwide annual school learning reviews. Some may view these meetings as summative in nature in that they are year-end reviews, but in a PLC, these meetings are formative since the overarching reason for the meetings is to develop focused plans for improvement, team by team and product by product.

The annual school reviews begin with a collaborative collection and analysis of data from all areas of student learning team by team, subject by subject, standard by standard. These data are collected and aggregated by the central office staff and presented in graphic formats to the entire faculty and the larger school community. Most important, everyone in attendance is asked to record comments and offer specific suggestions for improvement.

After each school has conducted its annual school learning review, a districtwide annual school learning review takes place. Presentations are given by school, rather than by team. These meetings not only highlight areas for future focus, but also provide the opportunity for multiple forms of recognition and celebrations! Teachers who work in a results-oriented PLC experience both professional satisfaction that comes with improved student learning and sincere and meaningful appreciation for a job well done!

The annual school review process serves as the initial step of the annual goal-setting process for the school district. The school review process allows for the collaborative identification of strengths, as well as patterns of areas that need attention. The results not only serve as the beginning step of the districtwide goal-setting process, they also serve to reveal areas that will need to be considered as the district begins its annual budget-building cycle. The annual school data review is truly the foundational step for a cycle of continuous improvement.

Epilogue

# Tying It All Together: Imagine Teaching in This School

DuFour, DuFour, and Eaker (2008) write, "In a PLC, collaboration is a systematic process in which teachers work together, interdependently, to analyze and impact professional practice in order to improve results for their students, their team, and their school" (p. 16).

Imagine teaching in a high-performing professional learning community. How would it differ from your current or past experiences? Perhaps the most striking difference would be this: rather than working in a culture of teacher isolation, all teachers in the school would be contributing members of collaborative teams. While it's true that many, if not most, teachers engage in some form of collaboration, in a PLC the collaboration is much more purposeful. Teachers have a *shared purpose* for being on a collaborative team, and that purpose is to improve learning for all students!

What collaborative team members *do* in a PLC goes far beyond collaborative conversations. They develop team norms—guidelines for how the team will do their work, day in and day out. They engage in a deep, rich study of the state and national standards and develop a guaranteed and viable curriculum for each student regardless of the teacher to whom he or she is assigned. They create rubrics and expectations for high-quality student performance, which naturally leads to the discussion of common scoring of student products and reporting of student progress. The point is this: if you are a teacher in a PLC, you are a contributing member of a collaborative team that is continually engaged in rich dialogue around what is essential for all students to know and be able to do—answering the first critical question of a PLC.

The team next moves to the second critical question, How will we know if our students are learning? Collaborative teams develop common formative assessments in order to monitor the learning of each student, skill by skill, on a frequent and timely basis. They aren't content with merely clarifying what students must learn. They pursue a cultural shift from an almost exclusive reliance on summative assessments to more frequent, collaboratively developed, common formative assessments. Simply put, being a teacher in a PLC means being part of a collaborative team that recognizes students are more apt to perform well on high-stakes summative assessments, *if the quality of their learning is regularly monitored along the way*—especially when the results of the assessments are used to provide students with additional time, support, or enrichment.

If you were to visit a grade-level team in a PLC during team collaboration time, you would observe teachers collaboratively analyzing student learning data and examples of student work. They would be discussing assessment results, item by item, as well as the effectiveness of the assessment itself. Teachers would be highlighting strengths in student learning, identifying areas of concern, and sharing instructional strategies that were used—learning from each other's strengths. They would be monitoring the learning of each student, skill by skill.

Since students learn at different rates and in different ways, teachers in a PLC answer the third critical question: What will we do if they haven't learned it? Some students, even our best students, will struggle with specific skills. When they do, they need additional time and support—as well as encouragement. Teachers in PLCs have the benefit of a systematic, schoolwide plan of layered interventions that provide students with help when they experience difficulty in their learning. They recognize it is their moral obligation to provide help to struggling students.

In this systematic plan, students benefit from ever-increasing focused support based on their level of need. Initially, most interventions occur within the classroom with reteaching or peer support. However, some students may need more intense interventions such as a tutor, or time in a computer lab, or a specific program for students who are experiencing difficulty.

Of course, not all students need additional time and support. Many students demonstrate proficiency in their learning. For that, the teams must answer the fourth critical question: What will we do if they've demonstrated proficiency? The schoolwide plan in a PLC also includes ways to enrich and extend student learning, stretching them far beyond proficiency.

Teams discuss issues such as grading and homework. They study effective grading and homework policies and practices and collaboratively address such questions as, What is the purpose of homework? and How much homework is appropriate? among many others.

Schools that function as PLCs embrace the assumption that improved *student* learning is inexorably linked to improved *adult* learning, and adult learning can best be accomplished by "doing the work" of a high-performing collaborative team. Thus, those who teach in a PLC engage in professional growth experiences that flow up from the learning needs of their students and their team rather than down from arbitrary and random ideas about what they need. Their learning is truly job-embedded and focused on the real world of classroom teachers.

Finally, imagine teaching in a school where the efforts and achievements of faculty and staff are publicly recognized and celebrated. In PLCs, those who are doing the work—day in and day out—know their hard work and incremental success are recognized and appreciated. Leaders do not leave recognition and celebration to chance or to others. They shape the culture of schools, and ultimately the behavior of those within them, through planned, purposeful, and most importantly, *sincere and meaningful* recognition and celebration of the behaviors they value the most.

# Appendix

# Examples of the Work of Teams

*Source: White River School District. Used with permission.*

## Learning Targets

### Grade 7 Math Expressions and Equations

Use properties of operations to generate equivalent expressions (7.EE.A1, 7.EE.A2):

- I can add and subtract linear expressions with rational coefficients.

- I can explain simplification of algebraic expressions—explain why $3x + x = 4x$, but $(3x)(x)$ is $3x^2$ OR why $3x + 2y$ cannot be simplified further but $(3x)(2y)$ can be simplified.

- I can draw representations for addition, subtraction, multiplication, and factoring of algebraic expressions and connect these drawings to symbolic representation.

- I can factor and expand linear expressions with rational coefficients.

- I can restate expressions to make sense of real-life situations (the perimeter of a rectangle can be $l + l + w + w$ or $2l + 2w$).

### Grade 4 Reading Standards for Informational/Literary Text

RL.4.3—Describe in depth a character, setting, or event in a story or drama, drawing on specific details in the text (e.g., a character's thoughts, words, or actions).

- I can identify characters, setting, and events in a story or drama.

- I can use specific details from the text to describe characters, setting, and events.

RI.4.3—Explain events, procedures, ideas, or concepts in a historical, scientific, or technical text, including what happened and why, based on specific information in the text.

- I can use specific events and ideas from what I read to explain what happened and why.

### Grade 4 Writing Standards

W.4.1—Write opinion pieces on topics or texts, supporting a point of view with reasons and information.

   a. Introduce a topic or text clearly, state an opinion, and create an organizational structure in which related ideas are grouped to support the writer's purpose.

   b. Provide reasons that are supported by facts and details.

   c. Link opinion and reasons using words and phrases (e.g., *for instance, in order to, in addition*).

   d. Provide a concluding statement or section related to the opinion presented.

- I can determine my opinion on a topic.
- I can state clearly my opinion on a topic in the introduction.
- I can organize my ideas to support my opinions with facts and details.
- I can link opinions and reasons in my writing.
- I can write a concluding statement to support my opinion.

## Honors Physical Science Syllabus

Welcome to Honors Physical Science!

Physical Science is a yearlong conceptual science course that covers a wide variety of topics from the physical world. These topics include matter, atomic structure, motion, energy, and space. A successful student in physical science will attend every class, pay attention during class, complete all coursework on time, and demonstrate knowledge on assessments. I am looking forward to working with students as well as parents to make sure everyone has a great year of learning.

### Text

*Physical Science Spectrum* by Holt

Each student will be assigned an online account for access online.

### Materials

Science notebook

Pen/pencils

Colored pencils

Glue stick

Scissors

Whiteboard marker

## Assignment Categories

Assessment 80%

Labs/projects 15%

Practice 5%

## Class Guidelines

Follow the Hornet Way!

Have pride in yourself, others, and your surroundings.

Show acceptance of others. Everyone is unique and deserves your respect.

You can show appreciation for others by treating those you interact with in a positive way. Remember, everyone learns at their own pace and style!

## Entry Task

We will have a short in-class assignment that we will complete at the start of every class period. These assignments are usually brief. Every day, the desk work assignment will be posted on the board. This assignment should be completed right away in your notebook when you enter class.

## CER Activities

We will learn through a variety of activities in this class. This includes lab activities. If you are behaving inappropriately in the lab or lab area, you will lose lab privileges and be asked to complete an alternative book assignment.

## Tests and Quizzes

We will have quizzes after each section of every unit and tests at the end of each unit. These tests and quizzes are weighted as 70% of your grade. You may retake a test or quiz by completing the test retake procedures.

## Grading Philosophy

### Practice Toward Standard

Practicing a skill is important for all learners; however, no one should be graded predominately on practice. Imagine learning to ride a bike. Most of us would receive 1s and 2s if we were scored on our first attempt at this new skill. Practice work in this class is scored on the four-point scale and weighted at only 5% of the student's total grade.

All homework and daily work fall into the "practice" category. The majority of practice work can be resubmitted by the student within one week to raise the student's grade in the course.

*Demonstration of Skill Mastery*

Assessments are designed to measure the student's level of mastery of a desired content skill. Assessments come in a variety of forms (tests, labs, oral examinations, products, etc.). Assessments are given after students have multiple practice experiences and have received detailed feedback from the teacher.

Assessments are weighted at 70% of the student grade. All assessments can be retaken/resubmitted, although, the retake often looks different than the original assessment.

*Opportunities to Show Skill Level*

Students are allowed multiple opportunities to show mastery of each skill. These opportunities are available to students who have shown continued effort to learn the content past the original assessment date. Retake requests must be submitted using the WRHS retake sheet.

## Understanding the Four-Point Scale

4—Mastery of skill (M)

3.6—Approaching mastery (AM)

3.3—Proficient in skill (P)

2.8—Approaching proficient (AP)

2.4—Basic skill standard (Ba)

2—Beginning (Be)

## Topics in Our Curriculum

### Semester I

**Engineering Design**

Students will be able to distinguish the difference between the scientific process and the process of engineering.

**Structure and Properties of Matter**

Students will be able to describe the structure of the atom and its influence on placement in the Periodic Table.

**Chemical Reactions**

Students will be able to understand that the creation of new material takes place as the result of chemical reactions.

**Forces and Interactions**

Students will be able to understand and calculate forces and interactions through Newton's laws of motion and gravity.

*Semester II*

## Energy

Students will be able to identify types of energy and how energy flows through a system.

## Waves and Technology

Students will be able to calculate wave speed and frequency and understand how waves are used in different technologies.

## Space Systems

Students will be able to understand the origins of the universe and the life cycle of a star.

## Earth Systems

Students will be able to understand the basic functions of global and local geology and how the Earth functions as a system.

This outline is a broad overview of the topics we will be covering in this course. Some topics may include more detail than others.

Student Signature: _____     Parent Signature: _____

Print Student Name: _____     Date: _____

# Unit Plans

| Linear Equations and Systems (8.EE.C) | | | | |
|---|---|---|---|---|
| Over the next month, you'll be studying equations, graphs, problem solving, and real-world scenarios that involve 1–2 data sets. While our data will grow at a constant rate, in high school you'll study data that grow in other ways. For example, the population of a large city may grow exponentially. | | | | |
| **Essential Questions** | | | | |
| ❑ Concept: How can I interpret solutions to linear equations and systems? | ❑ Skill: How can I solve linear equations and systems? | ❑ Application: How can I solve real-world problems involving linear data? | | |
| **Learning Targets** | | | Task 1 | Task 2 | Task 3 |
| **I can solve equations that have integers.** This means I can write out precise steps such as the Distributive Property, combining like terms, or inverse operations. Also, I can interpret my solution contextually. (DOK 1, 2) | | | | | |

Continued →

| | | | |
|---|---|---|---|
| **I can solve equations with rational coefficients.** This means I can extend my previous work to equations that have fractions or decimals. (DOK 1, 2) | | | |
| **I can predict an equation's type or number of solutions.** This means I can think strategically about an equation. Without solving it, I can determine whether the solution would be positive, negative, zero, or not exist. (DOK 3) | | | |
| **I can create equations that have infinitely many, one, or no solution(s).** This means I can fill in missing numbers to make the two sides of an equation always, sometimes, or never equal. Also, if I solve an equation that ends up with two identical or equal sides, I can interpret the result. (DOK 2) | | | |
| **I can analyze graphs of systems.** This means I can locate a point of intersection and explain what its coordinates mean. Moreover, I can make real-world decisions based on which line is higher on the graph. (DOK 2, 3) | | | |
| **I can solve a system by graphing.** This means I can use $y = mx + b$, or evaluate functions, to draw precise lines that intersect. Also, I can interpret my solution contextually. (DOK 1, 2) | | | |
| **I can create graphs that have one, zero, or infinitely many solutions.** This means I can use geo-boards to build lines that are intersecting, parallel, or collinear. Then, I can describe my lines with equations. (DOK 3) | | | |
| **I can model real-world scenarios with mathematics.** This means I can solve problems by drawing diagrams, collecting data in tables, analyzing graphs, or transforming given information into equations. (DOK 2, 3) | | | |

### Vocabulary to Master

| | | | | |
|---|---|---|---|---|
| coefficient | constant | distribute | infinitely | interpret |
| like terms | linear | point of intersection | precise | slope |
| Slope-Intercept Form | solution | Standard Form | system | *y*-intercept |

# Common Assessments

Name: _____     Date: _____     Period: _____

Algebra Unit 1A Assessment

Directions: Solve each equation for the given variable. Show all work to receive full credit.

## Beginning (BE)

1. $17 + x = 40$

2. $5 - x = 23$

3. $c/3 = -5$

4. $-3x = -81$

## Basic (BA)

5. $m/7 + 3 = -8$

6. $-5x + 2 = 17$

7. $4x - 7 = 29 - 2x$

8. $12x + 9 - 4x = 3$

9. $3(x - 4) = 0$

## Proficient (P)

10. $3(3x - 4) - 2 = 22$

11. $3 - 6x = -2 - 3x + 5$

12. If you tripled a number and added seven, the total would be 43. What is the original number? Write and solve an equation that represents this situation. Label your variable.

13. You went to the fair, and it cost $7 to get in. Each ride ticket you bought cost $2. If you spent a total of $30, how many tickets did you buy? Write and solve an equation that represents this situation. Label your variable.

## Mastery (M)

14. Look at the equation below. Is $x = -4$ the solution? Why or why not? Explain/justify your answer.

    $40 - 5x = -5 + 5(1 - 3x)$

15. The fine for speeding on the highways of most states is a function of the speed of the car. The speeding fine can be determined by a linear equation; where F represents the _fine in dollars_ and m represents the _number of miles the car is EXCEEDING the 70 mph speed limit_.

    In Washington, the speed limit on federal interstates is 70 miles per hour (mph). The fine for speeding on the Washington interstates is $10 per mile above the legal limit plus an additional $40. What would your speeding fine be if you were traveling 78 mph? Write the rule/equation used to determine the amount of a fine for speeding in Washington State. Show all work or explain in words how you arrived at your answer.

# References and Resources

Ainsworth, L., & Viegut, D. (2006). Common formative assessments: An essential part of the integrated whole. Thousand Oaks, CA: Corwin Press.

Becker, H. S. (1952). Social-class variations in teacher-pupil. *Journal of Educational Sociology, 25*(8), 461–465.

Bellon, J. J., Bellon, E. C., & Blank, M. A. (1992). *Teaching from a research knowledge base: A development and renewal process.* New York: Merrill.

Berliner, D. C. (1984). *Educational psychology.* Boston: Houghton Mifflin.

Berliner, D. C. (1986). In pursuit of the expert pedagogue. *Educational Researcher, 15*(7), 5–13.

Berry, L. L., & Seltman, K. D. (2008). *Management lessons from Mayo Clinic: Inside one of the world's most admired service organizations.* New York: McGraw-Hill.

Black, P., & Wiliam, D. (1998). The formative purpose: Assessment must first promote learning. In M. Wilson (Ed.), *Towards coherence between classroom assessment and accountability (103rd Yearbook of the National Society for the Study of Education,* pp. 20–50). Chicago: University of Chicago Press for the National Society for the Study of Education.

Blanchard, K. (2007). *Leading at a higher level: Blanchard on leadership and creating high performing organizations.* Upper Saddle River, NJ: Pearson.

Bloom, B. S. (Ed.). (1956). *Taxonomy of educational objectives: The classification of educational goals.* New York: Longman.

Borich, G. D. (2000). *Effective teaching methods: Research-based practice* (1st ed.). Upper Saddle River, NJ: Prentice Hall.

Brandwein, P. (1981). *Memorandum, on renewing schooling and education.* New York: Harcourt Brace Jovanovich.

Brookover, W. B., Beady, C., Flood, P., Schweitzer, J., & Wisenbaker, J. (1979). *School social systems and student achievement: Schools can make a difference.* New York: Praeger.

Brookover, W. B., & Lezotte, L. W. (1979). *Changes in school characteristics coincident with changes in student achievement.* East Lansing: Institute for Research on Teaching, College of Education, Michigan State University.

Brophy, J. E., & Evertson, C. M. (1976). *Learning from teaching: A developmental perspective.* Boston: Allyn & Bacon.

Brophy, J., & Good, T. (1974). *Teacher-student relationships: Causes and consequences.* New York: Holt, Rinehart & Winston.

Brown, D. J. (2013). *The boys in the boat: Nine Americans and their quest for gold at the 1936 Berlin Olympics.* London: Penguin Publishing Group.

Brualdi, A. C. (1998). *Classroom questions* (No. ED0-TM-98–02). Washington, DC: ERIC Clearinghouse on Assessment and Evaluation.

California State Department of Education. (1980). *Report on the special studies of selected ECE schools with increasing and decreasing reading scores.* Sacramento, CA: Office of Program Evaluation and Research.

Chalfant, E., & Wright, C. E. (Eds.). (2007). *The education of Henry Adams: A centennial version by Henry Adams.* Boston: Massachusetts Historical Society.

Clark, K. (1963). Educational stimulation of racially disadvantaged children. In A. H. Passow (Ed.), *Education in depressed areas* (pp. 142–162). New York: Wiley.

Conroy, P. (1972). *The water is wide.* Boston: Houghton Mifflin.

Conroy, P. (2010). *My reading life.* New York: Talese.

Cooper, H., & Baron, R. (1977). Academic expectations and attributed responsibility as predictors of professional teachers' reinforcement behavior. *Journal of Educational Philosophy, 69*(4), 409–418.

Cooper, H., & Good, T. (1983). *Pygmalion grows up: Studies in the expectation communication process.* White Plains, NY: Longman.

Cotton, K. (1988). *Close-up #5: Classroom questioning* (School Improvement Research Series). Accessed at http://educationnorthwest.org/sites/default/files/ClassroomQuestioning.pdf on January 6, 2015.

Curwin, R., & Mendler, A. (1988). *Discipline with dignity.* Alexandria, VA: Association for Supervision and Curriculum Development.

Curwin, R., Mendler, A., & Mendler, B. (2008). *Discipline with dignity: New challenges, new solutions* (3rd ed.). Alexandria, VA: Association for Supervision and Curriculum Development.

Davis, A., & Dollard, J. (1940). *Children of bondage: The personality development of Negro youth in the urban South.* Washington, DC: American Council on Education.

Deal, T. E., & Kennedy, A. A. (1982). *Corporate cultures: The rites and rituals of corporate life.* Reading, MA: Addison-Wesley.

Deutsch, M. (1963). The disadvantaged child and the learning process. In A. H. Passow (Ed.), *Education in depressed areas* (pp. 163–180). New York: Wiley.

DuFour, R., DuFour, R., & Eaker, R. (2008). *Revisiting professional learning communities at work: New insights for improving schools.* Bloomington, IN: Solution Tree Press.

DuFour, R., DuFour, R., Eaker, R., & Many, T. W. (2010). *Learning by doing: A handbook for professional learning communities at work* (2nd ed.). Bloomington, IN: Solution Tree Press.

DuFour, R., & Eaker, R. (1998). *Professional learning communities at work: Best practices for enhancing student achievement.* Bloomington, IN: Solution Tree Press.

Dweck, C. S. (2008). *Mindset: The new psychology of success.* New York: Ballantine Books.

Eaker, R., & Keating, J. (2008). A shift in school culture: Collective commitments focus on change that benefits student learning. *Journal of Staff Development, 29*(3), 14–17. Accessed at http://sustained-growth-leadership-development .wikispaces.com/file/view/Eaker+%26+Keating+Shift+in+School+Culture .pdf on January 8, 2015.

Eaker, R., & Keating, J. (2012). *Every school, every team, every classroom: District leadership for growing professional learning communities at work.* Bloomington, IN: Solution Tree Press.

Edwards, R. R. (1978). *A discussion of the literature and issues related to effective schooling.* Paper presented at the National Conference on Urban Education, St. Louis, MO.

Elmore, R. (2006). *School reform from the inside out: Policy, practice, and performance.* Cambridge, MA: Harvard Education Press.

Evans, R. (1996). *The human side of school change: Reform, resistance, and the real-life problems of innovation.* San Francisco: Jossey-Bass Education.

Fleming, E., & Anttonen, R. (1971). Teacher expectancy or My Fair Lady. *American Educational Research Journal, 8*(2), 241–252.

Fullan, M. (2005). *Leadership and sustainability: System thinkers in action.* Thousand Oaks, CA: Corwin Press.

Gagné, R. M. (1985). *The conditions of learning and theory of instruction* (4th ed.). New York: Holt, Rinehart & Winston.

Gettinger, M. (1989). Effects of maximizing time spent and minimizing time needed for learning and student achievement. *American Educational Research Journal, 26,* 73–91.

Glasser, W. (1993). *The total quality teacher.* New York: HarperCollins.

Glasser, W. (1999). *The quality school teacher: A companion volume to* The Quality School. New York: HarperCollins.

Glenn, B. C. (1981). *What works? An examination of effective schools for poor black children*. Cambridge, MA: Center for Law and Education, Harvard University.

Goleman, D. (1995). *Emotional intelligence: Why it can matter more than IQ*. New York: Bantam Books.

Goleman, D., Boyatzis, R., & McKee, A. (2002). *The new leaders: Transforming the art of leadership into the science of results*. Boston: Little, Brown.

Good, T., & Brophy, J. E. (1970). Teacher-child dyadic interactions: A new method of classroom observation. *Journal of Social Psychology, 8*(2), 131–137.

Good, T. L., & Brophy, J. E. (1974). Changing teacher and student behavior: An empirical investigation. *Journal of Educational Psychology, 66*(3), 390–405.

Good, T. L., & Brophy, J. E. (1978). *Looking in classrooms* (2nd ed.). New York: Harper & Row.

Good, T. L., & Brophy, J. E. (1980). *Educational psychology: A realistic approach* (2nd ed.). New York: Holt, Rinehart & Winston.

Good, T. L., Cooper, H. M., & Blakey, S. L. (1980). Classroom interaction as a function of teacher expectations, student sex, and time of year. *Journal of Teacher Education, 72*(3), 378–385.

Haley, A. (1965). *The autobiography of Malcolm X*. New York: Grove Press.

Hammond, L. D. (1997). *The right to learn: A blueprint for creating schools that work*. San Francisco: Jossey-Bass.

Hattie, J. A. C. (1992). Measuring the effects of schooling. *Australian Journal of Education, 36*(1), 5–13.

Hattie, J. A. C. (2009). *Visible learning: A synthesis of over 800 meta-analyses relating to achievement*. New York: Routledge.

Kanter, R. M. (2006). *Confidence: How winning streaks and losing streaks begin and end*. New York: Three Rivers Press.

Kotter, J. P., & Cohen, D. S. (2002). *The heart of change: Real-life stories of how people change their organizations*. Boston: Harvard Business School Press.

Kounin, J. S. (1970). *Discipline and group management in classrooms*. New York: Holt, Rinehart & Winston.

Kouzes, J., & Posner, B. (2006). *A leader's legacy*. San Francisco: Jossey-Bass.

Lehr, F. (1984). ERIC/RCS: Direct instruction in reading. *The Reading Teacher, 39*(7), 706–713.

Lent, R. C. (2012). *Overcoming textbook fatigue: 21st century tools to revitalize teaching and learning*. Alexandria, VA: Association for Supervision and Curriculum Development.

Levine, H., & Mann, K. (1981, April). *The negotiation of classroom lessons and its relevance to teachers' decision making.* Paper presented at the annual meeting of the American Educational Research Association, Los Angeles, CA.

Lezotte, L. (2005). More effective schools: Professional learning communities in action. In R. DuFour, R. DuFour, & R. Eaker (Eds.), *On common ground: The power of professional learning communities* (pp. 177–191). Bloomington, IN: Solution Tree Press.

Long, M. H., & Sato, C. J. (1983). Classroom foreign talk discourse forms and functions of teachers' questions. In H. Seliger & M. H. Long (Eds.), *Classroom oriented research in second language acquisition* (pp. 268–285). Rowley, MA: Newbury House.

Marzano, R. J. (2003). *What works in schools: Translating research into action.* Alexandria, VA: Association for Supervision and Curriculum Development.

Marzano, R. J. (2007). *The art and science of teaching: A comprehensive framework for effective instruction.* Alexandria, VA: Association for Supervision and Curriculum Development.

Marzano, R. J., Marzano, J. S., & Pickering, D. J. (2003). *Classroom management that works: Research-based strategies for every teacher.* Alexandria, VA: Association for Supervision and Curriculum Development.

Marzano, R. J., Pickering, D. J., & Brandt, R. S. (1990). Integrating instructional programs through Dimensions of Learning. *Educational Leadership, 47*(5), 17–24.

Mayer, G. R. (1995). *Preventing antisocial behavior in the schools.* Journal of Applied Behavior Analysis, 28, 467–478.

McDermott, R. (1976). *Kids make sense: An ethnographic account of the interactional management of success and failure in one first grade classroom.* Unpublished doctoral dissertation, Stanford University, Stanford, CA.

Mendler, A. N., & Curwin, R. L. (1999). *Discipline with dignity for challenging youth.* Bloomington, IN: Solution Tree Press.

Mendler, A. N. (2012). *When teaching gets tough: Smart ways to reclaim your game.* Alexandria, VA: Association for Supervision and Curriculum Development.

Miller, Z. (1996). *Corps values.* Atlanta, GA: Longstreet Press.

Mohr, K. A. J. (1998). Teacher talk: A summary analysis of effective teachers' discourse during primary literacy lessons. *Journal of Classroom Interaction, 33*(2), 16–23.

Morgan, E., Salomon, N., Plotkin, M., & Cohen, R. (2014). *The school discipline consensus report: Strategies from the field to keep students engaged in school and out of the juvenile justice system.* New York: Council of State Governments Justice Center.

Murphy, J. F., Weil, M., Hallinger, P., & Mitman, A. (1982, December). Academic press: Translating high expectations into school policies and classroom practices. *Educational Leadership*, 22–26.

Nanus, B. (1992). *Visionary leadership: Creating a compelling sense of direction for your organization.* San Francisco: Jossey-Bass.

National Commission on Teaching and America's Future. (2003). *No dream denied: A pledge to America's children.* Washington, DC: National Commission on Teaching and America's Future.

National Governors Association Center for Best Practices & Council of Chief State School Officers. (2010). *Common Core State Standards for English language arts & literacy in history/social studies, science, and technical subjects.* Washington, DC: Authors.

New York State Office of Education Performance Review. (1974, March). *School factors influencing reading achievement: A case study of two inner city schools.* Albany, NY: Author.

Passow, A. H. (Ed.). (1963). *Education in depressed areas.* New York: Wiley.

Peters, T. J., & Waterman, R. H., Jr. (1982). *In search of excellence: Lessons from America's best-run companies.* New York: Harper & Row.

Pfeffer, J., & Sutton, R. (2000). *The knowing-doing gap: How smart companies turn knowledge into action.* Boston: Harvard Business School Press.

Pierson, R. (2013, May). *Every kid needs a champion* [Video file]. Accessed at www.ted.com/talks/rita_pierson_every_kid_needs_a_champion?language=en on January 8, 2015.

Popham, W. J. (2008). *Transformative assessment.* Alexandria, VA: Association for Supervision and Curriculum Development.

Purkey, S. C., & Smith, M. S. (1982, February). *Effective schools: A review.* Paper presented at the National Invitational Conference, "Research on Teaching: Implications for Practice," Warrenton, VA.

Reeves, D. B. (2000). *Accountability in action: A blueprint for learning organizations.* Denver, CO: Advanced Learning Press.

Reeves, D. B. (2002). *The leader's guide to standards: A blueprint for educational equity and excellence.* San Francisco: Wiley.

Reeves, D. (2004). *Accountability for learning: How teachers and school leaders can take charge.* Alexandria, VA: Association for Supervision and Curriculum Development.

Ricks, T. E. (1997). *Making the Corps.* New York: Scribner.

Rogers, C. R. (1961). *On becoming a person: A therapist's view of psychotherapy.* Boston: Houghton Mifflin.

Rosenthal, R., & Jacobson, L. (1968). *Pygmalion in the classroom: Teacher expectation and pupils' intellectual development.* New York: Holt, Rinehart & Winston.

Rowe, M. B. (1969). Science, silence, and sanctions. *Science and Children, 6*(6), 11–13.

Rowe, M. B. (1986). Wait times: Slowing down may be a way of speeding up! *Journal of Teacher Education, 37*(1), 43–50.

Rutter, M., Maughan, B., Mortimore, P., & Ouston, J. (1979). *Fifteen thousand hours: Secondary schools and their effects on children.* Cambridge: Harvard University Press.

Santos, F. (2012). *Teacher survey shows morale is at a low point.* Accessed at www .nytimes.com/2012/03/08/education/teacher-morale-sinks-survey-results -show.html?_r=0 on February 3, 2015.

Saphier, J., Haley-Speca, M. A., & Gower, R. (2008). *The skillful teacher: Building your teaching skills* (6th ed.). Acton, MA: Research for Better Teaching.

Schrank, W. (1968). The labeling effect on ability grouping. *Journal of Educational Research, 62,* 51–52.

Schrank, W. (1970). A further study of the labeling effect on ability grouping. *Journal of Educational Research, 63*(8), 358–360.

Shaw, G. B. (2003). *Pygmalion.* New York: Penguin Putnam. (Original work published 1916)

Shouse, R. C. (1996). *School psychology of education.* Norwell, MA: Kluwer Academic.

Sinek, S. (2009). *Start with why: How great leaders inspire everyone to take action.* New York: Portfolio.

Stiggins, R. (2004). New assessment beliefs for a new school mission. *Phi Delta Kappan, 86*(1), 22–27.

Stiggins, R. (2005). Assessment FOR learning: Building a culture of confident learners. In R. DuFour, R. Eaker, & R. DuFour (Eds.), *On common ground: The power of professional learning communities* (pp. 65–83). Bloomington, IN: Solution Tree Press.

Tobin, K. G. (1984). Effects of extended wait time on discourse characteristics and achievement in middle school grades. *Journal of Research in Science Teaching, 21*(8), 779–791.

Tomlinson, C. A. (2010). Differentiating instruction in response to academically diverse student populations. In R. Marzano (Ed.), *On excellence in teaching* (pp. 247–268). Bloomington, IN: Solution Tree Press.

Tomlinson, C. A., & Allan, S. D. (2000). *Leadership for differentiating schools and classrooms.* Alexandria, VA: Association for Supervision and Curriculum Development.

Wagner, T. (2012). *Creating innovators: The making of young people who will change the world*. New York: Scribner.

Warner, W. L., Havinghurst, R. J., & Loeb, M. B. (1944). *Who shall be educated? The challenge of unequal opportunities*. New York: Harper.

Waterman, R. H. (1987). *The renewal factor: How the best get and keep the competitive edge*. Toronto, Ontario, Canada: Bantam Books.

Waters, J. T., & Marzano, R. J. (2006). *School district leadership that works: The effect of superintendent leadership on student achievement*. Denver, CO: Mid-continent Research for Education and Learning.

Weber, G. (1971). *Inner-city children can be taught to read: Four successful schools*. Washington, DC: Council for Basic Education.

Wiggins, G. (2010). What's my job? Defining the role of the classroom teacher. In R. Marzano (Ed.), *On excellence in teaching* (pp. 7–29). Bloomington, IN: Solution Tree Press.

Wiliam, D. (2011). *Embedded formative assessment*. Bloomington, IN: Solution Tree Press.

Williams, K. (2010, October 25). Do we have team norms or "nice to knows"? [web log post]. Accessed at www.allthingsplc.info/mobile/blog/view/90/do-we-have-team-norms-or-nice-to-knows on February 18, 2015.

Wilson, A. B. (1963). Social stratification and academic achievement. In A. H. Passow (Ed.), *Education in depressed areas* (pp. 217–236). New York: Wiley.

# Index

**Every School, Every Team, Every Classroom: District Leadership for Growing Professional Learning Communities at Work™**
*Robert Eaker and Janel Keating*
The PLC journey begins with a dedication to ensuring the learning of every student. Using many examples and reproducible tools, the authors explain the need to focus on creating simultaneous top-down and bottom-up leadership. Learn how to grow PLCs by encouraging innovation at every level. **BKF534**

**Learning by Doing: A Handbook for Professional Learning Communities at Work™**
*Richard DuFour, Rebecca DuFour, Robert Eaker, and Thomas W. Many*
Through continuous work with educators, the authors have created a more powerful, practical resource for moving forward in the PLC process. This book is an action guide for closing the knowing-doing gap and transforming schools into PLCs. It also includes seven major additions that equip educators with essential tools for confronting challenges. **BKF416**

**Solutions for Professional Learning Communities series**
Implement and sustain a high-performing PLC. These how-to guides—authored by renowned PLC experts—are packed with user-friendly solutions for you and your entire team. You'll discover practical, research-based strategies for committing to districtwide implementation, investigate why strong leadership is a crucial element of successful PLCs, and explore tools and techniques for monitoring progress to ensure far-reaching, lasting results.
**BKF667, BKF678, BKF676, BKF665, BKF668, BKF675**

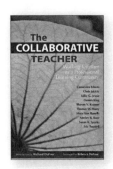

**The Collaborative Teacher: Working Together as a Professional Learning Community**
*Cassandra Erkens, Chris Jakicic, Lillie G. Jessie, Dennis King, Sharon V. Kramer, Thomas W. Many, Mary Ann Ranells, Ainsley B. Rose, Susan K. Sparks, and Eric Twadell*
*Foreword by Rebecca DuFour*
*Introduction by Richard DuFour*
Transform education from inside the classroom with this accessible anthology. Specific techniques, supporting research, and real classroom stories illustrate how to work together to create a guaranteed and viable curriculum and use data to inform instruction. **BKF257**

**Revisiting Professional Learning Communities at Work™: New Insights for Improving Schools**
*Richard DuFour, Rebecca DuFour, and Robert Eaker*
This 10th-anniversary sequel to the pivotal book *Professional Learning Communities at Work™* offers advanced insights on deep implementation, the commitment/consensus issue, and the human side of PLCs. Gain greater knowledge of common mistakes to avoid and new discoveries for success. **BKF252**

# "Tremendous, tremendous, tremendous!

The speaker made me do some very deep internal reflection about the **PLC process** and the personal responsibility I have in making the school improvement process work **for ALL kids."**

—Marc Rodriguez, teacher effectiveness coach,
Denver Public Schools, Colorado

## PD Services

Our experts draw from decades of research and their own experiences to bring you practical strategies for building and sustaining a high-performing PLC. You can choose from a range of customizable services, from a one-day overview to a multiyear process.

## Book your PLC PD today!
888.763.9045

Solution Tree